T0154361

READY FOR REVOLUTION:

THE CNT DEFENSE COMMITTEES IN BARCELONA, 1933–1938

READY FOR REVOLUTION:
THE CNT DEFENSE COMMITTEES IN BARCELONA, 1933–1938

AGUSTÍN GUILLAMÓN
Translated by Paul Sharkey

Ready for Revolution: The CNT Defense Committees in Barcelona, 1933–1938

© 2014 Agustín Guillamón.

This edition © 2014 Kate Sharpley Library and AK Press (Oakland, Edinburgh, Baltimore). Translated by Paul Sharkey. Special thanks to John Barker for indexing.

ISBN: 978-1-84935-142-3 | eBook ISBN: 978-1-84935-143-0
Library of Congress Control Number: 2013945489

Kate Sharpley Library   Kate Sharpley Library
BM Hurricane   PMB 820, 2425 Channing Way
LondonWC1N, 3XX   Berkeley, CA 94704
UK   USA
www.katesharpleylibrary.net

AK Press   AK Press
674-A 23rd Street   PO Box 12766
Oakland, CA 94612   Edinburgh EH8 9YE
USA   Scotland
www.akpress.org   www.akuk.com
akpress@akpress.org   ak@akedin.demon.co.uk

The above addresses would be delighted to provide you with the latest AK Press distribution catalog, which features the several thousand books, pamphlets, zines, audio and video products, and stylish apparel published and/or distributed by AK Press. Alternatively, visit our websites for the complete catalog, latest news, and secure ordering.

1st edition published by Aldarull Edicions (Barcelona) April 2011 as *Los Comités de Defensa de la CNT en Barcelona (1933–1938). De los cuadros de defensa a los Comités revolucionarios de barriada, la Patrullas de Control y la Milicias populares*

Cover design by Jared Davidson.

No more leaders, no more State
To profit from our battles.
Raoul Vaneigem, *La vie s'ecoule, la vie s'en fuit*

To live is to be militant.
Seneca, *Letters*

Morpheus: "I didn't say it would be easy, Neo. I just said it
would be the truth."
Larry and Andy Wachowski, *The Matrix*

TABLE OF CONTENTS

Translator's note

Since this translation is designed to make the original publication more accessible to readers with no Spanish, wherever the texts cited in the footnotes are exactly available in English versions, I have, as a rule, cited these English versions.

Where the citation is of untranslated texts in French, Catalan, or Spanish, and where specific publication/pagination details have been included, the citation has been left unaltered.

In the bibliography and elsewhere, where only the titles of cited texts have been given, without details as to their derivation, I have rendered these into English.

The purpose has been to banish exoticism and make the translated text more accessible to an English-language readership.

Glossary of terms used in the text

barriada – A district larger than a *barrio*: translated here mostly as "ward."

barrio – A district or quarter.

CAMC – Central Antifascist Militias Committee: improvised and cross-party agency formed by anti-fascist organizations and parties following the defeat of the army rebellion in Catalonia in July 1936.

CNT – National Confederation of Labour; anarcho-syndicalist labour federation headed by a National Committee and made up of local, *comarcal* (county), and regional federations.

comarca – The equivalent of a county.

DAS – Deutsch Anarcho-Syndikalisten (German anarcho-syndicalists in exile).

FAI – Iberian Anarchist Federation, founded in 1927 and headed by a Peninsular Committee representing Spain and Portugal.

faísta – Member/supporter of the FAI or of policies widely believed to enjoy FAI support.

Generalidad – Catalonia's home-rule government.

IWA – International Workers' Association a.k.a. Berlin International: the anarcho-syndicalist International to which the CNT was affiliated. Its Spanish initials are AIT.

NCDC – National Committee of Defense Committees.

NKVD – Soviet Secret Police.

paco – A slang term used for a sniper or Fifth Columnist.

pistolero – Gunman. The term was especially used to refer to goons hired by the bosses and authorities to "break" the CNT.

POUM – Workers' Party of Marxist Unification (non-Stalinist Marxists).

PSUC – Unified Socialist Party of Catalonia (Stalinists): the Catalan affiliate to the Comintern.

requetés – The ultra-Catholic and traditionalist Carlist militia.

SBLE -- Bolshevik-Leninist Section of Spain: tiny faction of Spain's official Trotskyists.

SIM – Military Investigation Service: the Republic's wartime security and counter-espionage agency, used to prosecute a Stalinist terror against deserters, draft-dodgers, and "defeatists," and enforcing collective responsibility against family members of "suspects."

sindicato libre – Free Trade Union: actually, mostly Catholic, conservative, and "yellow" unions sponsored by the employers to counter CNT influence.

sindicato único – The "one big union" embracing all the local workers, from whatever trades, skilled and unskilled; the key to local solidarity. Synonym for CNT unions.

treintista – A sympathiser with the signatories of the Manifesto of the Thirty; moderate anarcho-syndicalists opposed to the *faísta* line. *Treintistas* opposed to *faísta* adventurism, which might have damaging implications for painstakingly built union organizations.

UGT – Workers' General Union: socialist trade union; controlled in Catalonia by the PSUC.

Introduction:
Ready for Revolution

The photographic images of the Spanish revolution are implanted in our memories and too often taken for granted. Iconic figures like Durruti blinking at a notebook or standing smiling in a circle of comrades, Ascaso, rifle on his shoulder, enjoying a chat and a smoke in the bright Barcelona sun shortly before he is killed. Most of all, though, there are the crowds. Men and women with black and red caps in buses, on lorries, in hastily put together armored cars with CNT-FAI scrawled on the sides. Every one generating a sense of excitement and, yes, cockiness that is still palpable nearly eighty years later. We have had films, radio shows, interviews, so many anniversaries and so many books. Now, surely, the anarchist historical narrative of Spain is as familiar and understood as the photographs: initial revolutionary exhilaration and autonomy; then gradual repression by forces on the Left and, worst of all, a perceived betrayal of what the revolution had achieved by some anarchists who should have known better, but believed that the priority of the struggle was against fascism and not for the social revolution. What else do we need to know?

The smoke from Spain still hangs over all aspects of today's anarchism whether or not we like it—even for those who want to deny that what happened there has any relevance to the world today. For some, it has proved to be the end of something, the moving out of anarchism's home on the Left. For them, class struggle is moribund and bankrupt, something that should be subsumed by the struggle of the individual. They haven't yet announced, as George Woodcock maintained for many years, that anarchism died in 1939, but for those comrades at least a type of anarchism did. Less dramatically, others attempted to explain the circumstances that the CNT-FAI found itself in, suggesting that calls for anarchist revolution took no cognizance of what was happening both in Spain and in the world beyond it. They want us to examine carefully the hard decisions the organization had to take. Still others pore obsessively over the events. When did it go wrong? What could we have done differently in that place and on that date? Some comrades have spent time exploring all these areas. And still it goes on. This agonizing over, or even the outright dismissal of Spain as being of any importance, is not hard to understand. Rightly or wrongly, Spain has been seen by many of us as the only sustained period of time that anarchism actually helped bring about revolutionary change in the everyday lives of many, many people and, just as importantly, sustained that change. In parts of Spain, anarchists took on the army and won, and for many, that victory led to the creation of what we may call libertarian communism; a change in economic and personal relations that people could only have dreamed of a few years earlier. Capitalism had apparently been destroyed. Dreams had come true. All those discussions, all those articles, all those plenums, all those years of exile or imprisonment were not worthless. Yet we are left asking what went wrong? Was there some awful flaw in anarchism that has made it, like Bolshevism, a revolutionary dead end? Or was it a combination of circumstances and poor decision making by individuals that brought about the nightmare of 1939, the loss of everything, and the years of exile, repression, and resistance?

The CNT-FAI in 1934 was not a naïve and unsophisticated grouping filled with saintly militants driven by the purity, righteousness, and moral correctness of their mission. It was a hard-headed organization, shaped by its members' experience of strikes, insurrections, imprisonment, exile, cultural activities, and lives led in the working-class barrios and villages of Spain and elsewhere. It had a coherent sense of what was happening to capitalism in Spain and worldwide, did not exist in a purely intellectual and moral vacuum, and was well aware of the nature of the forces ranged against it. The CNT-FAI had its own legends and stories that carried tremendous weight in its decision making and was a remarkably complex group that we might be better off seeing less as one homogenous grouping but instead as several, whose membership changed according to the situations the organization found itself in and with the strategies it was using at the time. Many CNT-FAI members of whatever tendency were ferociously loyal to the organization and the comrades they had lost—García Oliver, for instance, spoke about the CNT as being "an enormous tomb which contains all the largely anonymous dreamers who believed they were struggling for social revolution"[1]—while their debates suggested the organization's continually evolving nature and refusal to become complacent or hidebound.

It is clear to see that, by 1934, the policy of "revolutionary gymnastics," which had been followed between 1932 and 1934, was a failure. The idea that repeated calls for insurrection would lead to an awareness of the repressive nature of the state, a growing confidence amongst the working class, and a series of rolling insurrections leading to revolution had left the CNT-FAI exhausted, some of its bravest militants in prison, and the organization basically weaponless. In itself, the tactic was not new to anarchism; Carlo Cafiero wrote as early as 1880, "Not only, then, are ideas born from deeds, they also need deeds in order to develop, to the point that they can inspire other deeds"[2] but, here, at this time and in these

---

1 Juan García Oliver, *Wrong Steps: Errors in the Spanish Revolution* (London: Kate Sharpley Library, 2000), 13.

2 Carlo Cafiero, *Revolution* (Edmonton: Black Cat Press, 2012), 64.

economic and social circumstances, such a strategy simply had not worked. We should be, perhaps, a little wary of being too dismissive of it, however. One has to think that the experience of, and belief in, insurrection did provide some with the confidence and tactical skill to take on the army and win in Barcelona. Yet the CNT-FAI's move away from its insurrectionary policies was a practical, rather than a moral decision, and the move to the Defense Committees helped both initiate and sustain the Spanish revolution in a profound and astonishingly extensive manner. Here was an organization whose competing tendencies, however they defined themselves, all understood that their reason for existence was to configure the best way to defeat capitalism and bring about libertarian communism, acting as conscious agents of their own change rather than waiting passively for it to happen, or for events to occur and reacting to them.

The CNT-FAI was always more than a trade union. It could be found in every aspect of working-class life; in its social activities, in its literature and culture, in its education and relationships. So when we talk about the Defense Committees being the "armed organizations of the CNT" (p. 27) we are talking about these groups being the Defense Committees of the working-class districts they were part of. Being an organic part of the community was a critical factor in all of this. Many Defense Committee members had grown up in the areas they represented. They knew the friends and enemies of the revolutionary movement and they knew the mood and tenor of their neighborhoods. They participated in rent strikes, they helped resist evictions, they financially supported families in times of illness, and prevented price gouging by greedy shopkeepers, together with a host of other activities. They understood the losses and small victories that made up working-class life and, when July 19th happened, they could move quickly into action against the army with the help of the working-class people they knew and whose community they were part of. Above all this was a planned and prepared response even if, at times, the situation appeared chaotic. Within a handful of days, the Defense Committees had the streets. Thanks to them, the bravery of the FAI action groups, and the courage of the working-class communities, events in Barcelona became something thrilling—a marvelous victory over the armed forces that prepared the way for libertarian communism. The Defense Committees had the skills, the support, and, yes, the power to make that happen.

Guillamón documents the rest of the story from here and all we would like to do is make one or two observations that we hope complement the narrative. Chapter 11, "The Barcelona FAI Radicalized by the Defense Committees," is a wonderful opportunity for the reader to see the various groups discussing the situation they find themselves in. It's rare to find this type of material in English that is not written from memory and in reflection long after the events described. The discussion leaps off the page and is full of contradiction, confusion, affirmation, and certainty, all served with a high level of sophisticated perception. There is an immediacy to it, not least because these are not the voices of the more sophisticated speakers and writers who we are used to reading, but those of the ordinary militant. Nearly a year had gone by since the possibilities of July 1936 and the experience of those months permeate the discussions. There can be no further assessment whether this is going to be a long or short war. It's the long haul and the atmosphere of the plenum is charged; something is going to happen, perhaps something already has, and we are privileged to be able to be there to sense it. This is radical history at its finest as the anarchists attempt to deal with the actions of the Stalinists, their other supposed allies, and the behavior of the CNT's "higher committees."

By 1937 it is clear that, as Guillamón's narrative recognizes, the tensions in the CNT had resolved into two clear positions that cut right through any other previous overlapping tendencies that might have existed. Now more than ever, the distinction between CNT and FAI was irrelevant. The ideological conflict within the organization was now between revolutionaries and those who wished to collaborate with other parties and groups. It was a tension between those who felt that the primary struggle was to maintain and extend libertarian communism and those who felt that the primary struggle was against Fascism and revolutionary change should be postponed until that overarching struggle was won. Many of the latter were soon on what Guillamón calls the "higher committees" of the CNT. When De Santillán talks about being in a collaborative mode we can, perhaps, understand the position of people like himself, Montseny, and others who see the struggle against Fascism as central to all actions and strategies. There is a logic there. Whatt is harder to understand is their inability to see the enormous potential of the Defense Committees and to observe their apparent complicity when the Stalinists and their friends refer to the Defense Committees as bandits and gangsters or dismiss those who refused to surrender to the primacy of the war against Fascism, as "uncontrollables." We should not, though, forget the loyalty of the Defense Committees to the CNT-FAI. The higher committees existed because the Defense Committees let them. Defense Committee members were usually too busy to take part in strategic debate on the war and, as a consequence, gave the higher committees free rein. The members of these higher committees were not lacking in self importance and saw a vacuum only they could fill. And fill it they did.

This book is not an easy read for those of us looking for a comforting re-enforcement of the purity of our anarchist ideal. Reality has an awkward habit of getting in the way, and at times it can be an unsettling read. Guillamón makes no attempt to hide the brutality that took place in those first few July days in Barcelona and the part the Defense Committees played in the settling of scores. The notion of anarchist-controlled prisons and the behavior of the CNT-FAI Investigation and Intelligence Services do not sit easily even as there is a distinct pragmatism about them. The real worry of the Liaison Committee of the Anarchist Groups in Catalonia, that members of the Durruti Column might well turn their guns on each other over the question of militarization, may well make us understand the passions that filled up those days in late 1936 but still leaves us unsettled. All this though is what very good history does. It makes us think, makes us interrogate our ideas and leaves us richer for it. It makes us want to find out more when we thought we knew enough.

In telling the story of the Defense Committees, Guillamón has made it incontrovertibly clear that the July days in Barcelona did not just happen. They had been planned for, and after the success of the working class communities against the armed forces and others, the Defense Committees were there to help administer food and welfare support, as well as to create libertarian forms of administration and support in a multitude of areas. Theirs is a remarkable story. If we want to find faults in their inability to coordinate or in their inability to sense, sometimes, what was happening on a national scale, we can. Sitting at our table, flicking through the Internet, we can find faults with nearly everything and, even if the faults are telling, we should be careful not to take away the reality of the magnificence of their particular achievements. For, as Guillamón writes, "The fighting, the killing, the suffering, and the dying was not done for the sake of a Republic or for democracy, but for the emancipation of labor and a better, freer, and fairer society, one that actually seemed within reach."

Agustín Guillamón has been editor of the magazine *Balance* since 1993. An ongoing investigation of events and personalities in the Spanish revolution, it has become a gradual recuperation of what we might call the "awkward squad"—those comrades from the revolutionary organizations who have been slandered by the neo-Stalinists and, more worryingly, sometimes, by members of their own organization looking to re-shape history and place themselves in the most flattering light. His book *The Friends of Durruti Group, 1937–1939* was published by AK Press in 1996 and *Ready for Revolution* is part of a trilogy that examines Spanish working-class anarchism up to and after the May Days of 1937. He describes his work as a historian as part of the "unveiling of the real history of the class struggle." A battle, if you like, against the amnesia that can easily envelop us.

This is a book that develops the work done in equally seminal texts such as Vernon Richards's *Lessons of the Spanish Revolution* (Freedom Press, 1972, enlarged edition), Stuart Christie's *We, the Anarchists* (AK Press, 2008) and Chris Ealham's *Anarchism and the City* (AK Press, 2010). Like them, *Ready for Revolution* stops us in our tracks and makes us re-assess and debate what we thought we knew. It is a beautifully researched book that is forcefully presented and is, without doubt, a major work of radical scholarship.

Kate Sharpley Library August 2013

1

From the Shapiro Report to the October 1934 Working Party Resolution

A confidential and not widely circulated report drawn up by IWA secretary Alexander Shapiro during a stay in Spain in 1932–1933 spelled out the essence and modus operandi of the defense committees, which were organized exclusively for the sort of front-line insurgent activity that Shapiro himself witnessed on 8 January 1933.[1] Shapiro's report was drawn up while the controversy between *faístas* and *treintistas*—over the suitability of impromptu, localized, serial uprisings—was still raging.[2] Shapiro offered a devastating criticism of the improvised character, lack of organization, and lack of groundwork in the January uprising. He was scathing in his denunciation of one person simultaneously holding positions on the CNT secretariat and the National Defense Council, on account of the confusion that this created. He showed how, in practice, the CNT had deferred to the decisions of the National Committee of Defense Committees (NCDC).

---

1 IWA, Report on CNT Activity (16 December 1932–26 February 1933).

2 The *faístas* agitated for uprisings regardless of objective circumstances, uprisings that would ignite the people through the example set by the revolutionary action groups. The *treintistas*, or reformists, took exception to FAI meddling in union business: they lobbied for trade union activity and a more grounded approach to laying the groundwork for a mass revolutionary uprising when circumstances were such as to favor its spreading across the state and society.

The Shapiro report, which had invaluable input from Eusebio Carbó, had this to say of the defense cadre in existence in 1933: "The main purposes of these defense cadres, which had been around for some time, were stockpiling arms for any eventual uprisings, organizing assault teams in various working class districts, and organizing troop resistance in their barracks, and so on."

Even during the uprising in Asturias,[3] the NCDC noted in a resolution that the insurrectionist tactics pushed by the Nosotros group, popularly known as "revolutionary gymnastics," had failed—and it pinned the blame on them for the CNT not being in a position to engage nationwide with the October 1934 uprising.[4] The time had come, the NCDC said, to look beyond these tactics: the danger and absurdity of ill-timed local insurrection launched without serious preparation had been amply proven—it left libertarians wide open to state repression and never spread to the populace around the country, a necessary escalation to successfully face down the state's military and repressive apparatus. Worst of all, that repression had dismantled the CNT's clandestine military machinery in the wake of the uprisings in January and December 1933. By the time October 1934 came around, when conditions for a revolutionary proletarian uprising were in place throughout the country, the anarcho-syndicalists were utterly spent and disorganized, weaponless, with their imprisoned militants numbering in the thousands.

---

3   Translator's Note: The reference here is to armed uprisings mounted by left organizations in many regions in October 1934 to preempt the accession to government of the CEDA party, which was regarded as "fascistic." The revolt was brutally suppressed. Interestingly, in the persecution of republicans and leftists, during and after the civil war, the Francoists tended to date the latter's subversion from October 1934 rather than 1936.

4   NCDC, "Resolution on the Establishment of Defense Committees" (11 October 1934).

They needed to bring intelligence and patience to their efforts, putting in the groundwork and arming themselves for the next opportunity, which was already taking shape with the recent crackdown on revolutionary actions. Hare-brained local short-termism, which paved the way to eruptions with no prospect of success, had to give way to intelligent and methodical planning for an effective and definitive insurrection.

The resolution's date, 11 October 1934, leaves no room for doubt about the influence that current historical events had on its drafting. Its clarity and analysis could scarcely have been more dazzling. However, more than seventy-five years later, the bourgeois historiography of liberals and Stalinists continues to peddle the self-serving line that the CNT used to explain away its failure to engage, aside from Asturias, in the insurrection of 1934, when in actual fact the true explanation was that it had been exhausted and weaponless: "May there be no repetition [in the future] of what happened recently, when, due to a widespread awareness that we were unprepared for a battle with only the slimmest chances of success, we had to stand idly by, racked with the pain of impotence and enduring intense criticism."[5]

Underpinning the NCDC's resolution of October 1934 was a determination to beef up the defense committees, overcoming their deficiencies, correcting mistakes, and above all, using the state's crackdown as a spur to carry on

---

5   Translator's Note: The CNT's line could be seen as "self-serving" because it was trying to counter the post-facto criticisms directed at it when the republicans in Catalonia tried to explain away their own failure by shifting blame to the CNT. The NCDC's focus was on the need to do away with "improvisation and hot-headed schemes" that actually hindered attempts to unleash a full-scale revolution. The CNT comment was backward-looking, the NCDC comment looked to the future. Explanation on the one hand v. remedial measures for the future on the other.

the struggle. The old tactics were dumped in favor of serious, systematic revolutionary preparedness:

In the absence of preparation, there is no revolution—and the more intense and shrewder the preparations, the more the revolution will prosper when the day comes. We must end the weakness for improvization and hot-headed schemes as the only [feasible] solutions in difficult times. That mistake, of trusting to the creative instincts of the masses, has cost us very dearly. One cannot just conjure up, as if through spontaneous generation, the necessary means to fight a war against a state that boasts experience, vast resources [in terms of armaments], and superior offensive and defensive capabilities.

The NCDC took the view that

The Defense Committees should be afforded the huge importance they hold for the CNT and libertarian revolution, a special emphasis being placed on constant monitoring of their structures, with an eye to moving beyond [improving upon] them, and funneling them the funds and morale and technical resources [aid] needed to render them more effective in promptly and directly achieving the desired goal.

The defense committees' clandestine militia had to be at all times subject to the orders and needs of the CNT: "The Defense Committees are to be an organizational form flanking the CNT." The resolution saw the defense committees as being made up of "volunteer militants," just as it saw participation in the specific organizations (i.e. the FAI and Libertarian Youth) as voluntary—without ever forgetting that the defense committees were the CNT's secret military organization, funded by the trade unions, which "will set a percentage of subscription dues to be handed over to them [the defense committees] on a monthly basis through the confederal committees of each locality or *comarca*."

The resolution even fixed a figure of "15% of weekly revenue," which it claimed was the standard in Aragon, Rioja, and Navarra, though this could be increased locally in response to urgent needs or circumstances. The bulk of the money was allocated to the different regional defense committees, which were to "distribute the gear acquired, not to the major contributing unions or localities, but wherever the need is greatest, in light of shortages or greater prospect of success."

With a very pragmatic and intelligent approach, the rationale was to act in accordance with the needs of the insurrection: "There will be places of strategic significance to the revolution which, because of protracted fighting, repression, or lack of libertarian milieu, will be in no position to contribute funding for equipment [armaments]. In order to remedy this deficit, they will deserve fellowship and support from our organizations, monitored by Regional Defense Committees."

The October 1934 NCDC resolution took the line that the grassroots groups cadre should be few in number, to facilitate their agility and clandestine operation, as well as to utilize each militant's character, expertise, and skills. Each group was to include a secretary, whose essential task was to liaise with other groups from the same barrio and to sponsor new groups. A second militant would make it his business to identify and register the names, addresses, ideological affiliations, personal details, habits, and danger of enemies within his group's allotted precinct. The reference to danger alluded to the profession or ideology of the enemy: "military, police, clergy, officials, bourgeois and marxist politicians, gunmen, fascists, etc., etc." A third militant was to study buildings and premises hostile to the labor movement and note their vulnerability and importance. The point being to draw up plans and compile figures for the human resources, items, and weapons found in "barracks, police stations, jails, churches and monasteries, political and employers' clubs, fortifications, etc." A fourth member of the group would look into locations of strategic and tactical note, that is, "bridges, underground passages, drains, sewers, houses with flat roofs, escape doors leading to different streets, fire escapes, or inner courtyards." The view was that a fifth member of the group should focus on public services: "lighting, water, garages, tram depots, the metro, transport routes, and their vulnerability to sabotage or seizure." A sixth would see to locating and assessing the vulnerability of places from which arms, money, and supplies might be procured for the revolution: "armories, private homes of weapon-owners, banks, loan offices, food and clothing warehouses, etc."

The reckoning was that six was the ideal number of militants to form a group or defense cadre, with the stipulation that, on occasion, an additional member might join them so as to cover matters "of the utmost importance." The resolution urged that, when it came to cadres, quality should take priority over quantity, and militants should be "discreet, active types." Confidentiality was everything.

So, in the wake of October 1934, the defense groups were characterized by small numbers (up to six militants, with very well-defined tasks). Dealings with other groups from the same district fell under the remit of the group secretary. These were intelligence-gathering and fighting groups that would play "the role of a righteous revolutionary vanguard" and "be a direct inspiration to the people." In other words, come the uprising, they had to be able to mobilize larger, secondary groups that would, in turn, mobilize the entire population.

The six-member defense group was the basic building block of this clandestine CNT military apparatus. It had a well-defined remit covering each barrio. In each barrio, an all-barrio defense committee was set up to coordinate all of the defense cadres, and a monthly report was forwarded to it by each group secretary. The secretary-cum-barrio delegate would prepare the summary for the District Committee, which would, in turn, forward it to the Local Defense Committee and "from there on to the Regional and National Committees."[6]

This organizational framework, suited to the larger cities, was simplified for villages, where the different groups would coordinate directly through the local committee. In the city of Barcelona, after 19 July 1936, every barrio set up its own supplies committee, coordinating with counterparts at district and citywide levels. At the root of these was the militant in each defense group whose mission was the provision of weapons and foodstuffs. These supplies committees, which lasted for several months, were interlinked with the Food Workers' Union, and set up numerous free food kitchens for militias and their families, as well as for the unemployed and needy.

The resolution also went into the detail about how and where "to establish defense groups or cadres, with personnel being drawn from the unions and distributed around the wards (barriadas) in industrial cities, allocating each a theatre of activity on a map of the city, a theatre from which they promise not to stray without express notification."

The detail and precision with which the defense committees were established are common knowledge. The resolution recommended that the group members be drawn

---

6 Translator Note: From the ground up, the ascending levels of group organization would have been barrio to barriada to locality (whole town/city) to province to region to national level. Some barrios might be quite small and depopulated depending on the built environment there, maybe accommodating just one defense group. These might be grouped with others into a barriada. Each ward committee would then liaise with and report to a local committee overseeing an entire town/city.

from the same trade union or profession "although this does not mean that they retain any ties to or dependency upon their union; they are at the exclusive disposal of the Defense Committees in the latter's fulfillment of their remit," because this "approach has the merit of making the militants banded together into defense committees the custodians of principle within the Union, as well as having them monitor the Union's performance internally and externally."

The NCDC resolution also outlined how the defense committees should be organized at the regional and national levels, incorporating labor sectors such as railwaymen, bus drivers, telephone and telegraph workers, postmen, and, ultimately, all whose occupations or organizations had a national scope—highlighting the importance of communications in any revolutionary uprising. Separate provision was made for infiltration work, propaganda, and recruitment of sympathizers within the barracks. After considering the need to discuss and continually hone insurrectionist tactics and plans through the defense committees at local, regional, and national levels—as well as endorsing the "working arrangement" (*trabazón*) with the FAI—the resolution closed with an appeal to CNT personnel to reflect upon the importance of consolidating, broadening, and improving upon an anonymous, secret CNT militia "confronting the police and military might of the state and the fascist or Marxist militias."

For the most part, the defense cadres were trade union cadres. From 19–20 July 1936 on, some of them set themselves up as *centurias* within the People's Militias and headed off immediately to tackle fascism on Aragonese soil. Thus, within various confederal columns, there are references to the metalworkers' *centuria*, the woodworkers' *centuria*, the construction workers' *centuria*, each made up of members from the same union.

The essential functions of the defense cadres were:

1. To procure, maintain, store, and train in the use of weapons. The defense committees' authority was rooted in being armed organizations. Their power was the power of the workers in arms.

2. Quartermaster functions, in the broadest sense, ranging from providing supplies to the populace and maintaining people's kitchens, through the establishment and upkeep of hospitals, schools, *ateneos*—and even, during the immediate aftermath of the people's victory, recruiting militias and provisioning the columns setting off for the front.[7]

Defense cadres had been around since shortly after the proclamation of the Republic and might be regarded as the armed self-defense action groups from the days of *pistolerismo* (1919–1923), now with an organizational overhaul and broader base.

In the 1930s, the unemployed were incorporated into the defense cadres on a rotational basis, in order to give them an income, pre-empt strike-breaking, and equip as many militants as possible with a knowledge of weapons. For those very reasons, and in order to prevent "professionalization," care was taken to ensure that their remuneration did not become permanent.[8] Throughout the years of the Republic, there were armed pickets and trade union action squads that protected demonstrations and strikes, or promoted local uprisings. On the other hand, the CNT's characteristic direct action prompted them to reject the Tri-partite (i.e.

---

7 Translator note: *Ateneos* or athenaeums were part of anarchism's cultural endeavors in Spain—a combination of clubhouse, reading-room, meeting-rooms, lecture hall, possibly hosting classes, amateur dramatics, and other "improving" pursuits for its self-educating clientele.

8 Chris Ealham, *Class, Culture and Conflict in Barcelona, 1898–1937* (London: Routledge, 2005). Also available as *Anarchism and the City: Revolution and Counter-Revolution in Barcelona, 1898–1937* (Oakland: AK Press, 2010).

union-state-employer) Arbitration Boards (*Jurados Mixtos*) and bureaucratic office negotiations: the violent activities of pickets were promoted as the only effective means of wresting better working conditions from an employer class that was running rampant.[9]

Implicit in the October 1934 NCDC resolution was an organizational and directional overhaul for the defense cadres that tacitly accepted the established criticisms of insurrectionist "gymnastics" levelled by Alexander Shapiro (1933) and the *treintistas* (1931).

---

9   Ibid.

2

The Local Revolutionary Preparedness Committee

In Catalonia, the practical implementation of this new structure for the defense committees was the subject of a working party resolution presented by the anarchist groups Indomables, Nervio, Nosotros, Tierra Libre, and Germen at the Plenum of the Barcelona Federation of Anarchist Groups, which met in January 1935. That resolution marked the foundation of a Local Revolutionary Preparedness Committee in Barcelona.[1]

The preamble to the report characterized the historical moment as "a time of immeasurable revolutionary prospects, primarily because of capitalism and the state's manifest inability to equitably solve pressing economic, social, and moral issues." It noted that the international policy since the end of the Great War had failed: "Upwards of fifteen years of ongoing work by economic leaders and as many experiments in various state-forms, including the so-called dictatorship of the proletariat, have not restored even minimal balance palatable to the broad masses, but have rather added to widespread unease and brought us to physical ruination and the brink of yet another war-mongering bloodbath." In the face of a truly bleak time in history—with fascism on the rise in Italy, Nazism in Germany, Stalinism in the Soviet Union,

---

1   Indomables, Nervio, Nosotros, Tierra Libre and Germen, "Resolution Presented to the Barcelona Local Federation of Anarchist Groups. Local Revolutionary Preparedness Committee" (Barcelona, January 1935).

an economic depression and massive, lingering unemployment in the United States and Europe—the report offered the hope of the revolutionary proletariat: "In the universal bankruptcy of ideas, parties, and systems, the revolutionary proletariat alone stands with its programme for overhauling the bases of economic and social reality, working arrangements, and solidarity." The resolution's optimistic authors saw Spain and the workers' movement as strong and capable enough to "wage definitive battle against the decrepit edifice of capitalist morality, economics, and politics."

Implicit in the authors' definition of the revolution was a searching critique of the childish policy (dropped in October 1934) of revolutionary gymnastics and improvization: "The social revolution should not be seen as an act of daring, like a Jacobin coup; it will be the consequence and outcome of an inevitable civil war of indeterminate length." In addition to this startlingly clear-sighted intuition of the civil war that would begin eighteen months later, there was an emphasis on the need to plan ahead by organizing the defense cadres along fresh lines: "If a modern coup d'etat requires great technical and insurrectionist preparation and resources, as well as people perfectly trained for the purpose, a civil war will, even more so, require a fighting machine that hasn't been cobbled together in the heat of the moment, but that is structured and articulated with as much planning and efficiency as possible."

It noted that there was plenty of manpower available, but equally that they lacked organization "for a sustained struggle against enemy forces." So what was needed was increased training. "The answer to this is the present Local Revolutionary Preparedness Committee that we are proposing." That committee would be made up of four people: two appointed by the Local CNT Federation and two by the Local Federation of Anarchist Groups. This four-man team would also set up an auxiliary commission. The chief task of this

Local Revolutionary Preparedness Committee was "to look into the means and methods of struggle, the tactics to be employed, and the linking of insurgent organizational forces." A clear distinction was made between established assault teams predating October 1934 and the new defense cadres. "The defense committees have hitherto been primarily organized assault teams; from now on they should be capable of grappling with the realities of modern struggle."

Revolutionary preparedness for a protracted civil war entailed fresh challenges not addressed by the tactics of the assault teams. "Given that it is not feasible to have advance access to stockpiles of the weaponry needed for a sustained struggle, the Preparedness Committee needs to look into how industries in specific strategic areas [...] can be converted to churn out war materials for the revolution." Here we see the source of the War Industries Commission formed on 7 August 1936 in Catalonia to conjure out of nothing a mighty war industry—thanks to the efforts of the workforce, and coordinated by the CNT's Eugenio Vallejo Isla, a metalworker; Manuel Martí Pallarés, from the Chemicals Union; and Mariano Martín Izquierdo. Even though the credit was later claimed by bourgeois politicians (like Josep Tarradellas) who had done their bit to make it a success, the venture "was entirely the doing of factory workers, technicians, and the accountable delegates that the CNT has placed in positions of leadership since the outbreak of the war."[2]

The CNT's regional committees were to be in charge of coordinating these Local Revolutionary Preparedness Committees. The latter could get together for special plenums to swap initiatives, news, and experiences. At the national level, meetings of regional delegates were also planned.

At no time was the revolutionary initiative to emanate from this Preparedness Committee: "It must always come

2 Memorandum on War Industry, Document No 4.

from the confederal and specific organizations, it being their business to determine the timing and take the reins of the movement." It would be up to the CNT unions and the anarchist groups to supply the funding, without "any compulsory overall levy being determined in advance." As to the "training of fighting cadres, in cities insurgent groups are to be raised on a ward-by-ward basis, as an unlimited number of nuclei, but those affinity groups eager to retain existing ties may also join the insurgent cadres, provided that they are subject to the oversight of the Preparedness Committee."

The NCDC's October 1934 resolution and the January 1935 resolution from the Barcelona anarchist groups stressed a new structure for the defense cadres, looking beyond the old view of them as mere assault teams and turning them into defense cadres with a strict remit covering revolutionary preparedness and grappling with matters of intelligence-gathering, armaments, tactics, and advance planning for a protracted civil war. What had been—prior to 1934—assault teams, were now cast in the role of intelligence-gathering combat cadres, cells of the future revolutionary army.

3

Differentiating between Defense Groups, Affinity Groups, and Action Groups

A distinction needs to be made between *defense* groups, *affinity* groups and *action* groups.

Since October 1934, the defense cadres had been the secret, anonymous militia of the CNT unions, handling everything from trade union defense to strike-picketing to attempted insurrections. They might be defined as the clandestine army of the revolution, entirely and seriously committed to matters of intelligence, armaments, training, strategy, and laying the groundwork for a workers' uprising. They were dependent upon the CNT, in the sense that the CNT unions funded them and the union militants supplied the personnel. This grassroots arrangement, made up of six-member groups, was in place, awaiting the mass incorporation of thousands of trade unionists, and also ready to accommodate secondary groups, such as affinity groups from the FAI, the Libertarian Youth, and the *ateneos*. But at no time were the defense committees FAI organizations, nor were they ever independent and autonomous: they were the armed organization of the CNT and wholly subject to decisions and initiatives emanating from the CNT's Regional (or National) Committee.

The CNT was more than just a trade union. In virtually every barrio in Barcelona there was a barrio committee that dealt with every aspect of a worker's social, cultural, and family life, creating a very well-defined and familiar space for struggle and solidarity that allowed for a natural relationship with neighbours, friends, and comrades, providing ideological training, information, and a springboard for activism.[1]

In the resolution he put to the May 1936 Zaragoza Congress on the matter of Libertarian Communism, Juan García Oliver set out his view of the revolutionary army: "We advocated the creation of a revolutionary army, which I believed it should be regarded as such from then on. Turning what we had done in Barcelona with the Confederal Defense Cadres into a tactic applicable throughout the length and breadth of Spain. That was more or less it."[2]

Garcia Oliver's stance on the revolutionary army ran into serious opposition within the FAI, which accused him of throwing his anarchist and anti-militarist principles overboard: "As I was making some remarks [at the Zaragoza Congress] on a number of matters, including the matter of the army, Cipriano Mera (a very fine comrade from the Construction Union in Madrid) called out: 'Maybe comrade García Oliver will tell us what color braid he would like!' Paradoxically, Cipriano Mera was the first to embrace militarization later and accept his Army braid."[3]

Affinity groups were the building blocks of the FAI's organizational structure. Essentially, these were groups of friends and/or militants, bound by ideological affinity, who took on tasks, principles, and tactics shared by the group—but which might conflict with those of other affinity groups. Especially notable, for its importance, was a clash between

---

1   Carles Sanz, *La CNT en pie. Fundación y consolidación anarco-sindicalista. 1910–1931* (Barcelona-Sabadell: Anomia, 2010), 10.

2   Freddy Gómez, "Interview with Juan García Oliver," recorded on 29-6-1977 in Paris (France). Pamphlet (in Spanish). Madrid: Fundación Salvador Seguí, 1990, 20. Available in English as Juan García Oliver, *My Revolutionary Life* (London: Kate Sharpley Library, 2008).

3   Ibid.

the Nosotros group and an anti-Nosotros bloc made up of a number of groups backing the Nervio group. The Iberian Anarchist Federation (FAI) was merely a common platform or coordinating body for affinity groups that were frequently at odds with its Peninsular or Regional Committee. In July 1937, the FAI turned itself into an anti-fascist party when an organizational overhaul replaced (or displaced) the affinity group as the building block of the FAI with a new, territorially-based organization which, in the case of Barcelona, shrank the local FAI to a mere 23 militants. The FAI hardly ever voted; and care was taken to ensure that plenum resolutions were adopted unanimously, a consensus being worked out among different positions in a text everybody could sign, or that awaited everyone's endorsement.[4]

The affinity group was transient, self-funding, decentralized, autonomous, and federalist. Clandestine conditions and natural inclination ensured that such groups were formed in order to carry out specific tasks, an ephemeral existence, after which they would dissolve. Some individuals might well meet up again in other affinity groups organized to carry out different specific tasks. This volatility and persistent clandestinity were required adaptations to unrelenting police repression, and mirrored anarchists' innate prejudice against any organizational structure—something that makes writing their history difficult. Even though there were occasionally affinity groups with longer life-spans, they were the minority. Normally, an affinity group was made up of a minimum of four and a maximum of around twenty comrades, at which point, if they exceeded twenty, they would split to form two separate groups. This was the case, say, with the Faros groups in the 1920s. The extreme autonomy enjoyed by affinity groups made them very independent of

---

4   José Peirats *De mi paso por la vida. Memorias* (Barcelona: Flor del Viento, 2009), 257.

the FAI. The Nosotros group, for instance, which used to address rallies as FAI spokesmen, did not formally join the organization until very late, towards the end of 1933 (according to some) or early 1934 (according to others). Affinity groups were also forever short of funds and material resources. Their aims were very broad and heterogeneous, covering a very wide spectrum of cultural, combinationist, recreational, or mutual aid interests ranging from the publication and distribution of scientific and literary materials, through drama, choirs, publications, debates, lectures, excursions, cooperatives, and so on—right up to maintaining an *ateneo* or a rationalist school.

Other affinity groups targeted trade unions (boosting the anarchist presence within them) or concentrated on prisoner solidarity work, or the funding of newspapers and *ateneos*. Affinity groups might emerge from trade unions, from the Libertarian Youth, or from the *ateneos*. Their main desire was to practice alternative ethical and social values in the here and now.

During the civil war, the affinity groups achieved their greatest presence and impact at meetings of Local Federations (especially in Barcelona), where they forcefully articulated their criticisms of and disagreements with the higher committees; but at the regional and national levels, it was these committees that ruled the roost. The organizational overhaul undergone by the FAI in July 1937 meant the bureaucratic marginalization of the affinity groups, which, although formally surviving, were no longer in a position to argue their cases at local plenums. This left them isolated and ineffectual. By then, the FAI was just another anti-fascist party, organized along territorial lines on the basis of individual members. The important results of this organizational re-structuring of the FAI was the enhancement of its propaganda machine, training people capable of holding down administrative and government positions, and (though this was never made explicit) reining in and overruling revolutionary affinity groups that were defiant and critical of the higher committees.

Back in the days of *pistolerismo* (1919–1923) action groups had been raised as self-defense teams from among trade unionists and from the ranks of the organization, since—in the face of brutal state terrorism, the militarization of the Somatén, and Sindicato Libre gunmen financed by the Catalan employers—their sole duty was to ensure the very survival of CNT militants and prevent the eradication of the CNT through the murder of some of its members and the resultant mass desertion of others.[5]

Following the murders of Salvador Seguí and Peronas (10 March 1923) an executive committee made up of Juan Peiró, Ángel Pestaña, Camilo Piñón and Narciso Marco[6] gave the go-ahead for forming action groups to retaliate against state- and employer-led terrorism by trying to kill Martínez Anido and the Carlist pretender Don Jaime.[7] Those targets were not killed, but Cardinal Soldevila was (4 June 1923), as was former governor of Bilbao, Regueral—and there were also clashes with gunmen from the Sindicato Libre and the Carlist requetés.

---

5   Translator's note: Dating back centuries in one form or another in Catalonia, the Somatén was an armed militia that tended to be of a conservative, authoritarian outlook, its members used as auxiliaries by the powers that be.

6   Juan García Oliver, *El Eco de los pasos* (Paris: Ruedo Ibérico, 1978), 629–633. See also Freddy Gómez, "Interview with Juan Garcia Oliver," 9. Come August 1931, all four members of that executive committee signed the *Manifesto of the Thirty* (Treinta), i.e. became *treintistas*.

7   CNT personnel had always been against personal attacks because historical experience had shown that they were futile. But in 1923, they decided to resort to this given how serious the situation was, but as an exception, in a controlled manner and on a temporary basis.

A secret National Plenum of Regionals, held in the summer of 1923 in Valencia, sounded the alarm about an imminent military coup d'etat and gave the go-ahead for preparations to confront the coup-makers, through hold-ups to raise funds to buy weapons and cast hand grenades. But by then it was too late to head off Primo de Rivera's coup d'état and the CNT was plunged into another long period of underground organizing and harassment, with its militants jailed and/or forced into exile.

The more radical trade unionists, or those workers who had been to the fore in some strike, were targeted by the bosses through the *pacto del hambre* (starve-'em-out) stratagem and, once sacked were never to be re-hired by any firm, thereby swelling the ranks of the action groups dedicated to carrying out hold-ups.

In the 1930s, these action groups were emphatically rejected by certain factions (the *treintistas*) for bringing the CNT into disrepute and confusing revolutionary activity with armed criminality; but, above all, because the years of *pistolerismo* had, all told, ended with the workers on the losing side. The state and the employers irrationally criminalized the action groups, not to mention the Sindicatos Únicos, the *ateneos*, and the affinity groups. Each Sindicato Único set up its own action groups as essential agents of direct action against mistreatment by foremen and employers,[8] against breaches of agreements, to man pickets, self-defense, and even to replace or shorten strikes where strike funds were frequently non-existent.

The state was a lot weaker in the 1930s than it is today: there was no social assistance, no unemployment pay, no sickness benefit, or old age pensions. Banks had fewer security measures and police resources and training were very poor.

8　And, on occasion, sexual abuse, especially in the textile industry where the workforce was overwhelmingly female.

Broad swathes of the population lived in utter poverty, divorced from any economic activity. Within this impoverished economy, street-trading loomed large, not just because it allowed a large body of street-hawkers to survive through popular solidarity but also because it kept the price of certain basic necessities in the working-class barrios low. Above all, it needs to be underlined that throughout the years of the Republic there was massive and uninterrupted unemployment—and that includes the civil war period. Strikers' demands, as well as vocal protests or direct expropriation of foodstuffs by the unemployed, invoking their "right to live," were always characterized as criminal by the police and the bourgeois press. So were the action groups. But according to popular ethics, the distinction between legality and illegality was meaningless in a wretched and forlorn world of rampant exploitation, where it was a struggle simply to eke out a bare existence.

The state's and employers' ferocious oppression recognized no distinctions between trade unionists, the unemployed, the needy, and gunmen: the courts and the police persecuted and made outlaws of them all equally. The difference between a gang carrying out expropriations to help prisoners or fund newspapers and an action group that was (literally) fed and sustained by the proceeds, was rooted exclusively in the final destination of the proceeds. Besides, life does not usually conform to the black or white of some abstract theoretical definition, and the actual spectrum of shades of grey can be infinite. Some action groups lived on the knife's edge between class struggle against the state, the bosses, and bourgeois society, on one side, and the millenarian or antisocial rebellion of the marginal, bohemian, and wretched on the other.

We should never lose sight of the priority the libertarian movement placed on a cultural outlook and efficient educational activity that shaped a lasting and extensive complex of *ateneos*, cooperatives, and rationalist schools—and cultural centers involving all these groups—which might also, temporarily and in exceptional circumstances, serve as action groups.[9] Thanks to a CNT resolution, during the days of *pistolerismo* (1920–1923), the average CNT militant owned a pistol (or knew how and where get one readily), since it was essential for self-defense purposes, and an effective way to reduce the numbers of militants murdered. Later, in the 1930s, a pistol gave its bearer a cachet of authority, commitment, and status among some of the lower classes who built and lived within an ethic and a society very different from that of bourgeois society at that time.

Political violence from the workers' movement was the product of the state terrorism that was firmly ensconced in institutions and recruited, in parallel with the police, from the ranks of the Sindicato Libre to form an organization of gunmen in the hire of the employers, tolerated and shielded by the civil governors.

Against this backdrop, reformist or social democratic organizations found it impossible to put down roots in Catalonia. The CNT's radicalism was a further by-product of state and employer terrorism. Seguí's murder in 1923 put paid to any inclination the CNT may have had to stick to pure trade unionism and compromise. In the 1930s, republicanism ran aground—due to troglodyte opposition from right-wingers and the Church—in its efforts to introduce the slightest meaningful reform, and because of its inability to resolve, let alone alleviate, the issue of mass unemployment that drove people looking for little more than a crust of bread to marginality, law-breaking, and insurrection. People's only weapon was their desperation.

Once the responsibility for Public Order had devolved to the Generalidad government, between late 1933 and January

---

9   There is a splendid scholarly study of such labor cooperativism in Marc Dalmau and Iván Miró, *Les cooperatives obreres de Sants. Authogestió proletária en un barri de Barcelona (1870– 1939)* (Barcelona: La Ciutat Invisible, 2010).

1934, the pairing of Josep Dencàs and Badía ousted more moderate nationalists from the Interior Department. Dencàs (operating out of the Interior Department) and Miquel Badía (from the Police Chief's office) enforced a brazenly fascist and racist policy of repression on the CNT.[10] They meddled systematically and decisively in strikes in an effort to break them, methodically manhandled and tortured anarchist prisoners in police headquarters, cracked down on the many hold-ups carried out by the action groups, and maliciously targeted the unemployed under "vagrancy" laws. At the same time, they breathed new life into the Somatén and sponsored the organization and arming of the *escamots* (the Catalanist militia) as anti-CNT paramilitary organizations. The events of 6 October 1934 and the resultant dissolution of the Generalidad government by the central government ended a dynamic that would most likely have resulted in a confrontation akin to the years of *pistolerismo*.

In May 1935, a plenum of anarchist groups condemned the action groups carrying out hold-ups, whether they were raising funds for the organization or for the survival of the robbers themselves, employed or not. Durruti argued that individual expropriation had had its day since collective expropriation—the revolution—was now imminent.[11]

"Investigative" journalists[12] fed the bourgeois, nationalist, racist denunciation of these action groups as mere

---

10 Translator's note: Dencàs and Badía were prominent members of the separatist wing of Catalanism, Estat Catala. These ultra-nationalists were admirers of Mussolini and distinguished themselves by their repression and obstruction of the CNT. When the October 1934 revolt in Catalonia failed, Dencàs made an undignified exit to Italy. Miquel Badía was assassinated (along with his brother) by anarchists in 1936, prior to the Army revolt.

11 Abel Paz, *Durruti, El proletariado en armas* (Barcelona: Bruguera, 1978), 310–315.

12 One thinks of Carles Sentis (now a centenarian), Josep María Planes, and "Tisner."

"Murcians" and "thugs," descriptions deliberately and contemptuously extended to the entire anarcho-syndicalist movement in order to discredit the CNT. There was a very real and worrisome danger of this wave of "private" hold-ups interfering with the people's preparedness for revolution.

The foregoing differentiation and theoretical schematization of defense groups, affinity groups, and action groups will do as a snapshot. But reality is more like a movie, complicated and subject to variation: so we need to remember that a snapshot cannot explain the shift from one category to the next, through the evolution of organizations and historical changes, and depending on whether groups were operating clandestinely, cashing in on a period when the CNT enjoyed legal status, or facing new prospects that opened up thanks to the "revolutionary gains" in July 1936.

This is what happened, say, to the San Martin Revolutionary Committee between 1936 and 1937. It was a somewhat special barrio committee to begin with, in that it seemed more radical than the rest, and its premises at No 7 Rambla Volart, were used by defense committees as a special holding and interrogation center. Following a serious incident created by Antonio Conesa in a comarcal hospital (resulting in his being arrested and standing trial), the core group driving the San Martin Revolutionary Committee's defense committee decided to reconstitute itself as an affinity group, the "El Nuevo Porvenir" affinity group, affiliated to the FAI. This proved to be an exceptional historical instance of an action group that had been the driving force behind a defense committee prior to July 1936 and then, after 19 July 1936, the engine driving a ward revolutionary committee, only to reconstitute itself as an affinity group and carry on with its activities.[13]

---

13 Brief on the criminal case against Antonio Conesa Martínez, José Conesa Martínez, and Antonio Ordaz Lázaro.

4

The Barcelona FAI Critiques the Nosotros Group's Notions of "Army" and "Power" (1936)

During the first half of 1936, when it was clear that military preparations for a merciless coup d'état were under way, the Nosotros group clashed with the rest of the FAI groups in Catalonia in heated arguments over two fundamental concepts. Those two concepts were the "seizure of power" and the "revolutionary army." The Nosotros group's pragmatism (more concerned with insurrectionary technique than any taboos) collided head on with *faísta* ideological prejudices, that is, the FAI's repudiation of what they called "anarchist dictatorship" and their deeply ingrained anti-militarism, which left everything up to the creative spontaneity of the workers.

The harsh attack on the "anarcho-bolshevik practices" of the Nosotros group was widely covered in *Más Lejos*, a magazine run by Eusebio C. Carbó, with Jaime Balius and Mariano Viñuales on the editorial team. *Más Lejos* published responses to a survey it had featured in its first issue, in April 1936, which boiled down to two questions about electoral abstentionism and a third question relating to the seizure of power: "May anarchists, under any circumstance, and SETTING ALL SCRUPLES TO ONE SIDE, prepare to take power, in whatever form, as a means of speeding their progress towards the achievement of Anarchy?"

Responses to the survey were received from Camilo Berneri, Pierrot, Paul Reclus, Isaac Puente, Amparo Poch,

"Nobruzán," Sébastien Faure, Federica Montseny, Evaristo Viñuales, Voline, Pierre Besnard, Fontaura, José Peirats, Armando Borghi, Ricardo Mestres, Juan Gallego, Melchor Rodríguez, Fernando Planche, José Pros, A. Shapiro, M. Nettlau, and Emma Goldman. The review's issue No. 9, its last, appeared on 2 July 1936. Virtually every response emphatically rejected the seizure of power, a notion that was considered Marxist and authoritarian, alien to anarchism. A few responses made more or less veiled criticisms of the Nosotros group's anarcho-bolsheviks, deeming the group to be outside of the anarchist movement. But none of the responses had any practical alternative to offer to this refusal to take power. It looked as if anarchist theory and anarchist practice had parted company, and this with a military coup on the horizon.

The June 1936 Anarchist Plenum

At the Plenum of Barcelona Anarchist Groups, held in June 1936, item five on the agenda was "The Anarchist Interpretation of Revolution," and the proceedings involved delegates from the groups Nosotros (García Oliver, Durruti and Francisco Ascaso), Nervio, Montaña, Indomables, Germen, Germinal, Seis Dedos, A, Justicia, Voluntad, and Solidarios, as well as delegates from the Local Federation and Peninsular Committee.[1]

The Peninsular Committee and Local Federation proposed an alteration to the agenda and that item five—which pitted the various groups attending against the Nosotros group—not be debated.

According to the Nervio group, the proceedings should concentrate, not so much on "basic issues," on which "we

---

1   Minutes of the Local Plenum of Barcelona Anarchist Groups held on the [illegible] of June 1936.

are all agreed," but upon "the terminology of statements made by García Oliver on a number of occasions."[2]

The Nosotros group believed "that it was up to those groups that have complaints about certain terms, positions, or concepts" to raise existing issues or problems "whereupon the Nosotros group will clear up whatever needs clearing up."

The A group cautioned "that we anarchists [already] see eye to eye on lots of basic points and have for years."[3] One of the most fundamental of those points was "destruction of anything signifying power, and that any group or comrade who thinks the concept has any usefulness cannot legitimately describe themselves as anarchist." The A group was accusing García Oliver of using the notion of power in a positive sense, thereby placing himself outside the borders of anarchism.

The Germen group drew a distinction between the various internal views of power and other matters within a specific organization and the sloppy use of such concepts in public discourse. Whereas the former was acceptable, the latter was not.

The Seis Dedos group, represented by E., made a very long speech, delving into reflections on "insurgencies and revolutionary upheavals in a number of countries and the genesis and development of same."[4] He cited the uprising in Bavaria involving "several anarchist comrades who tried to bring decisive influence to bear, from positions of power at

---

2   Nervio group: Santillán, Pedro Herrera, Jacobo Maguid, Germinal de Sosa, Adolfo Verde, Ildefonso Gonzalez, Jose Mari, Juan Rua, Vicente Tarin, Horacio Badaracco, and Simon Radowitzsky.

3   "A" group: Jacinto Toryho, Jacobo Prince, Abelardo Iglesias Saavedra, Federico Sabate, Miguel Tardaguila, Palmiro Aranda, Francisco Lopez, Juan Oso, and Jose Jimenez Sanchez.

4   Seis Dedos group: Manuel Escorza Del Val, Liberato Minue, Abelino Estrada, Jose Irizalde and Manuel Gallego. "E" refers to Escorza.

that." He stressed a number of passages from Bakunin that considered "the formation of a government and defending the revolution by means of decrees, if need be, but always under the supervision of the people." He pointed out that anarchists had been murdered by the Social Democrat Noske. He seemed to be coming to García Oliver's defense when he closed by saying that "The task of the daring and decisive minority is not to lead this upheaval but to stamp a properly anarchist brand upon it."

Speaking for the Nosotros group, García Oliver stated that "he had always operated within the bounds of anarchist discipline" because "at another Plenum of the Local Federation of Anarchist Groups he had explained and clarified his viewpoint and no [reproachful] motions were passed regarding his interpretation of these concepts."

However, he did concede that he had been asked by *Tierra y Libertad* to step back from propaganda activities with that paper, something that he regarded as serious in terms of "the arrogance behind such self-importance and, quite possibly, the nasty whiff of authority to boot."

With some solemnity, García Oliver declared "that on [some] occasions I have taken heed and even been measured in my language and the steps I have taken, but it looks as if the aim here is to get me to withdraw." He was not about to heed that demand from any quarter other than the Plenum itself, in which case he would abide by "such accords and not cause a split," nor try to weaken "the specific Organization."

García Oliver then launched into a full exposition of the notion of Libertarian Communism, stating that he had a hand in drafting the motion that, of all the motions put to the CNT congress last May and used in the drafting of the final motion on what Libertarian Communism meant, had the most anarchist content.

He spelled out "his ideas about seizing power." Step one would be to "discover how far we might go" and to decide "if we are setting our sights on infinity." That is, deciding whether "our aim is merely to act as fire-setters," or, "if, once the revolution breaks out and things expand widely enough to stretch to the furtherest horizon," we can, thanks to some "effective preparation," act as "channelers of that upheaval," competing with "other factions that also strive to harness this spreading upheaval."

He asserted that "The revolution does not exist to satisfy some aesthetic appetite but to resolve a series of outstanding social questions."

He explained that "though the upheaval might be triggered by force of arms, it must not be [...] armed men who grant new freedoms and new rights: that must be done by a national congress," and, until that congress meets, "armed force must be in anarchists' hands, lest it fall into the clutches of others."

García Oliver went so far as to speculate that, if a national congress fell short of achieving Libertarian Communism, "it would be our duty to cast that congress aside as unrevolutionary; we, as anarchists, must promote our revolution, on the understanding that, as anarchists, we cannot be mere onlookers but are supporters of Permanent Revolution."

Another comrade (Durruti? Ascaso?) from the Nosotros group asked whether the Plenum "is serious about making the Revolution"? A heated argument erupted and, after a while, an attempt was made to steer the debate back to the terms posed in the agenda.

Another comrade (Durruti? Ascaso?) from the Nosotros group dwelt upon "the interpretation of the Revolution" and said "that they had to be men. The time had come for action and daring and thus we cannot in any sense think along outmoded lines." He stipulated to the Plenum that "we cannot tolerate our efforts serving the purposes of forces other than our own." After various remarks about past events, he concluded "that our revolution must be anarchist if it is going

41

to be our revolution." He declared that "so far there has not been the slightest departure from principle. Quite the opposite. What we are out to do is harness our forces so that the Revolution may succeed."

Someone from A group stated that they had "never intended to finger any particular comrade." He argued that "The anarchist revolution cannot be anything other than the realization of the conditions for free co-existence" and rejected dictatorship of any sort: "At no time can we set about establishing any coercive authority. He agreed only to defensive action "in the event that other forces try to crush us." He quoted Malatesta to reaffirm his anti-authoritarian and anti-Nosotros stance: "We can never [...] achieve freedom by imposing it, and, therefore, we stand opposed to the statement by the member of Nosotros."

The Justicia group wanted to comment on a few things the Nosotros group had said "about measuring its language or holding discussions around cafe tables" and retorted that his own group "never met around a cafe table." He pointed out that "occupying public buildings symbolic of power is not the same as destroying them." He indicated that he was "against the formation of an Army [of the proletariat]," maintaining that "guerrilla teams or Defense Groups would be the Revolution's [best] defense." He declared that freedom could not be imposed through force, but only through persuasion.

The A group piped up to sarcastically say that "the Nosotros comrades deserve a more straightforward answer," especially regarding their thoughts about "taking power." They continued that comrades expressing qualms "about anarchist principles" were no longer comrades—and those who supported the seizure of power were no longer anarchists.

The Voluntad group indicated that it agreed with the A group but that there had to be an acknowledgment of "the need for imposition, since the revolution will not happen without it."

The Seis Dedos group, after confessing its own lack of experience, rambled on about the stances and ideas of the others, but could not quite decide on any of them. After this contribution, the chair asked that opinions be spelled out rather than "behaving as if we were in a cafe."

The Los Indomables group recognized "the abilities of the comrades whose views are under discussion here today." It took the line that "anarchists should not allow the revolution to be wrested from them." It acknowledged Durruti's claim that, once the revolution had broken out and there was no option but "to kill or be killed," it was reasonable to impose one's will "not to abandon anarchy but in order to reaffirm it." It completely rejected García Oliver's stance on power because "it was the very negation of anarchism." Likewise, it denied that there could be any common ground or collaboration between power, the army, and the people.

Francisco Ascaso expressed "his surprise at what he had heard tonight" and wondered "if this was the FAI of days gone by." He rebutted the criticisms leveled at the Nosotros group over the notions of "power" and "army," stressing the "membership's sense of responsibility" and the need for organization. The recording secretary was very careless and imprecise and reading the record does not allow us to quite gauge the position defended by Ascaso, who talked about Libertarian Communism, the coup d'état, and the need to reject any *ad hominem* arguments. He rejected any pressure from the press to get him to step down and argued that a coup d'état would "deny the people its chance to make the revolution." He talked about guerrilla warfare, about Russia and Durruti. And he concluded that the FAI was not whole-heartedly in favor of a revolution, "which is precisely why we need to come to some agreement."

The chair commented that "the García Olivers must end today" and that "we cannot say an act of contradiction [although maybe he said, or intended to say, *of contrition*]."

Los Solidarios called for "cafes to be closed down." The Germen group asked that a vote be put back or that "for unity's sake" the motion be tightened up. The Germinal group eventually plumped for drafting a resolution for the Plenum, not with an eye to getting the FAI to mend its ways, but so that "everything that [Garcia Oliver] has been saying about army and power should be repudiated."

According to García Oliver, the organization of the defense cadres, coordinated through *barrio* defense committees across the city of Barcelona, was the model to extend to the whole of Spain—with this structure being coordinated at regional and national level to form a revolutionary army of the proletariat. That army had to be complemented by setting up 100-person guerrilla units. Many militants opposed García Oliver's ideas, trusting more to the workers' spontaneity than to disciplined revolutionary organization. The anti-militarist, indeed pacifist,[5] beliefs of many affinity groups ensured that the Nosotros group's proposals (especially García Oliver's) were rejected almost unanimously.

So, the rejection of the proposal he would make on 21 July 1936, that they take power and "go for broke" after crushing the military uprising, which the vast majority attending the Plenum heard as a plea for an "anarchist dictatorship," had its precedent in this plenary held in June 1936, just a few days before 19 July 1936!

5   Dolors Marin, *Anarquistas. Un Siglo de movimiento libertario en España* (Barcelona: Ariel, 2010), 258–266.

5

The Worker Uprising of 19–20 July 1936: The Defense Committees See Off the Army

On the evening of 17 July 1936, the army rose in revolt in Melilla. The prime minister, Casares Quiroga, asked by reporters for his thoughts on the revolt replied with a wisecrack: "They've risen? Fine. Me? I'm off to bed." By 18 July 1936, the army mutiny had spread to the whole of Morocco, the Canaries, and Seville.

The Barcelona army garrison numbered some six thousand men, facing nearly two thousand Assault Guards and two hundred *Mossos d'Esquadra*.[1] The Civil Guard—and nobody knew for sure which side of the fence it would come down on—numbered about three thousand. The CNT-FAI could call upon about twenty thousand militants organized in ward defense committees and ready to take up arms. The CNT team sent to liaise with the Generalidad and loyalist servicemen committed to stop the coup-makers in their tracks, if it could have arms for just one thousand of its militants. But their negotiations with Escofet, the

---

1   Translator's note: The Assault Guards were a paramilitary police corps created by the Second Spanish Republic. Essentially dedicated to "public order" matters, the corps quickly found itself in confrontation with subversives and earned itself a foul reputation among those challenging the Second Republic from the left. The *Mossos d'Esquadra* were a small, Catalan, and largely Catalanist corps under the control of the Generalidad government of Catalonia.

superintendent of Public Order, and España, the Interior minister, proved fruitless. On the night of 17 July, the CNT's Juan Yagüe, secretary of the marine transport union, organized a raid on the armouries of some ships anchored in the port, coming away with about 150 rifles. To these were added, on 18 July, whatever had been recovered from armouries, watchmen, and sentries around the city. This tiny arsenal, stashed at the Transport Union HQ in the Ramblas, triggered a confrontation with the Public Order Department that insisted upon its being handed over. There was a danger of armed confrontation with the Assault Guard, and the CNT's own militants went so far as to threaten Durruti and García Oliver, who they deemed too conciliatory. The situation was resolved when a few useless old rifles were handed over to Guarner, Escofet's right-hand man, and a falling out between republicans and anarchists on the very eve of the army coup was averted.

From 3:00 AM on 19 July on, a swelling crowd pressed the Interior Department in the Plaza Palacio for weapons. There were no weapons for the people, because the Generalidad government feared a workers' revolution more than the army's revolt against the Republic. From the balcony of the Interior Department, Juan García Oliver urged CNT militants to get in touch with the defense committees in their respective wards or to march on the San Andrés barracks and wait for the first opportunity to seize the weapons stored there. Later, when the news broke of the revolt in Barcelona, people began fraternizing with Assault Guards after the latter, armed with both rifles and pistols, handed their handguns over to the civilians clamoring for them. At the same time Air Force lieutenant Servando Meana,[2] a CNT sympathizer who ferried news between El

---

2   Information lifted from the "Handwritten statement of Air Force Captain Servando Meana Miranda."

Prat airport and José María España, took it upon himself to give the anarcho-syndicalists the weapons stored at the Palacio de Gobernación, without consulting his superiors.[3] CNT personnel from the Chemical Workers' Union began manufacturing hand grenades.

At 4:15 AM on 19 July 1936, troops from the El Bruch barracks in Pedralbes took to the streets, making their way down Avenida 14 de Abril (known these days as the Diagonal) toward the city center. Workers posted near the various barracks were under orders to raise the alarm, but not to engage the soldiers until they had put some distance between themselves and the barracks. The Confederal Defense Committee was counting on it being easier to confront the troops in the streets than dug into their barracks.

Once the workers' insurrection against the army mutiny was under way, the Jupiter soccer ground on Calle Lope de Vega was used as a mustering point on account of its proximity to the homes of most of the anarchists from the Nosotros group and the huge CNT membership in the area. The Pueblo Nuevo Defense Committee had commandeered two lorries from the nearby textile plant and these were parked alongside the Jupiter pitch, the anarchists most likely using them as a clandestine arsenal. Gregorio Jover lived at No 276 Calle de Pujades. Throughout the night of 18–19 July, his quarters were turned into a meeting place for the members of the Nosotros group as they waited for word that the rebels had taken to the streets. With Jover were Juan García Oliver (who lived very near by at No 72 Calle Espronceda, almost at the corner of the Calle Llull), Buenaventura Durruti (who lived barely a kilometer away in the El Clot district), Antonio Ortiz (born in the La Plata barrio

---

3   Abad de Santillán delivered a hundred handguns to the Construction Union. See Diego Abad de Santillán, *Por que perdimos la guerra* (Esplugues del Llobregat: Plaza y Janes, 1977), 76.

in Pueblo Nuevo, at the intersection of Calle Independencia and Calle Wad Ras—known these days as Calle Badajoz and Calle Doctor Trueta), Francisco Ascaso (who also lived quite close by in the Calle San Juan de Malta), Ricardo Sanz (another Pueblo Nuevo resident), Aurelio Fernández and José Pérez Ibáñez aka "el Valencia." Jover's place overlooked the wooden walls of the Jupiter ground and those two lorries. At 5:00 AM, a runner arrived with news that the troops were starting to venture out of their barracks. Calle Lope de Vega and Calles Espronceda, Llull, and Pujades, surrounding the Jupiter ground, were filled with armed CNT personnel. About twenty of the most battle-hardened, tested in a thousand street fights, climbed onto the lorries. Antonio Ortiz and Ricardo Sanz mounted a machine gun on the flat bed of the lorry that moved out first. Sirens from the textile plants in Pueblo Nuevo wailed a summons to general strike and revolutionary uprising, spreading to other districts and to the ships anchored in the port. This was the pre-arranged signal for the fighting to start. This time the alarm sounded by the sirens literally meant taking up arms—"al arma"—to defend oneself against the enemy. With their red and black banners unfurled, the two lorries set off down the Calle Pujades for the Rambla de Pueblo Nuevo, with a cortege of armed men singing "Hijos del Pueblo" and "A las barricadas," egged on by residents crowding their balconies. They headed for Calle de Pedro IV, from there to the Construction Union headquarters in Calle Mercaders, and then to the Metalworkers' and Transport Union's premises on the Ramblas. Never had the lyrics of those anthems sounded so meaningful: "Though pain and death may await us, duty urges us on against the enemy. Freedom, our most prized possession, must be defended with faith and courage" and "In battle, the fascist hyena will founder on our bodies. And the entire people, along with the anarchists, will ensure that freedom triumphs."

From one of the two lorries stationed in the Plaza del Teatro, the Nosotros group, in revolutionary defense group-mode, oversaw the workers' response to the army revolt in Barcelona. Its control of the Ramblas kept the soldiers from the Plaza de Cataluña and the Atarazanas barracks—Captaincy General building from joining forces, while allowing swift movement through the secondary streets and back alleys of Chinatown and La Ribera to support the fighters in Brecha de San Pablo or on Avenida Icaria. Troops leaving their barracks on the outskirts had to be prevented from reaching the city center and linking up with the Captaincy—Atarazanas barracks, or seizing nerve centers like telephone, telegraph, or post offices, or radio stations.

The close personal relations between members of the Nosotros groups and a number of republican officers—especially in the Atarazanas barracks and among the Air Force personnel in El Prat—proved crucial on 19 July, with a significant arsenal at the Atarazanas barracks being handed over along with weapons stored at the Interior Ministry, as well as the ongoing aerial bombing of barracks under rebel control.[4] Collaboration between the CNT and the Air Force had already materialized several days prior to the military uprising in the shape of useful reconnaissance flights made over Barcelona by several members of the Nosotros group in planes piloted by officers Ponce de León and Meana—with the knowledge of the Air Force commander in El Prat, Díaz Sandino.[5]

There was precious assistance from gunnery sergeants Valeriano Gordo and Martín Terrer from the Atarazanas barracks, who had opened the gates to Calle de Santa Madrona, which allowed the entry of the armed anarchist groups and the arrest of virtually the entire officer corps, who were

---

4   Juan Garcia Oliver, "Ce que fut le 19 de juillet," *Le Libertaire* (18 August 1938).

5   Ricardo Sanz, "Francisco Ascaso Morio," type-written text.

marched out through the very same gates.[6] However, bursts of machine-gun fire from the nearby Dependencias Militares buildings gave Lieutenant Colubí an opportunity to escape and assume command of the resistance. The bolted gates of the extensive yards between the old, medieval Atarazanas building and the (since demolished) Training School building facing directly on to the Ramblas, where the Artillery Brigade had its offices and some officers their quarters, made the job allocated to the soldiers dug in there, of fending off the attackers, that much easier. The rebels regained control of the barracks, but the CNT had captured four machine-guns, some two hundred rifles, and several cases of ammunition. The crossfire between the Dependencias buildings and that part of the Atarazanas barracks overlooking the Rambla de Santa Mónica, plus machine guns set up at the foot of the Columbus monument, rendered them unassailable. Given that militants from the Metalworkers' and Transport Unions had struck out for Barceloneta, the anarcho-syndicalist forces left behind in the Plaza del Teatro decided to postpone the attack and moved on to the Brecha de San Pablo with weapons seized from the Atarazanas, leaving the area beyond the Ramblas (where the Dependencias Militares and Atarazanas Training School were) besieged by a group under Durruti's command, with artillery manned by Sergeant Gordo.

At around 4:15 AM, three squadrons from the Montesa Cavalry Regiment slipped out on foot from the barracks in Calle Tarragona. After an twenty-minute gun battle with the Assault Guards, the first squadron took over the Plaza de España with a machine gun platoon, and went on to

---

6   Though incorrectly mentioned in many books as a protagonist of the revolutionary events of 19 July, Sergeant Manzana was unable to participate in the fighting because he was locked up in the cells in the barracks and was not released until the afternoon of 20 July. See Márquez and Gallardo, *Ortiz: General sin dios ni amo* (Barcelona: Hacer, 1999), 101.

fraternize with the Assault Guards from the barracks at the intersection of the Gran Vía and the Paralelo, opposite the Hotel Olímpico (today's Catalonia Plaza Hotel). The Assault Guards and the cavalry squadron worked out a strange non-aggression pact and, over the course of the morning, reinforcements were allowed to emerge, unmolested, from the Assault Guard barracks, bound for Cinco de Oros and Barceloneta. At the time these reinforcements allowed the rebels to secure control of the Plaza de España, and later a company of sappers moved out from the Lepanto engineers' barracks, along the Paralelo, to the Atarazanas and the Dependencias Militares.

On Calle de Cruz Cubierta, the defense committee had thrown up a barricade outside the Hostafrancs mayor's office, sealing off the street. The rebel troops had two artillery pieces set up beside the fountain in the center of the Plaza de España, which had arrived in vans from the Docks barracks. The military fired a shell at the Hostafrancs barricade, but overshot the target, striking a small parapet above the entrance to Calle de Riego, claiming eight lives and wounding eleven. In a Dantesque scene, arms, legs, and chunks of human flesh dangled from trees, streetlamps, and tram cables. The head of one decapitated woman was hurled seventy metres. The rebels were in control of the Plaza de España up until 3:00 PM.

A second cavalry squadron, complete with machine gun platoon, and joined by a gang of rightists, were harassed on the Calle Valencia, but accomplished their mission, which was to take over the Plaza de la Universidad. They overran the university buildings, installing machine guns in the towers. They demanded that passersby show their papers, arresting CNT members or members of left-wing parties, including, among others, Ángel Pestaña. On the Ronda Universidad there was a gun battle with an armed POUM group. Over the course of the morning, the rebels were forced to retreat inside the university buildings, under pressure from a team of Assault Guards on whom they had opened fire, and POUM personnel who had taken the Seminary, from which they fired into the university gardens. Completely surrounded and after mass desertions, the rebels surrendered at 2:30 PM to a Civil Guard detachment, returning to the streets with the civilian prisoners they had taken as human shields.

At 4:30 am, a company of sappers left the Lepanto engineers' barracks on Gran Vía on the outskirts of Barcelona in Hospitalet de Llobregat (today's Plaza Cerdá, where the "court complex" is being built) and made its way to the Plaza de España where it mingled with the cavalry squadron controlling the area with its machine guns and its half battery, and with the Assault Guards, who had even pinned a proclamation of the state of war on the door of their barracks. Given that things were quiet there, they were ordered to the Dependencias Militares (today's Gobierno Militar, facing the Columbus monument). They proceeded along the Paralelo and Calle de Vilá y Vilá, as far as the Baleares wharf, when they ran into a company of Assault Guards coming in from Barceloneta.[7] The company was routed, caught in the crossfire between the Atarazanas and the cavalry squadron. A small team was left behind in Atarazanas but the majority ensconced themselves in the Dependencias Militares and made ready to hold the building. The first victory had gone to the rebels and Escofet had lost control of the Paralelo. The rebels secured their control of the medieval shipyards, the Customs House, and the three-chimneyed power plant, which meant they controlled the Paseo de Colón and lower

---

7   At 6:00 AM, a company of Assault Guards had been ordered to head for the Paralelo, but after an unexpected brush with a company of engineers outside the Atarazanas barracks, it sustained heavy losses, including the officer in charge, Captain Francisco Arrando (brother of the Alberto Arranda who headed the Security and Assault troops).

part of the Paralelo. In order to break through this choke hold and cut off the rebels in the Plaza de España from those in the Atarazanas, workers from the Woodworkers' Union and from the Pueblo Seco Defense Committee quickly threw up a huge barricade on the Brecha de San Pablo, between El Molino and the Chicago tavern.

The third squadron, having ventured out of the cavalry barracks on Calle Tarragona, had been assigned the task of consolidating the rebels' control of the Paralelo, in order to connect its own barracks with the Captaincy General. But nearing the Brecha de San Pablo, they were halted by intense gunfire from a monumental barricade in the form of two walls of rubble and sandbags across half the avenue. The military only managed to take the barricade and the CNT Woodworkers' Union headquarters on Calle del Rosal by sticking to the Mola Plan and using women and children as human shields.[8] They then set up three machine guns: one outside the La Tranquilidad bar (at 69 Paralelo, beside the Victoria theatre), a second on the roof of the building adjoining El Molino, and the third on the Brecha de San Pablo barricade. All three were put to full use. It was now 8:00 AM. It had taken the third squadron two hours to capture the barricade defended by the Pueblo Seco Defense Committee and militants from the Woodworkers' Union. But the workers continued to harry the troops from the far side of the Brecha, from the terraces of nearby buildings, and

---

8   The Plan drawn up by General Mola, the director of the military revolt against the republican government, laid down the use of terror by the rebels as the only effective means of coping with massive popular opposition. It explicitly provided for threats to be made against the children and wives of resisters, as well as for mass shootings. Being outnumbered, the rebel military and fascists needed to resort to terror right from the outset in order to cow the enemy, waging a war of extermination that had previously been waged in the colonial wars in Morocco.

from all intersections. By 11:00 AM, the third squadron had gained control of the entire Brecha, after five hours of fighting. However, an attempt by the troops stationed in the Plaza de España to reinforce their colleagues in the Brecha was halted outside the Avenida Cinema (at 182 Paralelo) due to sniping and harrying activity against them from the perimeter walls of the show grounds adjacent to the Paralelo and from Tamarit. CNT personnel decided to mount a counterattack on the Brecha, indirectly, from Calle Conde del Asalto (now the Nou de la Rambla) and elsewhere. But this proved fruitless. Residents of Pueblo Seco threw up barricades on Calles Mata, Cabanes, Blai, and Concordia to defend their barrio. About ten Assault Guards who had been mobilized in the Brecha by an officer siding with the military mutineers, decided to throw in their lot with the masses. Shortly after that, CNT reinforcements from the Plaza del Teatro, having stormed the Hotel Falcón—where they had come under fire—headed for the Ramblas via Calle de San Pablo. Reaching an agreement with the carabineros barracks that it would not take sides, they emptied the Santa Amalia women's prison and made their way up the Calle de las Flores towards the Ronda de San Pablo, assailed by the fire of the mutinous troops. With a small team carrying machine guns captured from the Atarazanas barracks, Ortiz managed to get to the far side of the Ronda, quickly erecting a small barricade that offered shelter from the three rebel machine guns in the Brecha. The anarchists swung up onto the balcony and set up their machine guns on the roof of the Chicago tavern (the building that houses the Caixa de Catalunya today). These provided cover for a whirlwind attack on the Brecha, simultaneously coordinated from Calle de las Flores, from both ends of Calle Aldana, from Calle de las Tapias, and from the Pay-Pay café on Calle de San Pablo (which faced the Sant Pau del Camp romanesque church, where they had slipped into a back door through a flanking manoeuvre from Calle

Huertas. The captain commanding the troops beside the machine gun posted in the middle of the Brecha was gunned down by Francisco Ascaso, the leading and best positioned of the attackers advancing across open ground. A lieutenant tried to take command and continue the defense, only to be shot down by a corporal from his own side. That was the beginning of the end of the engagement. By between 11 o'clock and midday, the third squadron was defeated and the Brecha de San Pablo was back in the workers' hands. Meanwhile, Francisco Ascaso was jumping with joy and waving his rifle over his head. García Oliver could not stop shouting "We're a match for the army!" In that crucial location in the city the anarcho-syndicalists—including Francisco Ascaso, Juan García Oliver, Antonio Ortiz, Gregorio Jover, and Ricardo Sanz—had defeated the army after than six hours of fighting. A tiny number of soldiers who had retreated inside El Molino were still holding out, but they finally surrendered at around 2:00 PM after using up all their ammunition.

The Badajoz Infantry Regiment (from the Pedralbes barracks) headed for the Captaincy building after being summoned by General Llano de la Encomienda, although their plan was to place themselves under the command of General Goded who was already flying from Palma de Mallorca to Barcelona to take charge of the army mutiny. As it reached the Gran Vía, Captain López Belda's company carried on down Calle Urgell as far as the Paralelo, where it came under gunfire and made its way from there to the Atarazanas barracks, the Columbus monument, and Captaincy, where it provided reinforcement for the troops already there. López Belda and his sappers were the only rebel troops to successfully accomplish their mission, in this case, reinforcing the Atarazanas barracks and Captaincy.

The remainder of the column, led by Major López Amor set off down the Gran Via for the Plaza de Cataluña, engaging the Montesa Regiment, which had already occupied the Plaza Universidad, in a firefight. After that mistake was cleared up, one company headed down the Ronda de San Antonio towards the Captaincy building, but near the San Antonio market, faced harrying action from defense committees who could not allow them to reinforce the troops in the Brecha. They were forced to duck inside Los Escalopios where they surrendered after an hour of fierce resistance.

After leaving some men to hold the University, the rest of the troops under López Amor poured into the Plaza de Cataluña from Calle Pelayo and the Ronda Universidad, shouting "Long live the Republic!" They were surrounded by a curious, expectant crowd unsure whether they were loyal troops or mutineers. Some shots were traded between the rebel troops and the Assault Guards, but white handkerchiefs were produced, the shooting ceased, and the Guards and soldiers hugged and fraternized. The mass of armed civilians managed to break up the troop formation by mingling with the soldiers. Ambiguity, sly tactics on both sides, the Guards' indecisiveness, the workers' suspicion, and exceedingly close physical proximity made for an unbelievable and dangerous mess.

The square was occupied by Assault Guard units and by numerous armed, militant workers in and around the Ramblas, the Telephone Exchange, and the Puerta del Ángel. Major López Amor issued orders to ask the largely CNT-affiliated civilians for their papers, but given that there was no way to detain them all, he decided to herd them away from the area and to set up machine guns on each side of the square: on the roof of the Maison Dorée (on the corner of Calle Rivadeneira—now occupied by Sfera), on the ground floor of the Cataluña Cinema (roughly where Habitat is now), in the Hotel Colón (presently a building owned by Banesto and playfully and enjoyably overrun by "anti-system" groups from 25 to 29 September 2010), and at the Casino Militar (now swallowed by El Corte Inglés)—with two small

7.5 calibre guns at the center of the Plaza Cataluña. López Amor then headed for the Telephone Exchange, intending to take it over and monitor communications. After ten minutes of bewilderment, the Assault Guards' initial cooperation, encouraged by the treachery of their commanding officer, Lieutenant Llop, turned into outright hostility.

López Amor ordered the two guns in the center of the square to open fire on the Telephone Exchange. Communications were all but severed by three salvoes. The gunfire in and around the building spread. Amid the confusion, a team of Assault Guards captured López Amor outside the Casino Militar. Assault Guard companies and armed workers ensconced themselves in Fontanella, the upper floors of the Telephone Exchange, the Puerta del Ángel, and the Ramblas.

By then Calles Pelayo, Vergara, and Ronda Universidad had been overrun by worker militants and the military was successfully cut off: ultimately, the latter had no choice but to retreat into the Hotel Colón, the Maison Dorée, the Casino Militar, and the ground and first floors of the Telephone Exchange, from which they held off the attacks of citizens and Guards. The middle of the square was no-man's-land. The troops had been prevented from making their way down the Ramblas to the Atarazanas barracks and Captaincy building, or via Fontanell and the Portal del Ángel to the Via Layetana police station or the Generalidad Palace. The Telephone Exchange and nearby radio stations had also been denied the rebels.

The Telephone Exchange workers cut the lines linking the Captaincy to the mutineers' barracks. It was not long before popular forces had overrun the Casino Militar and the Maison Dorée, thanks to a joint plan by Assault Guards and workers who had used the metro tunnels to secure their positions. Resistance from the rebels, now controlling only the artillery-pounded Hotel Colón and the lower floors of the

Telephone Exchange, ended at 4:00 PM, when they surrendered in the face of a belated but decisive attack by the Civil Guard, with help from Assault Guards and an enthusiastic populace encouraging them. A massive crowd packed the street corners, metro exists, and adjacent streets. White flags appeared at the Hotel Colon, and the people's wrath could be contained no longer. The field gun that Lecha had dragged from Claris boomed again. From the Ramblas, Durruti and Obregón (the latter perishing in the attack) led a massive, daredevil onslaught of anarcho-syndicalist militants, recapturing the lower floors of the Telephone Exchange. At the same time, Civil Guards and workers, with the POUM's Josep Rovira leading the way, burst into the Hotel Colón, capturing the officers there. The square was strewn with dead bodies. Here too the army was defeated.

From the Gerona barracks, or the Santiago Cavalry, at the intersection of Calle Lepanto and the Travesera de Gracia, near the San Pablo Hospital, three fifty-man squadrons deployed on foot at around 5:00 AM, with machine-guns mounted on cars. Their mission was to take over the Cinco de Oros (today's Plaza Juan Carlos I), where the Paseo de Gracia meets the Diagonal, and then make their way to the Plaza Urquinaona and the Arco del Triunfo. They faced light gunfire, as they progressed along Calles Lepanto, Industria, Paseo de San Juan (known then as Calle Garcia Hernández), and Calle Córcega. But waiting for them at the Cinco de Oros were several companies of Assault Guards, a cavalry squadron and a machine-gunner section, along with a host of worker militants posted on rooftops, balconies, trees, and porticoes—armed with automatics and hand grenades. The rebels, not bothering with the precaution of a scouting party, were surprised by the heavy gunfire that swept their front ranks, taking a heavy toll of men and officers. Colonel Lacasa, commanding the Santiago regiment, retreated with his surviving officers and some soldiers into the Carmelite monastery where the Diagonal meets Calle Lauria. With active assistance from the friars, they made the place impregnable thanks to the machine guns they installed on the lower floors and the roof. A Civil Guard detachment dispatched to take them on joined them instead. Around the monastery, the colonel set up forward positions at the intersections of Calles Córcega and Santa Tecla, Claris and Diagonal, and Menéndez Pelayo (now Torrent de l'Olla) and Lauria, but in view of heavy losses, they were forced to withdraw by the late afternoon. By nightfall, the rebels inside the monastery had agreed to surrender to the Civil Guard at daybreak the following day.

A short distance away, where Calle Balmes meets the Diagonal, half an hour after the battle at the Cinco de Oros had started, four lorries from the San Andrés Artillery depot, carrying about fifty gunners bound for the Plaza de Cataluña, were ambushed, halted, and wiped out by worker and Assault Guard gunfire. Their weapons and artillery were seized by the defense committees.

The mountain artillery regiment at the Docks barracks on Avenida Icaria had played host to the plotting of the army revolt. Two small lorries with sizable artillery pieces managed to leave the barracks and make it to the Plaza de España. The rumble of one gun, set up in the center of the square, announced that the gunners had taken to the streets. At 6:00, a column was organized under Major Fernández Unzué, its objective being to seize the Interior Ministry and then the Generalidad Palace. Back in October 1934, the very same officer, commanding a single battery, merely had to start firing at the Generalidad Palace for Companys's Catalanist rebellion to immediately hoist the white flag and surrender. The barracks was bombed by a plane shortly before they left, inflicting casualties and damaging morale. Nonetheless, three batteries took to the streets, without waiting for the two companies from the nearby Alcántara Infantry Regiment that were supposed to have provided them with cover. Textbook strategy had it that batteries should have infantry cover, since horse-drawn artillery pieces were sitting targets, having to proceed slowly down the middle of the street, but the officers were convinced that the rumble of an opening salvo would send the "rabble" scurrying for cover.

Meanwhile, in Barceloneta, excitement among local residents and dockworkers had turned into a single-minded cry for arms. Major Enrique Gómez García from the Assault Guards barracks in Barceloneta decided, once conflict was imminent, to distribute guns to anyone who would guarantee to return them by leaving a trade union or political party membership card. The first rebel battery, led by Captain López Varela, managed to proceed without difficulty past the San Carlos bridge (no longer there), which crossed Avenida Icaria and the railway tracks, before a bunch of Assault Guards, and workers armed by Assault Guards, stationed near the Barceloneta bullring (also gone), on the bridge itself, on railway cars and sidings, and on the nearest balconies and rooftops unexpectedly opened fire. A swarm of worker militants from Pueblo Nuevo, Barceloneta, and from the Transport and Metalworkers' Unions on the Ramblas quickly joined in.

All three batteries were caught in a crossfire, each of them keeping the others from making any headway. López Varela managed to set up his machine guns, and four more big guns from his battery, and began shooting, still pressing on towards Barceloneta. After two hours of defensive fighting, the rear batteries, stalled and continually pinned down by well-entrenched attackers, sustaining many casualties, managed to head back to barracks in a chaotic retreat marked by terror and a stampede of the livestock carrying munitions, which were exploding as they were struck by the gunfire. At the very entrance to the barracks they sustained fourteen casualties by two strafing planes—which were less successful at bombing the interior of the barracks a bit later.

López Varela's battery, with its retreat now cut off, could not get beyond the junction of Avenida Icaria and Paseo Nacional, which was blocked by a huge, two-metre-tall barricade, thrown up by dockworkers using the customary cobblestones and less traditional sacks of carob beans, in addition to wood and five hundred tons of paper spools. These had been unloaded by forklift in half an hour by from the *Ciudad de Barcelona*, anchored in the nearby "moll de les garrofes," the usual landing point for carob beans brought by schooners from coastal towns of Castellón and Tarragona. The battery faced mortar fire coming from the roof of the Interior Ministry as well as heavy rifle and machine-gun fire from the Naval School and the Depósito Franco. The military were firing at barricades and at the crowds, opening terrifying holes in both. But the barricades were rebuilt and the crowd merely intensified its onslaught. The rebels' position was becoming untenable. At 10:00 AM, word came to withdraw, but their retreat turned into a *Via Dolorosa*: as the soldiers tried to retreat, the paper spools, converted into roving barricades, closed in, rolled by unarmed workers, while others, well-shielded behind the spools, hurled grenades and kept up unrelenting gunfire. A final onslaught was launched against the thirty-odd men cowering behind their field guns and dead horses, and hand-to-hand fighting broke out. A wounded López Varela was removed to the Interior Ministry with the rest of the captive officers, while their soldiers fraternized with the people. Several guns and a range of weaponry had been captured. It was not even 10:30 AM.

The Docks barracks was under siege, with a barricade erected a hundred metres from its main gate. The Alcántara Infantry Regiment was easily repelled twice, although a few soldiers did manage to duck unexpectedly inside the barracks, which did not change the desperate situation of those under siege, who eventually surrendered to some Assault Guard officers, who took charge of the prisoners around 8:00 PM. Overnight, the barracks was captured by the Barceloneta and Pueblo Nuevo defense committees, who encountered no resistance.

Two barracks stood adjacent to the Ciudadela Park: the Quartermaster barracks, which stood by the Republic, so much so that it was trusted to filter out and keep an eye on the two Civil Guard *tercios*; and the Alcantara infantry barracks, where the officer corps was split between sympathizers and opponents of the revolt, and this latter barracks espoused an oddly non-committal stance and typically soldierly caution, the upshot being that the troops were very late in taking to the streets after 9:00 AM, on instructions from General Fernandez Burriel. One company was given the task of aiding the besieged Docks artillery barracks, but failed in the face of an armed crowd that soon drove it back inside its barracks. A second company was assigned with occupying the Radio Barcelona studios at No 12 Calle de Caspe. Hemmed in at the Plaza Urquinaona, the troops tried desperately to reach Calle Caspe via Calle de Lauria, but after an hour of tough fighting, found itself all but smashed, some of them managing to duck inside the Hotel Ritz, where, after coming under artillery fire, they surrendered.

The barracks of the Seventh Light Artillery Regiment and the Artillery Depot were both at the far end of the Calle San Andrés del Palomar. The rebels orchestrated a joint defense of both buildings, relying on the cooperation of civilian personnel, most of them monarchists who had reacted badly to the harangue addressed to them by Captain Reinlen, with its closing cries of "Long live Spain!" and "Long live the Republic!" Some thirty thousand rifles were stored at the Artillery Depot.

In the wake of that first sally by the four lorries wiped out at the Diagonal and Calle Balmes intersection, a second was organized by another group: its mission was to back up the Badajoz Infantry Regiment (which by then had retreated into a number of buildings on the Plaza de Cataluña, unable to make any further headway). This second team was made up of one battery (four guns). It reached Calle Bruc via Calle de la Diputación at 7:00 AM, after a six kilometre march with hardly any setbacks—only to be ambushed at the intersection of the two streets by a bunch of Assault Guards and armed workers.

The gunfire alerted some nearby Assault Guards guarding the Public Order Department in the Via Layetana, some who had arrived in the Plaza de Cataluña from the Cinco de Oros, as well as some of the popular forces laying siege to Hotel Colón and the Telephone Exchange. The battery made its way along Calle Diputación as far as Calle Claris, but when it tried to turn down the latter and cross the Gran Vía, heavy rifle and machine-gun fire erupted, the troops and horses taking heavy casualties. With the artillery and machine guns set up in the square formed by Calle Diputación, Calle Claris, Calle Lauria, and the Gran Vía, they opened up on the crowds, which regrouped and counter-attacked every time. The battery's seventy soldiers were facing a much more numerous enemy—well-positioned on rooftops, doorways, and balconies—whose enthusiasm was not diminished by artillery fire. Two Assault Guard companies arrived to help the popular forces, while a third refused to engage and quietly returned to its barracks in the Plaza de España. Hundreds of workers continually joined the fight. The rebel battery's situation was becoming more and more difficult. Still, after two hours of fighting, the carnage caused by its cannon fire was ghastly. The artillery was shielded by a line of machine-guns, rendering it inaccessible to all assailants. The Assault Guards backed off, thinking that they were not properly equipped to tackle artillery. One group of CNT militants used novel and risky tactics to mount a final, successful attack: climbing onto the flatbeds of three lorries they sent hurtling at top speed towards the line of machine guns, and then leaping from the vehicles, hurling grenades. The sheer unexpectedness of this broke through the protective shield of machine guns, which the militants then turned on the artillery. By 11:00 AM, the fighting was over. While the rebel officers surrendered to the Assault Guard, the anarcho-syndicalists seized the machine-guns and one piece of artillery, which they dragged laboriously towards the Plaza de Cataluña.

At the Captaincy building on the Paseo de Colón, the generals and high-ranking officers who were the divisional commanders of Catalonia resembled something from a comic opera. By that point, nobody was paying heed to General Llano de la Encomienda, the supreme divisional commander, who was loyal to the Republic. But at the same time, no one had the gumption to overrule him and assume command. The rebel general Fernández Burriel allowed Llano to carry on issuing orders and receiving phone calls in his office. It was all white-gloved preening, posturing soldiery, and palaver about honor. When General Goded, after declaring a state of war in Majorca and easily overrunning the island, arrived in Barcelona by sea-plane at about 12:30 to head up the revolt in Catalonia, he could not fathom why Llano de Encomienda was still a free man, and why the General Staff had yet to centralize the rebels' operations. Goded's journey from the Naval Air Base to the Captaincy building had been punctuated by the sound of intense gunfire and the distant thunder of artillery. After he and General Llano exchanged curses and mutual death threats, Goded had to confront the existing military situation. He made a fruitless phone call to the Civil Guard's General Aranguren, seeking his obedience. Aranguren, who was in the Interior Ministry building, accompanied and discreetly watched by España, Pérez Farrás, and Guarner, declined to throw in his lot with the rebels. Goded then ordered the Alcantara Infantry Regiment to make another attempt to help the artillery troops at the

Docks barracks. He could not understand how the latter had left without infantry protection. Given the demoralization caused by the constant bombing and strafing by aircraft, he sent a courier to order the sea-planes that had ferried him from Majorca to bomb El Prat airport. But by the time the courier reached the Air Base with his orders, the sea-planes had already left for their base in Mahón—in view of the blatant hostility of the seamen and Air Force personnel. It was 2:30 by then and defeat looked all but certain for the rebels. So Goded then tried to bring reinforcements from Mallorca, Zaragoza, Mataró, and Gerona. He was unable to get Mataró and Gerona on the phone; nor could he send anyone there because the tires of his armoured vehicle had been shredded by shrapnel. Zaragoza and Palma were too far away to offer effective assistance. And the Alcántara Infantry Regiment had also failed to accomplish its mission: it had easily been fended off in its second attempt to get closer to the Docks barracks, and the soldiers who had successfully ducked inside the barracks were not enough to break the siege.

A motley crowd of Assault Guards in unbuttoned tunics or in shirt sleeves and militant workers with gleaming rifles, helmets, and cartridge belts they had wrested from the enemy, dragged the cannons captured at the Diputación and Claris intersection down the Via Leyetana, hell-bent on attacking the divisional HQ. Dockworker Manuel Lecha, a former gunner, set up the artillery in Plaza Antonio López to shoot point-blank at the Captaincy building, while the batteries captured on Avenida Icaria tried indirect shots from Barceloneta. It was 5:00 PM. Watching these preparations, Goded called España, the head of the Interior Department, pompously insisting that the latter surrender, and got, by way of an answer, half an hour's grace to decide to give himself up, with an assurance that his life would be spared. At the end of that time, the artillery would start firing. The artillery fire began at 5:30 PM. Forty cannon rounds and increasingly closer rifle fire left no doubt about the imminence of an attack. A white flag appeared and both sides stopped shooting. But when a loyalist officer stepped up to accept the surrender, the machine guns at the Captaincy building erupted again. The fighting was renewed and the doors were about to give way when the white flag appeared again. This time, however, the attackers did not cease fire: they demolished the doors and surged into the Captaincy. It was 6:00 PM. Major Pérez Farràs, at some risk to his own life, managed to protect General Goded from a lynching in which a number of officers in civilian clothes perished, and to spirit him away to the Generalidad Palace, where Companys persuaded him to broadcast a cease-fire over the radio microphones set up there: "Luck has gone against me and I am a prisoner. So, if they wish to avoid bloodshed, the soldiers who accompanied me are hereby released from all commitment." That was at 7:00 PM. His message was taped and broadcast by radio stations across Spain every half hour, with notable propaganda impact.

So overwhelming was the people's success that a number of buildings fell on their own, without a shot, like ripe fruit. The warden of the Modelo prison opened the gates for the inmates, in anticipation of a riot and a likely storming of the prison. The Construction Union had its headquarters at 26 Calle Mercaders, as did the CNT Regional Committee, the Local Federation of Unions. Just opposite was the Labor Board, at what is now 34 Vía Layetana. The adjacent building, now 32, was the Casa Cambó. Both buildings were taken over by CNT personnel without a fight, since they had been utterly abandoned and left with their furnishings and archives intact. Together, both buildings became known as "CNT-FAI House," and until the end of the war were the headquarters of the regional committees of the CNT, the FAI, the Mujeres Libres, the Libertarian Youth, the editorial offices of news bulletins in multiple languages, and, among many other committees, the Barcelona Defense Committee.

The few men guarding the barracks and the San Andrés artillery depot, most of them civilian rightists and monarchists, could see the swelling crowd closing in around the barrack. Around noon, the air force strafed and bombed he barracks and the training school, taking care not to set off the arsenal and causing a few casualties among both soldiers and those besieging them. The planes made another three or four of their raids, killing or wounding more people and doing tremendous damage to the morale of the defenders, which was compounded by news of the army revolt's disastrous fate in Barcelona. After dark, the defenders, civilian as well as military, left the barracks in dribs and drabs and made a run for it. Facing no resistance now, the CNT defense committees from San Andrés, Horta, Santa Coloma, San Adrián, and Pueblo Nuevo attacked the barracks and training school before daybreak, seizing the entire arsenal stored within—some thirty thousand rifles. The Barcelona proletariat had now successfully armed itself. The Assault Guards, sent in by Escofet to prevent that from happening, backed off from an armed confrontation with the workers.

The barricades thrown up outside the barracks in order to contain the besieged rebels now held the Assault Guards at bay. Enforcing bourgeois order was by that point out of the question: the situation had taken a really revolutionary turn. Had those Assault Guards fired on the people, they would instantly have been signing their own death warrants.

In actual fact, after 6:00 PM, with the Plaza de Cataluña captured once and for all, and with Goded having surrendered at the Captaincy building, the rebellion had been effectively defeated. That just left mopping up the last few holdouts. With scarcely any manpower, utterly demoralized, and susceptible to increasing desertion, the remaining barracks either surrendered or were stormed over that evening and night. This is what happened, for instance, to the Bruc barracks, guarded by a small platoon of rebels in Pedralbes.

That afternoon a plane dropped some leaflets explaining that the troops had been disbanded and the rebel officers had stood down. This led to the desertion of almost all the troops. The few remaining officers decided to hand the barracks over to the Civil Guard, although it was stormed shortly after that by CNT workers, who encountered no resistance. They christened it the "Bakunin" barracks.

By 20 July only two rebel positions were holding out: the Carmelite monastery and the Atarazanas barracks and Dependencias militares.

A huge crowd had been laying siege to the Carmelite monastery since daybreak, impatiently breaking through the cordon of Assault Guards. Those under siege had announced the night before that they intended to surrender, but they had not stopped firing at any attempt the besiegers made to get any nearer. In the eyes of the masses surrounding the monastery, the monks' active complicity with the rebels—who had been given refuge, medical assistance, and food—was certain proof that the clerics had also been manning the machine guns that had cut down so many of them. Around noon, Colonel Escofet arrived in command of a Civil Guard company; he parleyed with the rebels over their immediate surrender. The gates opened and, from outside, the officers could be seen inside, getting chummy with the hated monks. An angry mob, pushing past the Assault and Civil Guards, invaded the monastery beating, knifing, or gunning down monk and military alike at point blank range, and then went on to mutilate the corpses. Colonel Lacasa's corpse was decapitated, Captain Domingo's was decapitated, mutilated, and cut up with a saw, and Major Rebolledo's castrated. Unnamed militants broke up a popular procession that was celebrating the victory with the colonel's head on a stick. A taxi ferried the sliced up remains of Captain Domingo to the zoo for tossing to the wild animals.

At the far end of the Ramblas, in front of the Columbus monument, was the Dependencias militares building. Across the street to the right was the Atarazanas barracks, split into two areas separated by wide yards (that were, in turn, divided by walls and reinforced doors): the Maestranza (gone now, but that overlooked the Rambla de Santa Mónica), which was still resisting, and the former medieval shipyards, which by then had been captured. The Dependencias building (now the Military Government building where Salvador Puig Antich was tried in 1973) housed all of the division's ancillary services: the courts, hearing rooms, prosecution division, mobilization center, etc.

The crossfire set up among the Dependencias, the Columbus monument, and the Atarazanas rendered them impregnable. The balcony of the Atarazanas, which overlooked the Rambla, had a wide firing angle that took a deadly toll on the attackers. The siege had begun on 19 July. By daybreak on the 20th, with the coup now broken across the city, all available resources were mustering on the Rambla de Santa Mónica to await the final assault. A 7.5 calibre gun under the command of Sergeant Gordo relentlessly pounded the old Atarazanas blockhouse, while the lorry that had come from Pueblo Nuevo, the machine gun on its flat-bed shielded by mattresses, reversed toward the barracks, sending bursts of machine-gun fire all the while. The situation was becoming untenable for the besieged, about a hundred and fifty men: 110 in the Dependencias and about 40 at the Atarazanas. Two cannons and two mortars on the wharf were added to the siege. Aircraft relentlessly strafed and dropped bombs. Hand grenades were thrown from the balconies. The exhaustion of their ammunition made the soldiers in the Dependencias decide to surrender. Having negotiated with the Interior Ministry for the safe passage of the officers' relatives in the building, they ran up the white flag shortly after noon and allowed the Assault Guards inside.

The anarchists laid siege to the rebel's final redoubt at the Atarazanas barracks, shooing away offers by the Civil Guard and POUM militants to participate in the final assault. The CNT Defense Committee, the old Nosotros group in full, was outside the Atarazanas, their minds made up to take it. The anarchists closed in on the barracks, some darting from tree to tree for cover, others "behind the paper spools as they rolled forwards." In one ill-advised rush, Francisco Ascaso was killed by a bullet in the head. Shortly after that, the re-sisters inside the Atarazanas surrendered, hoisting a white flag. Seeing this, the libertarians clambered over the walls and burst inside, opening up on the officers and mingling with the ordinary ranks. That was a little before 1:00 PM.

6

The Revolutionary Ward Committees, the People's Militias, and the Revolutionary Situation in July 1936

Even as the army mutineers were being defeated, on 19 and 20 July 1936, the members of the defense committees were styling themselves and becoming known as "the militians." With no transition at all, the defense cadres became People's Militias. The skeleton structures of the defense cadres had allowed them to expand by recruiting additional cadres. It was simply a matter of making room for the thousands of worker-volunteers who joined the battle against fascism, which now extended into Aragon. The confederal militias were at the forefront of the armed units that set off to seek and defeat the fascist enemy. They were the revolutionary proletariat's armed organization. Their example was imitated by other worker columns, including those of bourgeois extraction. Given the absence of any unified proletarian army, as many militias surfaced as there were parties and organizations.

The defense cadres now underwent a double transformation. They became the People's Militias that established a front line in Aragon in the initial stages, triggering the collectivization of land in liberated Aragonese villages; and they also became the revolutionary committees that enforced the "revolutionary new order" in each barrio of Barcelona and every village in Catalonia. Their common origins in the defense cadres ensured that the confederal militias and the revolutionary committees were always very cohesive and interrelated.

In the wake of the victory over the fascist army revolt in Catalonia, each barrio's (or village's) defense committee set itself up as ward (or district) revolutionary committee, under a wide variety of names. In Barcelona, these barrio revolutionary committees were almost entirely made up of CNT personnel. Local revolutionary committees, by contrast, were usually formed by accommodating every one of the worker and anti-fascist organizations, mirroring the make-up of the Central Antifascist Militias Committee (CAMC).

In each ward or district, these revolutionary committees—especially during the seven weeks following 19 July 1936—performed the following functions:

1. They commandeered buildings for use as committee headquarters, supplies depots, and *ateneos*, or rationalist schools. They seized and maintained hospitals and newspapers.

2. They searched private homes to requisition weapons, foodstuffs, cash, and valuables.

3. They mounted armed searches of all suspect premises, the aim being to arrest "*pacos*," "sleepers," priests, right-wingers, and fifth columnists. (Remember that sniping in Barcelona carried on for an entire week).

4. In each barrio, they set up recruitment centers for the Militias, which they armed, funded, kept supplied, and (until mid-September) paid using their own resources. They maintained, even after May 1937, an intense and ongoing bond between each ward and its militians on the front lines, welcoming them home during their leave.

5. In addition to the safe-keeping of weapons at the defense committee headquarters, there was always some space or warehouse where the district supplies committee was set up, requisitioning foodstuffs from rural areas by means of armed coercion, barter, or purchase with vouchers.

6. They imposed and collected a revolutionary tax in each barrio or district.

The way committees did this—by intimidating individuals or firms through personal letters with receipts attached, or through blunt armed threats—facilitated the arbitrary action of a few opportunistic or unscrupulous people. The bourgeoisie and property owners always saw such taxation as "a hold-up," since it was not being carried out by state agencies and, in the few instances involving abduction or death threats, it was inhumane. Which is not to say that the levy was not fair, necessary, and appropriate under those revolutionary circumstances, being one way to cover the costs of the war, the volunteer militias, the defense committees themselves, the free canteens, the hospitals, the schools, arms purchases abroad, public works schemes providing work for the unemployed, etc.

The provisions committee would set up a people's canteen which, at the outset, was free for militians, their families, and the unemployed. But within months, as foodstuffs became scarcer and more costly, it introduced a voucher system, subsidized by the barrio or district revolutionary committee. The defense committee's headquarters always had a room for the safe-keeping of weapons and, on occasion, a small jail where arrested persons could be held temporarily.

The revolutionary committees performed important and wide-ranging administrative services, covering everything from the issuance of vouchers, food stamps, safe conduct documents, passes, setting up cooperatives, performing marriages, supplying and maintaining hospitals, through to the seizure of foodstuffs, furnishings, and buildings, funding rationalist schools and *ateneos* run by the Libertarian Youth, paying militia members or their families, and so on.

The ward revolutionary committees were coordinated at the Regional Committee's headquarters, where the secretaries of each of the ward defense committee would meet. In addition, there was the standing Confederal Defense Committee based at the Casa CNT-FAI.

For things that exceeded the remit of the ward revolutionary committee—matters relating to the confiscation of large sums of cash and valuables, or anything relating to arrest, intelligence-gathering, and investigation—they could turn to the CNT-FAI Investigation Service run by Escorza from the Casa CNT-FAI.

So, in Barcelona, the ward defense committees were subordinate to the following higher committees:

1. In regard to the recruitment of militians (in July and August 1936) and supplies for the people's militias (up until mid-September), they were answerable to the CAMC.

2. In regard to supplies of foodstuffs and basic necessities, to the Central Supplies Committee.

3. In regard to the trouble-shooting and resolution of problems, to the CNT Regional Committee, which gave the orders and policies for them to follow. This had to do with the defense cadres' famous dependency on the trade unions and the loss of autonomy agreed to in the 1934 Working Party Resolution.

4. They coordinated and shared experiences with the Barcelona Defense Committee, which was simply an organizational tier above the district committees. And barely functional.

5. For intelligence, investigation, hunting down the fifth column, and other armed 'police' work, they deferred to the authority and experience of the CNT-FAI Investigation Service.

The basic, clandestine, armed organization of the CNT were the defense cadres, organized along territorial lines that were clearly defined in respect to other groups, their six members performing very specific functions in terms of intelligence, espionage, and investigation. In times of insurrection, these cadres were flanked by secondary groups of trade union militants, FAI affinity groups, members of *ateneos*, etc. After 19 July, intelligence-gathering, spying on the enemy, and investigating the strength and leadership of the class enemy were overseen by the CNT-FAI Investigation Service, while other matters were thrashed out at meetings at the Casa CNT-FAI among the secretary-delegates of each barrio committee and the Regional Committee.

The Investigation Service was led by Manuel Escorza from an attic at the Casa CNT-FAI and he had its own investigation patrols at his disposal; these were not answerable to the Control Patrols.[1] Escorza handled the intelligence gathering and investigation side of things for the various barrio-level revolutionary committees. His Investigation Service was a far reaching intelligence and counter-espionage network that reached beyond Spain into France and Switzerland. Counter-espionage work abroad was overseen by Liberato Minué, Escorza's brother-in-law. The intelligence network widened and reached down into the investigation committees already found elsewhere, into virtually every defense committee, and into the various confederal columns.[2] It incorporated

---

1   See "Control Patrols" in glossary.

2   Given the intelligence-gathering and investigatory duties of the defense cadres, as outlined in detail above, it was only to be expected that after 19 July 1936 the (barrio and local level) revolutionary committees retained these functions as part of

itself into various different collectives as well. For instance, the DAS group (of exiled German anarcho-syndicalists) was authorized by the CNT-FAI Investigation Service to research the activities of Nazi groups in Barcelona, thereby operating as a German investigation patrol for a number of months.[3]

Power in the Streets

The real power to implement and make determinations was in the street: it was the power of the proletariat, wielded by the local, defense, and workers' control committees, spontaneously commandeering factories, workshops, buildings, and property; organizing, arming, and shipping the volunteer militias they had recruited to the front lines; burning down churches or turning them into schools or warehouses; setting up patrols to extend the class war; manning barricades, now class borderlines, monitoring passersby and displaying the committees' power; operating the factories without bosses or directors, or converting them for war-time production; commandeering cars and lorries or foodstuffs on behalf of the supplies committee; carrying out *paseos* targeting bourgeois, fascists, and priests; supplanting obsolete republican town councils, and imposing their absolute authority over everything in each locality, without waiting for instructions from the Generalidad or the Central Antifascist Militias Committee (CAMC).[4] The

---

their regular and routine responsibilities, drafting reports that Escorza then took it upon himself to marshal and bring together under the CNT-FAI Investigation Service.

3 The payroll of the CNT-FAI Investigation Service, dated 24 October 1936, contains the names of the German anarcho-syndicalists "Fernand Gotze" and "Arturo Levin."

4 Translator's note: A *paseo* is a leisurely stroll. In Civil War contexts, it refers to taking someone away to be murdered elsewhere, something akin to being "taken for a walk or a ride" in a gangster context.

distinguishing feature of the revolutionary situation was the fragmentation of power.

As we have seen, from early morning on 19 July, the Nosotros group had set itself up as the Revolutionary Defense Committee in order to lead the revolutionary uprising. Most of its members then naturally became column delegates, like Durruti and Ortiz, or took on leading posts with the CAMC, like García Oliver, Aurelio Fernández, and Marcos Alcón, embodying the transformation of the defense committees into People's Militias, i.e., into a "revolutionary army."

On the night of 19 July there was no authority more real than that of the "federation of barricades," with the immediate goal of defeating the rebels. Disbanded or confined to barracks, the army and police vanished from the streets after 20 July 1936. Their place had been taken by People's Militias made up of armed workers fraternizing with discharged soldiers and uniform-less Guards in a single victorious bloc that had become the vanguard of the revolutionary insurrection.

Over the following week, while the CAMC was still only provisional, barrio committees popped up as expressions of the power the defense committees had secured. These coordinated with one another to form a genuine city-wide federation that exercised full power in the streets and factories, and everywhere else, in the absence of an effective city council, Interior Ministry, or Generalidad. The dozens of barricades erected in Barcelona were still in place come October, controlling vehicular traffic, and asking for documents and the general pass issued by the various committees to enforce, defend, and monitor the new revolutionary situation, and above all as an identifying feature of the committees' new power.

In Barcelona, in the absence of instructions from any organization, and with no coordination beyond whatever revolutionary initiatives the moment required, the defense committees-turned-barrio revolutionary committees organized the hospitals that had been overwhelmed by the flood of wounded; set up people's canteens; commandeered cars, lorries, weapons, factories, and other spaces; searched private homes, arrested suspects; and established a network of supplies committees in every barrio. The latter was co-ordinated through a Central Provisions Committee for the city, in which the Foodworkers' Union built up a consider-able presence. The revolutionary contagion spread to every segment of society and to every organization that sincerely backed the new revolutionary situation. This was the only real power wielded by the CAMC, which was presented to the people-in-arms as the anti-fascist agency that had to di-rect the war effort and enforce the revolutionary new order.

On 21 July, a Plenum of Locals and Comarcals had re-jected the option of seizing power, which was construed as dictatorship of the anarchist leaders rather than as the im-position, coordination, and extension of the power that the revolutionary committees were already wielding at street level. On 23 July, a joint and secret meeting of the higher committees of the CNT and FAI closed ranks in favor of col-laborating with the CAMC, and agreed to plan a Plenum on the 26th to overcome resistance from the rank and file.

The first two anarchist columns set off on the 24th, under the commands of Durruti and Ortiz. Durruti made a speech over the radio warning of the need to stay vigilant against a potential attempted counter-revolution. The revolutionary situation in Barcelona had to be preserved until they could "go for broke" once they had taken Zaragoza.

On 25 July, Companys dropped in at the Navy School to upbraid members of the CAMC over their ineffective han-dling of public order; he was greeted with indifference by García Oliver who threateningly dismissed him.

On the morning of 26 July, at a Regional Plenum, the deci-sion made by the CNT-FAI higher committees on 23 July and at the earlier Regional Plenum on the 21st—that the CNT-FAI should collaborate in the CAMC—was ratified. The plenum confirmed, unanimously, that the CNT would stick by its stance and play its part in the new class-collaborationist body known as the CAMC. The plenum also set up a Provisions Commission answerable to the CAMC, to which the different supplies committees that had popped up everywhere were to defer.[5] It also ordered a partial end to the general strike. A summary of the main accords reached at this Plenum was published in the form of a Proclamation, to ensure that they were generally known and abided by.[6] The CAMC gathered on the evening and night of 26 July to map out and structure itself into several departments: War, Barcelona Militias, Comarcal Militias, Provisions Commission, Propaganda, Authorization and Permits, Control Patrols, Military Health, Transport, and Subsidies.

Juan García Oliver took on responsibility for the War Department. Abad de Santillán, with help from Miret and Pons, would see to the militias's supplies. Aurelio Fernández was appointed head of the Investigation Department, or (much the same thing) the real chief of the revolutionary police, assisted by José Asens (FAI) and Tomás Fábregas (Acció Catalana party) who directed the Control Patrols. Marcos Alcón (Durruti's replacement) took over the Transport Department with help from the UGT's Durán Rosell (a replacement for Antonio López Raimundo, who died on the Huesca front). Josep Miret (Unió Socialista and then PSUC parties) and Joan Pons (Esquerra) were in charge of the Comarcal Militias Department. Jaume Miravitlles (Esquerra) took charge of the Propaganda Department and

---

5 Rather than coordinating these supplies committees that had been created from below by the revolutionary committees, they were done away with so that the CAMC might oversee from on high.

6 This Proclamation is reproduced in A. Guillamón, *Barricadas en Barcelona* (Barcelona: Ediciones Espartaco, 2007), 224–225.

Josep Torrents (Unió de Rabassaires) of Provisions. Rafael Vidiella (standing in for José del Barrio, the delegate from the Karl Marx Column) joined the Investigation Department headed by Aurelio Fernández. Joan Pons Garlandi (Esquerra) was put in charge of the Authorization and Permits (passports) Department. Artemi Aiguadé Miró (Esquerra) headed up Military Health. Josep Tarradellas took over the crucial Economy and War Industries Department. The Guarner brothers, Díaz Sandino and Pérez Farrás, were appointed as military advisors. Lluis Prunes, the Generalidad's Defense minister, soon stepped down from his theoretical and largely ineffective (unrecognized) post as chair of the CAMC.

Right up until the CAMC's dissolution, García Oliver was the outstanding presence and he was constantly at loggerheads with the Generalidad government—although their clashes became less intense, less significant, and of less interest as the weeks went by, on account of the Regional Committee's withdrawal of its support from García Oliver, as well as the inefficacy of the CAMC and the CNT's very early but secret decision to dissolve it. The most serious clash was of course García Oliver's vetoing of the Casanovas cabinet put forward by Companys on 31 July 1936, a line-up that included two counsellors (ministers) from the PSUC—Joan Comorera and Rafael Vidiella—and one (Josep Calvet) from the Unió de Rabassaires. García Oliver's ultimatum, which included the threat to do away with the Generalidad because the new cabinet was an attack upon the very existence of the CAMC, finished with Companys backing down, tinkering with the line-up (until it was whittled down to republicans alone) within days of publishing a decree announcing its formation.

The stance of the CNT-FAI top committees was incoherent, unsustainable, and contradictory. Their ideological principles prevented them from joining the Generalidad government, but they also did not want to see that government threaten the CAMC, preferring that it defer to a body that was not and had no desire to become a revolutionary government and alternative to the Generalidad. The CAMC was not in complete control, but it had no desire to see others rule either. The anarcho-syndicalist leaders wanted to freeze the existing revolutionary situation. One can call this *dual power* only by forgetting that real duality implies a fierce, inexorable contest between two opposing forces, each out to destroy its rival. In Catalonia's case, it was more appropriate to talk about a duplication and complementarity of power between some Generalidad government departments and the CAMC—at times, irksome, ineffective, and irritating to everyone. García Oliver's threat to the formation of a Casanovas cabinet sought simply to preserve this duplication. Anarcho-syndicalist participation in the business of government through the CAMC proved unsatisfactory. But no one yet dared to suggest, to the armed libertarian membership, a direct entry into government. When reality crashes into principles, it is normally the latter which give way.

Meanwhile, the CAMC launched the New Unified Schooling Council (CENU) on 27 July 1936, the War Industries Commission (on 7 August 1936), the Control Patrols (11 August 1936), and the Economic Council (11 August 1936). These were milestones in a trend towards reducing the CAMC to an exclusively military remit. What was actually going on was a process of subsuming all revolutionary initiatives into the machinery of government. These mixed commissions enjoyed a large measure of autonomy and decision-making authority as well as a sizable worker presence—extending even to chairmanships and other leadership positions—but they were at all times organically integrated into the various domains of the Generalidad government, which was growing in prestige, presence, and authority, to the permanent detriment of the CAMC and the revolutionary committees. The most notable instance involved the War Industries Commission, where Tarradellas assembled a team of experts such as Colonel Jiménez de la Beraza, Air Force Major Miguel Ramírez, and Artillery Captain Luis Arizón. They, along with highly skilled workers like metalworker Eugenio Vallejo (a pioneer, since 20 July, in setting up an incipient war industry) brought with them the cooperation and enthusiasm of various trade unions and committees, managed to conjure out of absolutely nothing a war industry that was churning out remarkable (but insufficient) batches of war materials in barely a few months.[7]

The Control Patrols

That summer in Catalonia, the success of the July 1936 worker uprising to counter the army rebellion produced a revolutionary situation in which the armed proletariat imposed a class crackdown on bourgeois individuals and symbols (entrepreneurs, priests, fascists, and former *Sindicato Libre* gunmen), expropriating their assets, smashing their repressive forces (the Army and police), and suppressing the Church. This was a spontaneous, violent, festive worker suppression of the bourgeoisie and the Church as immediate reprisal for their attempt to enthrone a military dictatorship by force of arms. Later, on 11 August 1936, the Control Patrols were set up as the police arm of the Central Antifascist Militias Committee (CAMC).

The Control Patrols outlived the CAMC: they were not disbanded until early June 1937, a month after the incidents known as the "May Events" of 1937. They were made up of

---

7   On 26 July, Durruti had commissioned Vallejo to establish a war industry. He set about coordinating the metalworkers' and chemical workers' unions together with the miners of Sallent and converting civilian production to an armaments industry. CNT-member Vallejo worked effectively with Tarradellas in the medium term, but the implicit message was that the initially revolutionary venture was under the oversight of the Generalidad.

eleven sections covering every *barrio* in Barcelona. At their inception, they numbered some seven hundred men and eleven chiefs, one for each section. Some of them were drawn from the requisitioning patrols and others from the defense committees, although many of the latter were loath to operate as "police" on ideological grounds, leaving the way open for the entry of less reliable personnel. Besides, only half of the patrolmen were CNT card-holders or from the FAI: the other half belonged to other organizations serving on the CAMC: the POUM, the Esquerra Republicana de Catalunya (ERC), and the PSUC, for the most part. Only four section delegates out of eleven belonged to the CNT: the four from Pueblo Nuevo, Sants, San Andrés (Armonía), and El Clot. Another four belonged to the Esquerra, three to the PSUC, and none to the POUM.

The Control Patrols were answerable to the CAMC Investigation Committee, headed by Aurelio Fernández (from the FAI) and Salvador González (from the PSUC), the latter a replacement for Vidiella. Its Central was at No 617 on the Gran Vía, run by two Patrol delegates, José Asens (FAI) and Tomás Fábregas (Acció Catalana). The patrolmen's payroll (they were paid ten pesetas a day) was covered by the Generalidad government. Even though arrests were made by every section, and some detainees were questioned at the former Casa Cambó, their central prison was located in the former Poor Clares convent of San Elías.

At San Elias a court had been set up with the task of passing summary judgment on detainees.[8] Normally, the panel had the participation of the Arias brothers (Aubí and Bonet) from the FAI, África de Las Heras and Salvador González (PSUC), Coll (ERC), and Barceló from the

---

8   This Emergency Revolutionary Court was "formalized" at the meeting of the Patrols Secretariat held on 3 January 1937. It was made up of Torrents (from the POUM), Bonet (CNT), and Chueca (UGT).

POUM. This court operated independently. From time to time Aurelio Fernández, Manuel Escorza, Vicente Gil (aka *Portela*), Dionisio Eroles, Riera, and José Asens took a hand in the court's activities on account of the positions they held.[9] Detainees were briefly interrogated with no judicial guarantees of any sort.

Manuel Escorza del Val was in charge of the CNT-FAI Investigation and Intelligence Services, a body controlled, not by the CAMC but by the CNT and FAI regional committees—which is to say it was a libertarian agency that, in keeping with Escorza's suggestion to the 21 July Plenum, was out to create an autonomous, independent, armed CNT force that might one day "boot out" the Generalidad government. Later, Escorza headed up the Special Investigation Brigade attached to the Security Council.

The CNT-FAI Investigation Service carried out intelligence, repression, and espionage activity. It was led by Manuel Escorza who, ensconced in his attic at the former Casa Cambó, had seized the archives of the Fomento del Trabajo and the Lliga Regionalista, which gave him access to enough names, details, connections, and addresses to carry out an efficient "mopping up" of right-wingers, clergy, and persons out of sympathy with the "revolutionary new order." He would draw up deadly lists each day for the CAMC's Control Patrols or the various anarchist investigation committees—not just in Barcelona but across Catalonia—of persons to be arrested and questioned: these faced essentially two fates, release or execution. In addition, Manuel Escorza took it upon himself to research and nominate the most suitable people for various positions of responsibility within the CNT, which gave him huge influence within the CNT's higher committees.

---

9   At the 3 January 1937 meeting of the Patrols Secretariat, questions were raised about Riera's participation in interrogations on the grounds that "he had nothing to do with the Patrols nor with Investigation."

At the Hotel Colón and the Equestrian Club, with the aid of Joaquín Olaso, África de las Heras, and Victorino Sala, Salvador González set up a PSUC prison and repressive network like Escorza's. The Esquerra's Josep Soler Arumí did likewise at the Centro Federal in the Paseo de Gracia, and had the dismal honor of being the first to systematically use torture on detainees.

Following the May Events and the disbandment of the Control Patrols in early June 1937, all the anarchist prisons disappeared. By 1938, all the chekas belonged to the PSUC or to the SIM (a Spanish version and arm of the NKVD). Once the Stalinists got their wish and the Negrín government formed on 17 May 1937, state terror began slowly to be enforced. The propaganda claimed it was targeting the fascists' virtually non-existent and weak "fifth column," but in fact the full brunt was borne by revolutionary minorities and the workers' movement—which was mainly anarcho-syndicalist in Catalonia.[10] The relocation of the republican government to Barcelona in November 1937, in addition to the almost complete nullification of the Generalidad government power, and the resultant squabbles with representatives of the Catalan petite bourgeoisie, was the final consolidation within Catalonia of a regime of state terror. This was a state riddled with Stalinists, who had wormed their way into every key post throughout its apparatus. In it, the SIM enjoyed the cooperation and connivance of the Negrín government, its police, and its Army; courts made according to the Stalinists' recipe; and an extensive network of chekas that could torture or murder with utter impunity.

By 1938, the move from the revolutionary situation of July 1936, and a working class attack on the bourgeoisie

---

10 According to Gero (aka Pedro or Pere), these minorities were dangerous not so much on account of their lack of numbers but for their ability to set political aims for the proletariat.

and the Church, to a state dominated by home-grown and soviet Stalinists enforcing state terror against revolutionary minorities and the anarchist movement was complete.

...arricade erected on 19 July 1936 outside "El Molino" on the Paralelo. The CNT
...efense committees and the CNT Woodworkers' Union defeated the army mut...
...eers at this point.

Barricade thrown up on the Ramblas, junction with the Calle Fivaller (the Ca[lle] Ferrán or Fernando today). Note the protective tape on the plate glass window[s].

Sandbags protecting a doorway on the Ramblas. On the wall there is a poste[r] announcing a Friends of Durruti meeting to be held at the Goya Theatre.

Barricade erected in the Gracia barrio in May 1937. The display windows are artistically decorated with tape, installed as protection against flying glass in the event of bombardment.

Durruti, here on the Aragon front.

Barricade erected in May 1937 in the Plaza Dostoievski (the Plaza del Ángel these days) at the end of the Calle Llibreteria. This photo shows the view one would have had of the barricade on emerging from the doorway behind which Camilo Berneri lived, and looking to the right in the direction of the Generalidad Palace. It was facing the UGT's Water, Lighting and Power (electricity) Workers' Union. This barricade was erected by PSUC militants as a defense against anybody meaning to approach from the Via Layetana with the intention of attacking the Generalidad.

The same barricade, the view from the Calle Llibreteria. In the background, beneath a banner there is a poster that says "UGT Water, Lighting and Power Workers' Union" on a building located on the Via Durruti (Via Layetana). To the left, between two pillars, stands the entrance to where Berneri lived in the middle of the Plaza del Ángel (aka Plaza Dostoievski), in apartment 2B, first floor. The photo clearly shows that the entrance to the building where Berneri lived was wide open to crossfire coming from the PSUC barricade and the balconies of the UGT union premises.

Furthermore, it can be seen from the photo that the entrance to where Ber
neri lived was surrounded by a barricade stretching from the Via Durruti
(today the Via Layetana) as far as the middle of the Plaza Dostoievski (today's
Plaza del Ángel). No one could have entered or exited via that doorway with
out leave from whoever was in charge of the barricade. Machine-guns had
been erected on the roof of the building, aimed towards the Via Durruti and
the Casa CNT-FAI, located at a range of some two hundred metres.

Thus the location was entirely under PSUC-UGT control: from the Call
e Llibreteria barricade, the barricade in the Plaza, and from the UGT union
premises. As a basic safety precaution the Stalinists would have checked
and searched all of the apartments in the building where Berneri lived, it
being at the heart of the stalinist defense arrangements.

Berneri and Barbieri were in the worst possible location, at the worst
possible time.

The Italian anarchists were identified in the course of an initial visit (on
Tuesday 4 May at 1.00 a.m.), as they lived in the building; during a second
visit (at 3.00 p.m. on Tuesday 4 May) their weapons (three rifles) were confis
cated and they were ordered not to leave the building. On the third occasion
(Wednesday 5 May 1937, at 6.00 p.m.) their visitors returned with "orders
from above" to arrest Berneri and Barbieri.

Berneri's corpse was found on the night of 5–6 May 1937 very near to
the Generalidad Palace and barely fifty metres from the Plaza del Ángel.
Barbieri's corpse was found on the Ramblas.

No one but the stalinists could have arrested them and no one but the
stalinists could have murdered them and only a very few people could have
handed down the order from above that they were to be executed.

C.N.T.   **F.A.I.**

Agrupación "Los amigos de Durruti"

¡TRABAJADORES..¡

Una Junta revolucionaria. - Fusilamiento de los culpables.

Desarme de todos los Cuerpos armados.

Socialización de la economía.

Disolución de los Partidos políticos que hayan agredido a la clase trabajadora.

No cedamos la calle. La revolución ante todo.

Saludamos a nuestros Camaradas del P.O.U.M. que han confraternizado en la calle con nosotros.

VIVA LA REVOLUCIÓN SOCIAL... ¡ABAJO LA CONTRARREVOLUCIÓN!

Leaflet distributed on the barricades on 5 May 1937 by the Friends of Durruti.

Said leaflet as reprinted in the 6 May 1937 edition of La Batalla (the POUM mouthpiece).

Comité de Defensa Barriada de Pueblo Nuevo

Se autoriza al portador para dejar-
le libre el paso por las barricadas para
que siga su camino.

EL COMITÉ

Barcelona 25 Julio 1936

A barricades pass, issued by the Pueblo Nuevo Defense Committee on 25 July 1936.

AGRUPACION LOS AMIGOS DE DURRUTI
A LA CLASE TRABAJADORA

1 Constitución inmediata de una Junta revolucionaria integrada por obreros de la ciudad, del campo y por combatientes.

2 Salario familiar. - Carta de racionamiento. Dirección de la economía y control de la distribución por los sindicatos.

3 Liquidación de la contrarrevolución.

4 Creación de un ejército revolucionario.

5 Control absoluto del orden público por la clase trabajadora.

6 Oposición firme a todo armisticio.

7 Una justicia proletaria.

8 Abolición de los canjes de personalidades.

ATENCION TRABAJADORES

Nuestra agrupación se opone a que la contrarrevolución siga avanzando. Los decretos de orden público, patrocinados por Aiguadé, no serán implantados. Exigimos la libertad de Maroto y la de los camaradas detenidos.
Todo el poder a la clase trabajadora
Todo el poder económico a los Sindicatos
Frente a la Generalidad, la Junta revolucionaria

A Friends of Durruti poster, put up on walls and trees lining the streets of Barcelona in late April 1937.

CNT

Sindicato de Hospitalet barriada de la(Torr...

Este Sindicato ruega a la COMISION DE ABAS...

de esta localidad facilite el pasage gratis...

te obrero en paro forzoso a su pueblo natal...

Hospitalet(Torrassa)

S.U. de...
BAR...
LA TO...
C.N.T...

ATENEO OBRERO CULTURAL DEL POBLET
COMITÉ REVOLUCIONARIO

Rogamos a los compañeros del c...
que faciliten pasage al compañe...
se a GANDIA poia de VALENCIA.
al objeto de acompañar a su h...

EL...

C.N.T.   F.A...

Autorizamos al portador del prese...
Amalia Montero Lopez   para...
pueda circular libremente hasta T...
(Valencia)
Barcelona 3 Agos...
EL COMITE DE BARRIADA...

C.N.T.   F.A...

...os al portador del pres...
Jardi Velasco para...
...cular libremente hasta...
...ia)
...lona 3 Agosto de 19...

C.N.T.

COMITE DE DEFENSA...

El comp...
está autorizado para poder v...

Barcelona 4 de Agosto de 19...

C.N.T.   F.A.I.

Autorizamos al portador del present...
...urelia Garcia Martinez   para qu...
pueda circular libremente hasta...
Salvacante de Cuenca
Comite de Gracia
4 de Agosto 1936

A selection of passes and permits issued by a range of committees.

Comité de defensa de San Adrián del Besos

Certificamos que Salvador Pardo Prech y José Robert Cardona, pertenecen a las milicias Antifacistas de esta localidad.

Autorizamos para que puedan trasladarse a Valencia por asuntos de familia comprometiéndose a regresar para el día siete de los corrientes

San Adrián del Besos 3-8-36

El Comité

Comité Revolucionario

de la Barriada de Gracia.

Vale de libre circulación del

Coche núm. 83244 B.

Barcelona 2 Agosto 1936

Milicia Antifeixista
Barriada Hospital General de Cataluña

Este comité recomienda al compañero José Fol Bataller — miliciano, estuvo en Lérida, cayendo enfermo, para que pueda trasladarse a Gau a ser posible gratuitamente.

El Comité

— 5 AGO. 1936

COMITÉ DE DEFENSA ANTIFAGISTA
DE LA
BARRIADA DE
SAN PABLO
Avda. GAUDÍ

C. N. T.   F. A. I.

Autorizamos al portador

Joaquina Gimenez L...

pueda circular libremente

Valencia).

Barcelona 3 de Agosto

A. I. T.

CENTRO.

...es
...mens, f. Caspe

El Comité.

U. H. P.

C. N. T.   U. G. T.

Comisión de Abastos

Camioneta

Autorizamos al ~~coche~~   núm. 51,972

matrícula de Barcelona libre circulación hasta

prov. de Barcelona ida y vuelta y ~~Besos~~

para abastecer de mercancías a dicha población.

Departiment de Vi...

Papiol, 3 de agost   de 1936

Joan Gené   El Comité Revolucionario.

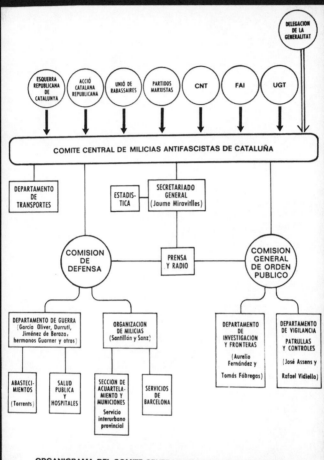

ORGANIGRAMA DEL COMITE CENTRAL DE MILICIAS ANTIFASCISTAS
mostrando las conexiones o relación de sus servicios

Organisational profile of the CAMC.

A pass bearing three stamps: Office of the Secretary of the CNT Regional Committee, the Barcelona Local Trade Union Federation, and the Anarchist Groups of Catalonia.

Seal of the Barcelona Local Defense Committee.

7

The Assembly-Driven Modus Operandi of the Defense and Supplies Committees

On Saturday 22 August 1936, there was a meeting at the Casa CNT-FAI between the top libertarian committees. The CNT's local and regional committees, the Militias Committee, the FAI Committee, and the Barcelona Local Defense Committee were all in attendance, as were Jover and Toryho.

It was agreed that the Local Committee would look to the Shopworkers' Union to recruit a secretary "who will service every meeting held by the Committees, and who will be paid."

Santillán stated that "the issue of the cards that are to carry just one picture" had now been settled. He announced that "besides the 600 militians, the remaining Control Patrols are to be made up of volunteers who, as such, are not to receive payment."[1]

At the same time it was agreed that "a sort of billet (so to speak) will be set up to ensure that volunteer comrades are fed, and later some arrangement can be worked out so that, without insulting them, the comrades may receive one or two pesetas a day for cigarettes and papers."

On the one hand were the Control Patrols, paid ten pesetas a day and drawn from every one of the anti-fascist organizations—CNT, PSUC-UGT, ERC, and the POUM. And, on the other, were the defense committees in each barrio, with

---

1   The Control Patrols started out with an initial 711 patrolmen.

a headquarters in each ward of Barcelona; the latter would be supplied with food and a daily allowance of two pesetas for incidentals. These defense committees were exclusively CNT organizations.

Jover and the FAI Peninsular Committee believed that "some of the guards posted on these premises cannot be justified and serve no purpose and propose reducing them to an absolute minimum."

Ramos proposed that they appoint a key-holder for the Casa CNT-FAI, his task being to monitor comings and goings "with the aid of an armed comrade."

The Local Federation moved, and its motion was carried, that the guard on the Casa CNT-FAI be whittled down to twelve comrades "operating in six-man shifts." It was left to Serapio to organize this.

Toryho asked for two assistants, one of them a driver. His request was granted.

The Peninsular Committee was insistent that "the standard wage should apply to all comrades working on the various Committees."

Germinal disclosed that some comrades had guaranteed him that they could furnish him with all manner of weaponry "planes included; the only thing missing is sufficient capital to pay for it."

The Defense Committee reported that "at various meetings held around Barcelona, it was agreed that, before giving up their weapons to send to the front lines, they want the government-controlled armed corps to disarm first."

This statement from the Barcelona Defense Committee, *speaking for the revolutionary committees at barrio level*, made at meetings of the higher committees held in the Casa CNT-FAI, is extraordinary important. For a start, note the meeting-based character of it and how it was organized in every Barcelona barrio, and also the refusal to disarm unless the old police forces, still viewed as class enemies under the orders of the Generalidad government, disarmed first. The revolutionary barrio committees, with their supply and defense sections, were the *alma libertas* of the social revolution in progress.[2] We have already seen how they functioned on the basis of assemblies and possessed arms captured in the uprising in July, arms that they were refusing to give up as long as the old forces of repression remained extant. The barrio committees were immersed in a class warfare that neither entertained nor countenanced anti-fascist deals with the government or with bourgeois organizations.

Jover indicated that he agreed with the arguments put forward at the ward level and "pointed out to the Militias Committee that it was responsible for what we have heard and what may happen." Meaning that the counterrevolution was in the barracks of the forces of repression.

The secretary of the Local Federation of Unions reported that some comrades from the Gracia ward had made it their business to investigate issues relating to the provisioning of the Aragon front militias. They had uncovered reprehensible acts in Lérida, and had warned that, unless such nonsense was ended, they would raise a "*centuria,* or whatever they could, and head toward Lérida."

Santillán, from the CAMC, tried to calm things "by making clear that he was well aware of outrages, and that he had gone to Lérida and had severely punished the scoundrels busily carrying out the aforementioned outrages."

The Defense Committee from the Central ward revealed that it knew for a fact "there is a huge amount of war munitions" where the government forces were quartered, proposing, with comrade Jover (who also took part

---

2   *Alma libertas,* meaning the "bread of freedom," was the inscription that appears on the book held by the Statue of Liberty at the Biblioteca Publica Arus at No 24, Paseo de San Juan in Barcelona.

in the proceedings), they make "a painstaking investigation to clarify this matter, since Santillán assures us it is all fantasy."

The revolutionary barrio committees insisted that the government forces of repression be disarmed. That was a basic principle for those who had spearheaded the July insurrection. Santillán was lying when he argued that those forces were not armed. Besides, why were they not being dispatched to the front, appropriately officered and monitored by militians? What were they doing, armed, in the rearguard?

The proceedings were wound up at 10:30 AM.

That initial session of the top libertarian committees might be summed up as: the CAMC and its anti-fascist unity agreements versus the class war of the barrio committees.

From the end of August 1936 onwards, the San Andrés ward's Antifascist Revolutionary Committee levied a revolutionary tax by sending out a form. The top of the form was a letter, or communiqué, addressed to an individual or company, and the bottom, much smaller part, served as a receipt or proof of payment.[3]

The communiqué read:

Citizen XXX

For days now, our brothers have been fighting on distant soil, offering their blood, and even their very lives, to slay the stinking octopus FASCISM, which aims to crush the proletariat in its many and most loathsome tentacles. These lives offered in defense of the freedom and rights of the producer class require your disinterested cooperation until such time as the fight ends and the Sun of

---

3   I have consulted upwards of a hundred documents filled out in the names of firms or individuals and held at the Salamanca Archive.

the JUSTICE AND EQUALITY to which we shall all have equal title shines its light.

The CNT and the FAI invite you, and hope you will not turn a deaf ear to its appeal, to, insofar as your means allow, help to swell the fund set up so that our bold and selfless defenders are better equipped to see this glorious struggle through to its conclusion, and so that their families and the bereaved are appropriately cared for.

Barcelona, 23 August 1936.

The date-stamps ranged from that date in August 1936 through 27 October 1936.

The counterfoil read: "Citizen XXX has contributed XXX pesetas to the fund launched by this CONFEDERATION." And at the foot of a very brief letter there was this note: "This form should be returned to the union premises at No 146, Calle S. Andres, or will be collected."

Both the letter and the receipt recorded the reference number allotted to each donor, and on the dotted line was a seal that, when the form was torn, remained half on the letter and half on the receipt.

This revolutionary levy was justified as necessary if militians, who received no soldier's pay from the Generalidad prior to mid-September, were to be outfitted, and their families—and the families of the unemployed—tended to.

The counterfoils indicate a wide range of sums donated: two pesetas, three pesetas, five pesetas, ten pesetas, fifteen pesetas, twenty pesetas, twenty five pesetas, fifty or one hundred pesetas, five pesetas payable weekly, nothing (with "ten per cent of my pay having been agreed"), or the rather more non-committal "not donating; will do so when possible."

The Sants barrio's Supply Commission was set up at the instigation of the fighters, the day after they had defeated the rebel military, as a way of resolving the supply issue facing the workers in arms.[4] "Urgent necessity prompted us to take steps to provide everything needed to feed those fighting for freedom on the barricades. Widening our focus, in that time of widespread confusion, we decided to include the non-combatant, but needy population."

So, the supplies committees were a way of meeting the short-term "incidental" needs of combatants—auxiliary methods of getting food to the armed men doing the street fighting and serving on the barricades. A second, ethical consideration broadened their remit to include the needy and indigent population, which normally included the families of the many unemployed, and the families of militians who, being mobilized for war, were unable to report to their workplaces or be breadwinners for their families.

The "procedure" employed by these supplies committees or commissions was "requisitioning from a range of establishments those products and food items" needed to meet "the needs of the this ward's population."

Within a few days of the victory over the military, "an assembly of militants reiterated its confidence in these comrades" serving on the acting Supplies Committee "until another meeting of revolutionary personnel was held, which agreed to establish the present Supplies Commission made up of fifteen comrades chosen from those at the meeting, said Commission being authorized to expand in accordance as needed—which they did, bringing new individuals on board who, while not union members, were well-known, long-standing militants bringing the experience of their years of struggle to the project."

This information about the mechanics by which the Supplies Committee was set up is very interesting, and can be extrapolated to other wards around the city: a supplies

---

4   "Memorandum presented by the Sants ward's Supplies Commission to its Unions," *Solidaridad Obrera* (25 August 1936), 6–7.

committee improvised during the insurrection would be ratified at a gathering of militants and subsequently added to at another assembly "of revolutionary personnel," the choice falling essentially upon CNT union members who might be joined by older, respected anarchist militants. No barrio and no locality was without its Supply Commission, because it was set up to deal with a pressing and vital problem, providing food, that nothing and nobody was likely to resolve unaided—much less the Generalidad government or any other state or political agency.

It needs to be stressed that these gatherings were CNT gatherings: not open barrio assemblies, but gatherings of the trade union and revolutionary militants of each ward.

Looking back from 25 August, on the basis of the documentation available to him, the author of the article assessed the work done by the Sants Supplies Committee "despite the unforeseen difficulties presented by any period of revolutionary upheaval":

Week one: 6,000 meals distributed daily.
Week two: 10,000 meals distributed daily.
Week three: 6,000 meals distributed daily.
Week four: an average of 5,000 meals distributed daily.

In order to cope with so many daily meals, it was obliged "to go ahead and set up communal canteens as the only way to meet the needs of the working population." The places where people could eat for free were set up "in the Hotel No 1, Plaza de España; in the Orfeón in Sants; in the Luis Vives Schools; on the premises of 4, Calle Torre Damians; in the Las Corts ward and Plaza del Centro; in the Manufacturing Trades local; and the La Pergola Saloon at the Exposition grounds."

The Sants Supplies Committee or Commission justifiably bragged that, during the month they had taken charge of the people's canteens, efficiency had been so high that it was the only time the Sants *barrio's* needy population "had not gone to bed with their basic needs unmet."

The members of the Committee noted the huge difficulties they had to resolve vis à vis governmental agencies in order to keep the barrio supplied, though this was not intended as "any sort of criticism of our comrades" on the Central Supplies Committee.

In light of the "ordinance published in the *Diario Oficial* and confirmed by our representatives on the relevant committees," which gave the go-ahead for "militians to be paid a maintenance allowance," it was anticipated that the demand from militians' families would cease. But the Supplies Committee warned the unions that this did not spell an end to its operations, since they still had to serve the families of the many unemployed.

Thus, the supplies committees had been created as the answer to a military necessity and to attend to the defense committees' basic quartermastering needs. Following the success of the workers' uprising, those supplies committees took it upon themselves to tackle the problem of feeding the militians, militians's families, and the unemployed in every barrio or village. Free, communal canteens were set up. After a decree was passed arranging for militians to be paid (it only became effective in mid-September 1936), the need to provide for militians' families evaporated, but there was still a need to assist the families of the unemployed, as well as hospitals, clinics, and sanatoriums.

Analyzing the three documents cited above, we can conclude that the defense and supplies committees were no longer clandestine agencies, created by and for the insurrection and subsequently adapted to recruit and maintain the People's Militias that marched off to fight in Aragon or performed the roles of "revolutionary police" and rearguard militias. They had also stopped being simple suppliers of the people's canteens that supported the families of those workers volunteering on the front. By mid-August the defense and supplies committees (or sections) of the revolutionary *barrio* committees had taken on a public, assembly-based role. And not people's assemblies open to all and sundry, but assemblies of the (CNT) militants in their barrio.

The frictions between the higher committees and such gatherings of *barrio* militants emerged that early on. The top committees' proposal for disarmament had been rejected by the assemblies of the defense committees. Assemblies of the supplies committees had ratified and broadened the line-up of each barrio's supplies committee, even as they broadened and diversified their theatre of operations. These revolutionary barrio committees were also collecting a revolutionary levy to fund the People's Militias, the people's canteens, and other pressing needs. They were genuine committee-governments. In Barcelona, these revolutionary barrio committees were potential agencies of working-class power.

8

From the CAMC'S Military Failure to Militarization

With the establishment of a series of technical commissions and Councils (covering the Economy, Provisions, etc.), the CAMC was progressively transformed into an agency specializing exclusively in matters of defense and public order. This increasingly distanced it from any claim that it constituted a revolutionary government capable of replacing the Generalidad government. However, this refusal to become a revolutionary government irreparably doomed any hope that the CAMC might lead and centralize the war against fascism, due to its political inability to become the sole organizer and leader of the new army. The makeshift militias had been formed without any single directing agency. Rather than a single proletarian army, militia columns were formed around the different parties and trade unions, as the private armies of each organization, with all the ensuing problems of coordination, homogenization, and centralization. Within a few months, this structure enabled the Stalinists and Generalidad government to consolidate their creeping counter-revolution. If the CNT leaders had abjured an "anarchist dictatorship," how were they supposed to push through an anarchist army? Besides, lack of revolutionary theory, programme, or perspectives led the higher committees of the CNT, overwhelmed by the revolutionary initiatives of the grassroots committees, to resort to constant improvization that, when coupled with an optimistic belief that the war would be over in a few weeks, prevented them from properly gauging the future implications of their bad decisions.

Thus the CAMC turned its back on what had been, at its inception, its number one aim: setting up volunteer worker militias, keeping them supplied, and directing the war effort. Chronic lack of weapons and munitions—which were distributed, not to the front lines and columns where they were needed, but where Party leaders decided based on their ideological affinities—was used to discredit rival militias and boost one's own reputation. The watchword "going for broke once we take Zaragoza" backfired on its promoters since, unless Zaragoza was taken, the anarchists could not even think of mounting a coup, and the implication of this was that the supply of arms to the anarchist militias needed to be choked off. The inability to impose a single command on the militias led to serious shortcomings in their organization and operation since there was not the slightest coordinating and planning of military operations between the different militias manning the same front.

So, the CAMC also failed in the military sphere. The 24 October 1936 decree militarizing the militias laid the ground-rules for the Republic's bourgeois army. The only option open to militians was to resist the inevitable militarization which, by March 1937, had become a fact of life.

Meanwhile, the revolutionary situation in the streets was unmoved by the anarcho-syndicalist leadership's calls for collaboration. The diffuse power of the different local committees spread throughout Catalonia, with varying degrees of power and autonomy, and in some places led to a complete break with republican legality and the balance of power that existed in Barcelona between the Generalidad and the CAMC. Thus, in Lérida the CNT, the POUM, and the UGT had taken over the running of the city and had set up a People's Committee from which republican forces were excluded, the intention being to establish an authority based solely on workers' organizations. Both Josep Rodes (POUM) who held down the position of public commissar, and

Joaquín Vila (UGT), the serving Generalidad delegate, used their positions for the benefit of the People's Committee of Lérida, as did Francisco Tomás (FAI), exploiting his role on the new People's Intelligence Committee.

These local revolutionary committees had set themselves up as out-and-out city-states, or committee governments,[1] imposing fines and taxes, recruiting militians for the front, setting up control patrols to enforce their authority, carrying out public-work schemes funded by revolutionary taxation as a way of sorting out mass unemployment, expropriating factories and workshops that were then collectivized, imposing a new rationalist educational model, seizing buildings and foodstuffs, buying arms abroad, maintaining free hospitals and canteens, and much more. Town councils were replaced by these local committees and the Generalidad was denied the slightest influence. Throughout Catalonia, without the CNT's issuing any instructions to this effect, bourgeois firms and properties were systematically expropriated along with churches and monasteries, even as the CAMC in Barcelona was dividing up barracks, printshops, newspapers, and a number of buildings and hotels between different organizations. The CAMC's suggestions were followed by the local and barrio committees, as long as they did not contradict revolutionary interests, but they ran into tremendous resistance when they were seen as compromises with the bourgeoisie and the Generalidad government. At the same time, the CAMC had to rely on these local committees if it wanted to see its plans implemented. The conflict within the CNT-FAI leadership between those for and those against collaboration extended into troubled relations between the CAMC and local revolutionary bodies. The Generalidad

---

1   G. Munis uses this expression in his book *Jalones de derrota, promesa de victoria* (Barcelona: Muñoz Moya, 2003).

government merely legalized the social and economic fait accompli of the collectivizations and "revolutionary gains" as its only way of building the prestige and acceptance it lacked. The CAMC was scarcely in a position to govern or ordain anything outside of the city of Barcelona, without the acquiescence of the local committees or trade unions. The latter's weakness was that they could not consolidate themselves as a genuine alternative authority across the whole of Catalonia without the coordinating and marshaling support of a labor organization, much less in defiance of all the existing organizations.

The CAMC and Generalidad coincided in their policy of reaffirming the old town councils against the local revolutionary committees, a policy pursued very effectively by the Comarcal Militias Department headed by Josep Miret and Joan Pons. That department removed recruitment and organization of militians from the local committees—who had been doing the job unsolicited for several weeks—and assigned it to comarcal commissions based on the new territorial boundaries in Catalonia. This comarcal arrangement made it easier to control the various local committees: they each had to send a delegate who would be operating well away from local revolutionary pressure.

So, not only was the CAMC not a revolutionary government coordinating local committees, but it actually regarded the latter as diminishing its authority. And the higher CNT committees not only backed the strengthening of the Generalidad, but indeed applauded the weakening of the local committees. Which is why they let the PSUC's Miret and the ERC's Pons get on with things. It was another serious mistake by the CNT leadership because undermining the local committees eroded the real base upon which CNT authority depended, beyond the city of Barcelona.

In Barcelona, the revolutionary ward committees, where the real authority of the CAMC was rooted, set themselves up in the headquarters of each barrio's defense committee, overseeing thirteen supply warehouses, as well as a number of commandeered buildings, prominent among them the Hotel Numero Uno in the Plaza de España; the Monumental Bullring; Los Escolapios on the Ronda de San Pablo; the Campo Sagrado tram depot; the San Andrés, Pueblo Nuevo, and Pedralbes barracks; the Francia train station, and the Northern train station.

In 1975, Marcos Alcón, from the Nosotros group and a CAMC member, revealed a revolutionary initiative made by several defense committee delegates after the dissolution of the CAMC. It was meant to bolster and increase the power of the defense committees:

The CAMC had already ended. We had our counsellors in Catalonia's Generalidad government. And that is how things stood when a commission representing the Barcelona defense committees came to have a word with me—a commission made up of Daniel Sánchez and Ángel Carballeira from the Gracia district, and I think it was Trapote from the Central district and some others I cannot recall. They told me the following: "The defense committees met last night. We analysed the situation and share the belief that the revolution is being strangled by the higher committees. So, it was agreed that we should go to the Casa CNT-FAI and toss out the members of the committee, and we are here to propose that you become the new regional committee secretary." Although I agreed with them that we had been making too many concessions, I couldn't have been more surprised. But I was one of those militants belonging to the cadres of authoritative voices that I was speaking about earlier, and the "responsible" militant in me bridled. And I answered them: "I agree absolutely with what you say: Let's kick over the traces. But this is not the way to go about it. *The cure could be, would be, worse than the disease.*"[2]

Alcón's account encapsulates the contradictions of the CNT membership, as well as their continual retreats from principle in the face of governmentalism, retreats imposed by an ideology of anti-fascist unity that looked no further than winning the war on fascism. It also encapsulates the impotence of the grassroots membership and the defense committees, who had spearheaded the revolutionary events of July 1936, and who, months later, would take on Stalinism in May 1937; they were incapable, however, of grappling with "responsible" higher committees. They also were not in any position to replace those higher committees, because they were now performing functions essential to a movement wholly subsumed into the machinery of the state. The CNT was such a motley organization that, in actual fact, it encompassed "several CNTs." Yet even this was not as important as the widening gulf separating the local and barrio committees from the higher committees.

Against Militarization

Twenty-six September 1936 saw a Generalidad government formed that included anarchist "counsellors." The termination of the CAMC was formalized on 1 October 1936.

A decree on 9 October—with a follow-up released on 12 October—announced that all the local committees that had emerged on 19 July 1936 were being disbanded and that their places would be taken by new town councils. Despite resistance from many local committees to their disbandment, and several months of delay in the appointment of the new councils, this was a death blow from which they would

---

2   Marcos Alcón "Remembering 19 July 1936," *Espoir* (20 July 1975).

not recover. The resistance from the CNT membership, who ignored the desires of the higher committees or the orders from the Generalidad government, posed a threat to the anti-fascist agreement. The anarcho-syndicalist leaders were caught between the pressure of a membership loath to obey them and the accusation, coming from all the other anti-fascist forces, that the government's decrees had to be implemented and enforced, thereby bringing "the uncontrollables" to heel.

That was the true legacy of the CAMC and its nine weeks existence: the shift from local revolutionary committees wielding all the power on the streets and in the factories, to their dissolution—to the sole advantage of fully re-established Generalidad authority. Similarly, the decrees signed on 24 October[3] regarding militarization of the Militias as of 1 November and the promulgation of the Collectivization decree completed the appalling record of the CAMC: namely, the shift away from worker militias made up of volunteer revolutionaries to a classic bourgeois army, subject to the monarchy's military code of justice and directed by the Generalidad; the shift away from expropriation and workers' control in the factories to a centralized economy controlled and steered by the Generalidad.

The delayed implementation of these decrees, caused by the quiet but fierce resistance of the CNT rank and file, which was still armed, ensured that the Generalidad government prioritized disarming the rearguard, fomenting a propaganda campaign against so-called "uncontrollables," and leading to a secondary goal summed up in the mantra-like slogan "Arms to the front."

The strong resistance coming from the anarcho-syndicalist grassroots to militarization of the militias, to

---

3 As published in the Generalidad's *Boletín Oficial* of 28 October 1936.

Generalidad control of the economy and collectivized firms, to the disarming of the rearguard and the dissolution of the local committees manifested itself in the several months by which actual implementation of the Generalidad government's decrees on these matters was delayed. In the spring of 1937 that resistance crystallized as an enormous malaise, exacerbated by unhappiness with the progress of the war, inflation, and the dearth of basic necessities. It culminated in widespread criticism by the CNT membership of the CNT-FAI higher committees' partnership in government, and of the anti-fascist and collaborationist policy of their leaders, who stood accused of having frittered away the revolutionary gains made on 19 July.

In October 1936, the decree militarizing the People's Militias generated huge discontent among the anarchist militias of the Durruti Column on the Aragon front. After protracted and bitter arguments in March 1937, several hundred volunteer militians based in the Gelsa area made up their minds to quit the front and return to the rearguard.[4] It was agreed that militians opposed to militarization would be relieved within a fortnight. They then quit the front, *taking their weapons with them.*

Once back in Barcelona and in the company of other anarchists (who argued for continuing and deepening the

---

4   "Not only did they refuse to be militarized, but they also ignored the insistence of both Committees [the CNT and FAI regional committees] that they dump their weapons and quit the front [...] since there was no way of reconciling the differences of opinion existing within the Durruti Column [...] in that there was such tension between the two factions that there were fears that this might result in a bloody clash [...] the bulk of the comrades from the Gelsa *agrupación* have quit the front in defiance of the views and accords of the specific and confederal organizations," in FAI, "Report presented by this Liaison Committee of the Anarchist Groups of Catalonia to the comrades of the region" (March? 1937).

July revolution) and against the CNT's collaboration with the government, the Gelsa militias decided to launch an anarchist organization separate from the FAI, the CNT, or the Libertarian Youth. Its mission would be to channel the anarchist movement along a revolutionary path. And so a new group was formally constituted in March 1937 after gestating for several months since October 1936. Its steering committee decided to take the name the "Friends of Durruti Grouping," which invoked the shared background of the former Durruti Column militians—though, as Balius correctly observed, this wasn't any sort of reference to the thinking of Durruti himself, but rather to his status as a popular legend.

To a greater or lesser extent, revolutionary opposition to militarization of the People's Militias showed itself in all the confederal columns, especially the Iron Column, which decided on a number of occasions "to pop down to Valencia" to give the revolution a boost and confront counter-revolutionary elements in the rearguard.

In February 1937 there was a gathering of confederal columns dealing with the militarization issue. Threats that columns not consenting to militarization would be denied arms, food, and manpower, coupled with the belief that the militians were about to be transferred to other already regularized units, made an impact. Many felt it was better to accept militarization and then adapt it flexibly to their own column. In the end, the ideology of anti-fascist unity and CNT-FAI collaboration in the business of government—in defense of the republican state—triumphed over the resistance to militarization, which was in the end accepted even by the recalcitrant Iron Column.

9

The Defense Committees, All or Nothing at All. From Potential Organs of Worker Power to Mere Armed Adjuncts of the Trade Unions

From late November 1936 until early December 1936, the CNT debated the role that defense committees should take in Barcelona.

The barrio revolutionary committees had not assumed any effective power, nor had they even coordinated with one another autonomously, having instead done so though a deferential Barcelona Defense Committee instigated, monitored, and funded by the Local Federation of Unions. So by the end of November these potential organs of power, thrown up in the barrios of Barcelona with the July 1936 uprising, found their roles reduced and abolished because the CNT had taken the governmentalist route.

By then the CNT had joined the Barcelona and Valencia governments. With the revolutionary path blocked, the ward revolutionary committees watched as the barrio defense committees and ward provisions committees were dismantled and annihilated, either taken over by the trade unions or subsumed into new bodies.

The function determines the agency. With no revolutionary coordinating, leadership, or administrative functions to perform, and no authority to wield, the defense committees, even if they were potential agencies of power, were fated to decline, undermined and subordinated to the trade unions.

At 10:00 AM on 29 November 1936, a Barcelona Plenum of Trade Unions and Wards convened: in attendance were representatives from the Printing Trades, Liberal Professions, Leatherworkers, Petroleum-workers, Public Services, Chemicals, Foodstuffs, Distributive Trades, Aviation, Communications, Transport, Construction, Health, Metalworking, Light and Power, Fishing Industry, Automobile, Municipal Officers, Railways, Public Entertainments, Glassmakers, Marine workers, and Peasant unions. Also in attendance were the defense committees from the following wards: Sarriá, Pueblo Nuevo, Prat Vermell [today's Zona Franca], Sants, Central, and Gracia, as well as the Local Defense Committee.[1]

At Doménech's suggestion it was agreed that the Foodstuffs and Distribution unions, along with the Supplies Department, headed by himself, would form a commission to devise a swift and effective solution to improve the supply situation in Barcelona city. A proposal that other unions also should be on the commission was rejected.

The discussion then moved to Item 4 on the agenda—"What is to be the status of the Defense Committees?"—with an introductory report from the Local Defense Committee outlining the activities of the defense committees.

Railways acknowledged the Local Defense Committee as having the same status as the various union delegations present, pointing out that "the Ward Committees will in all matters be answerable to that [Local Defense] Committee" which would have control of weapons stored on union premises. The unions would monitor their militants. A mandatory

---

1   Minutes of the Plenum of Unions and Wards held on 20 September 1936, opening at 10:00 AM.

ten *céntimo* stamp would be introduced in order to fund the Confederal Defense Committee.

Municipal Officers moved that the defense committees be empowered to appoint a delegate to the Local Plenum of Unions, but that each trade union "shall keep track of its members' weapons." As for finances, it agreed that "things should continue as they have been to date."

Foodstuffs was of the view that the defense committees should present all issues to the unions and that the latter would have "their own weapons in storage, monitored by the Local Defense Committee." The defense committees' expenses would be paid on a pro rata basis and each Ward Committee would oversee "all of its component groups."

Aviation declared that "the defense committees are vital in the wards, with all their prerogatives and obligations monitored by the Local Federation" of trade unions. Weapons and manpower had to be overseen by the ward defense committees.

Health was of the view that the defense committees, being made up of one delegate from each trade union, "must abide by trade union accords." Arms needed to be in the custody of the trade unions.

Liberal Professions thought that the defense committees were "the Organization's armed wing" and that they had to "abide by the unions' decisions, except in extreme cases."

Leatherworkers believed that "since the Defense Committee comrades are part and parcel of the trade unions," it was up to the latter to discuss current circumstances and determine what action to take. It expressed support for "the need for arms to be under the control of the Defense Committee." As for the financial side of things, it came down in favor of a pro rata payment.

Printing Trades saw the defense committees' mission as the armed defense of the CNT with the Local Defense

Committee liaising with the unions. It was up to the defense committees to control existing weaponry. "The ward defense committees ought to be made up of delegates from the unions embedded in those" barrios. There had to be a genuine working arrangement between the wards and the trade union headquarters in the barrios. The defense committees ought to be funded by the Local Federation of Unions.

Petroleum-workers made the point that "the defense committees should administer everything that falls under their jurisdiction." As to their funding, each union should hand over ten percent of its revenue.

Weaving & Textiles took the line that they should be acknowledged as having an existence of their own, "which they have had since the moment they were formed." They should control their weapons themselves. And the union to should sort out the financial side of things.

Distributive Trades defined the defense committees as defenders of the revolution "in accordance with the Organization's guidelines and norms." They should be organized along the same lines as the unions and embrace the principles of the CNT. It was up to the Local Federation of Unions to exercise "absolute control of said [defense] committees, of the comrades who serve on them [as well as of] any weapons they have." Funding should come from all the unions on a pro rata basis.

Communications endorsed Distributive Trades' suggestion. Transport abstained as the matter had not been on its agenda and thus there had been no debate on the issue. Metalworking thought that there was a need "for the functions of the defense committees to be defined." Fishing Industry contended that the defense committees had to retain the character they had when they were created and that the unions should have final say on anything they proposed.

The Local Defense Committee explained the work done by the defense committees "and the manner of their creation."

Glassworkers argued that it was time for the defense committees to disappear as they had served their purpose. Their members should rejoin their unions and any functions they were performing should be taken up by the Local Federation of Unions.

Marine-workers suggested that the membership of the defense committees should be appointed by the trade unions. A lively debate ensued favoring retention of the defense committees, with only Glassworkers dissenting. "The motion from the Distribution Union as outlined above" was carried unanimously, save for Glassworkers' opposing vote.

Delegations from the ward defense committees requested the right to contribute to the discussion.

The Sants Barrio Committee stated that the unions should consult the defense committees on matters of armed struggle, and it should be for the defense committees, rather than the trade unions, to oversee weapons and manpower in each barrio.

The Gracia barrio committee agreed with Sants, adding that the defense committees should be granted fresh investigation and monitoring powers at barrio level.

The Pueblo Nuevo barrio committee reported "comprehensively and clearly on the work done in this ward," asking for "arms and manpower to be controlled at ward level, backing its contention with clear arguments, and explaining how to carry it out." It asked the CNT unions to decide what percentage of defense committee slots should be set aside for UGT members.

The Local Federation of Unions, after a number of clarifications, called upon the gathering to decide once and for all "the situation and powers of the defense committees." Regarding the UGT, it explained that existing agreements granted it "thirty percent of the places on a ward-by-ward basis."

Transport broadened the debate to include the ward supplies committees, arguing that they should be retained until there were new bodies to replace them. In its view, the functions of the barrio-level supplies committees ought to be taken over by the Foodstuffs and Distribution Unions in concert with the Local Defense Committee "assuming, of course, that the ward defense militants can be brought on board." The Organization should make sure that positions of responsibility were filled by able comrades specialising in such tasks.

This was strictly a trade union outlook, which did not look kindly upon the importance the defense and supplies committees had acquired at the barrio level. They felt that, once the revolutionary uprising and its aftermath were over (both being exceptional, temporary phases), their functions should be taken over by the trade unions.

Distribution, agreeing with Transport's syndicalist viewpoint, suggested that "until a restructuring [of the ward supplies committees] has taken place," they should be controlled by the defense committees which were already under the thumb of the unions. The meeting endorsed this view.

The San Martín barrio committee requested that the mission of the defense committees be specified and asked if they might sit in on trade union plenums.

The Local Defense Committee gave a run-down of "this Committee and the work currently weighing upon its members."

Public Services suggested that comrades appointed by the Organization to positions of responsibility should "attend the meetings of their respective union militants," since that way the unions could monitor their actual policies. This was agreed.

Following a debate about weapons permits, a proposal was passed agreeing that the Local Federation of Unions and the Local Defense Committee would issue and stamp a "weapon license" that would then be distributed by the unions. The unions would keep a detailed copy of permits issued—compiling lists of names, addresses, wards, whether the weapon was a rifle or handgun, its calibre, and so on—for forwarding to the Local Defense Committee. At all times, the work of the defense committees would be under the supervision of the Local Federation of Unions.

The discussion then shifted to general business, with a notable warning from Distribution about the need to keep a tight rein on careerists stepping into unmonitored positions of responsibility, noting the existence of outside elements who acquired their union card after taking up their post.

What was being discussed was the measure of the ward defense committees' autonomy vis à vis the trade unions. Suggestions ranged from acknowledgment that the Local Defense Committee had an identity of its own and complete independence, acknowledging them as the ARMED WING OF THE CNT, through to their full and comprehensive subordination to the dictates of the Local Federation of Unions, which would not only be to debate matters and determine actions but also store weapons, control manpower, and fund the defense committees.

Though no limit was set to this ranking: it might or might not extend to the storage of weapons, to control over the men brandishing them, the determination of actions, possible exceptions to the trade unions' oversight of the defense committees, a sliding scale of supervision. The Local Federation of Unions oversees the Local Defense Committee, the latter the ward committees, and they the groups in each barrio...what was actually at stake was what sort of a working arrangement there should be in each barrio between the unions and the defense committees, or, if you like, how to structure the CNT's armed organization in each and every barrio and throughout the city of Barcelona.

Ultimately, the decision was to acknowledge the specific characteristics of the ward defense committees and the work of the Barcelona Defense Committee as the armed wing of the CNT in the city, albeit under the absolute control of the Local Federation of Unions.

On 2 December 1936, during the evening and night time hours, there was a meeting of the higher libertarian committees attended by the CNT's Regional and Local committees, the Defense Committee, the CNT-FAI Investigation Service, the Patrols, Public Order, and the Victims of Fascism Support Committee.[2]

For the Regional Committee, Mas reported on the Generalidad government crisis "prompted by the plan for a new army." He proposed that they come to a joint agreement that might later be endorsed by a Plenum of Locals and Comarcals [committees], and remarked on the discontent there was about the "winding up of the Law Commissions."

According to the Regional Committee, the essential issue was the widespread defiance of the calls to disarm: "In which the wards are our worst enemies."

Fábregas reported that Reverter was in Montjuic.[3] There was talk of the Estat Catalá conspiracy and "its plans for eliminating all the department chiefs for disagreeing with

---

2 A gathering of committees held on 2 December 1936.

3 Translator's note: Andreu Reverter was a playboy Catalanist appointed by Companys as Commissar-General of Public Order in Catalonia. He seems to have been linked to the more separatist wing of Catalanism. In the autumn of 1936, some police officers were intercepted while trying to smuggle gold bars into France. Some sort of a deal was struck between Reverter and Companys, Reverter was freed from custody but his body was later found on the roadside outside Manresa. His killers have variously been identified as FAI gunmen and henchmen of Companys from the Public Order Corps. The whole thing is a bit murky and mysterious. Given Reverter's position, small wonder that it was thought his arrest might be of interest to the plenum.

them" He stated that "Companys pretends to be sick [so as] to be unavailable to anybody." He noted the CNT's disagreement with Sandino's military scheme. And volunteered that this was all part of a "general onslaught" on the CNT.

Santillán called for discipline, citing the example of how the Aguiluchos, Ascaso, and Rojinegra columns had been unified on "one united front," whereas the PSUC's Libertad Column "seeking to go it alone, was seized by panic [and] rushed the train in order to get back here—and had to be compelled by force to return to the front lines." Then again, he gave his view that "decrees should not be accepted when it is known in advance [that the masses will not abide by them], as in the case of the collection of weapons."

Eroles reported that Companys had hinted to him about "the need to make changes." The cabinet crisis, according to Eroles, had been bubbling under the surface for a long time, and the CNT's opposition to the military scheme was merely a hypocritical pretext to force a crisis. Canela endorsed Eroles's account, stating that Companys had mentioned to him a long time ago that he had it in mind to form a CNT-UGT-Rabassaires cabinet.

Juanel took the floor to contradict Fábregas's line of argument, denied that the CNT was behind the cabinet crisis, and concluded that "we have to persuade the masses of the necessity for a united command."

Portela spoke up to reiterate what Santillán had already said, that is, that the CNT department chiefs should only agree to and commit themselves to "what we can deliver," recognizing that a mistake had been made in agreeing to disarm the rearguard; they had no way of getting their own members to comply, especially the revolutionary committees in the wards.

Doménech noted the differing outlooks among the committees in attendance and could see no option but to "tread a middle path." He stressed the contradiction between the

CNT's joining a government, when the tradition and education of the membership had always focused on rebelliousness and "living with no government and no distinctions; and now, through these alliances we have made, and despite our shrouding our actions in mystery, we serve in governments, class differences still pretty much exist and now, to cap it all, we are out to impose a steely discipline and blind obedience to a unified command." Doménech closed by saying "there is no way out of this bind."

Juanel spoke up again to move that responsibility be centralized and to argue for the necessity of discipline. Santillán argued that fascism had "regrouped" and formed a bloc that they needed to smash. But without an equivalent force, it would be impossible. The Defense Committee (Campos and Canela) countered Juanel and Santillán, claiming that "The Organization cannot and should not be controlled by four comrades, which seems to be the intention." If anybody made such an attempt, he would have to face down "the wards and [the] Unions."

At this get-together of the higher committees, again we see reference to revolutionary ward committees (and the trade unions) as guarantors of the revolutionary process, in opposition to fascism, in opposition to the Generalidad government, and most especially in opposition to the CNT-FAI's own higher committees.

The Regional Committee talked about working out some makeshift solution and resolving things at a later date. The Local Federation raised "the need to determine where we stand *vis-à-vis* the Generalidad Council" regarding the new military organization. Toryho asked why the Estat Català plot had not been reported. Magriña suggested that, in the future, "the comrades representing us on the Security Council should deliver detailed briefings "on completion of their service." In view of the lateness of the hour, the meeting was adjourned.

At the morning get-together of the higher committees, the militias of Madrid had been condemned for rejecting militarization; at the afternoon session, it was the ward committees that were criticized for rejecting disarmament. The rift between the higher committees and the grassroots membership was plain and showed every sign of growing into the abyss of a split.

A Plenum of Barcelona militants was held at 5:00 PM, on 5 December 1936.[4]

The first item for discussion was the output of the War Industry. The Local Federation reported the calamitous situation in every front-line unit, insisting that "determined and effective action be taken, and some solution to the issue be worked out."

Agustín, a member of the War Industry Monitoring Committee, gave the history of the Committee's performance, highlighting the names of García Oliver and Torrens as guarantees of the quality of the work done. He pointed out that the responsibility for shortcomings in the stream of provisions to the fronts lay with the distribution chain. Chiva added to this "the Via Durruti's lack of capacity," that is, the shortcomings of the old Central Provisions Committee, and the rivalry and lack of coordination currently found among the different Departments and their differing political persuasions. Somebody [name not recorded in the minutes] spoke up to say that they were not there to listen to reports from the War Industries Committees about past shortcomings "but to discuss and offer fresh proposals" to resolve the matter. Virgili said that empowering a Plenum of Militants "to override the accords of the Trade Unions" was not on, as if the criticisms coming from Chiva and Agustín struck him as having gone too far.

---

4   Minutes of the Plenum of Militants held in Barcelona on 5 December 1936.

The reminder that a Plenum of Militants could not amend the accords of a Plenum of Unions (and, by extrapolation, that a trade union plenum could not tinker with the accords of a regional plenum and a regional plenum in turn could not tinker with a national plenum) highlighted a basic bureaucratic mechanism of control. Criticisms and suggestions emanating from the rank and file membership were prey—just as they would have been in any other faction, whatever its ideological persuasion—to filtration, selection, and amendment, as they climbed up through the ranks, so that by the end, the Organization's final accords belonged to the same old bureaucrats, barely a few dozen individuals in office for years on end.

Santillán issued a reminder that "we are in collaborative mode" and that there was a "lamentable duplication in two committees supplying the front lines, an anomaly that must be sorted out through the amalgamation of the pair of them."

Next, he read "a plan for the reorganization of War Industry deliveries to the front lines," endorsed by representatives of the CNT and the UGT.

Busto expressed disagreement with the current tactics of the Organization "which allows for the UGT to edge the CNT out of the positions it holds."

The CNT had a sacrosanct regard for the UGT as a trade union. Stalinist candidates had only to run as UGT representatives rather than as PSUC representatives for them to win acceptance as partners in a government based on trade unions. The expansion of the UGT at the company level was the result of an unbelievable blind spot on the part of the CNT, which allowed any opponent of collectivization-socialization, or of CNT management, to mount their opposition as a UGT member and, almost always, with representation equal to that of the CNT, even though the UGT in some firms was a tiny minority or utterly non-existent.

Juanel called for an ironing out of differences and for the War Department to be recognized as having sole responsibility for the War Industries and supplying the front lines.

Fleche, who claimed to represent all of the front lines in Aragon, declared "that the comrades have been left to their own devices and there are differences between the various columns fighting in the front lines," although he did not detail whether or not those differences were due to ideological affiliation.

At the suggestion of the panel chairing the meeting, the scheme read by Santillán was passed, provided it had the prior agreement of the comrades currently directing and administering the War Industries.

Discussion then moved on to another item on the agenda: What freedom of action should the ward committees enjoy?

The secretary of the Local Federation of Unions raised a few anomalies regarding the performance of the tenants' defense committees formed at the ward level. It also railed against "other committees that pay no heed at all to the Organization's accords."

Agustín replied that the Local Federation was mixing up two separate issues—the tenants' committees and the defense committees—and indeed had not been specific and clear about which sort of committee was performing badly or well. He thought "that each committee, according to its character, has a specific function to perform. For instance, the Ward Defense Committee's task is to oversee the arming and defense of the ward, and has no right at all to meddle in the rent issue."

Prieto defended the performance of Gracia's Tenants Committee.

Ponce declared that "it is not true, as the Local Federation has claimed, that there are Revolutionary Committees in existence, for there are only Defense Committees." Nonetheless, he reckoned that "the functions and responsibilities of the Ward Defense Committees should be spelled out."

Briones, on the other hand, fervently defended the defense committees and "sees a danger to the revolution if their powers keep being eroded." Chiva too expressed support for "control of gear and armed men being left to the Ward Defense Committees."

Rubio spoke up in favor of the defense committees' performance. Segundo Martínez, a chairperson, moved: "That the matter of the defense committees be put to the Unions and that the defense committees defend their position at that time." This proposal was carried.

It was also agreed that the Tenants' Defense Committee's right to control all the buildings in Barcelona be recognized and that comparable bodies at ward level liaise with it.[5] The proceedings were brought to a close at 8:30 PM.

The barrio revolutionary committees, which emerged in Barcelona with the triumph of the workers over the army and fascist revolt, had, over those first few weeks, taken on many responsibilities, as already detailed, turning into genuine committee-governments.

But the CNT's higher committees, their prime aim being to win the war over fascism, decided to collaborate with the rest of the anti-fascist parties and organizations—later embracing governmentalism, joining the Generalidad government, and the Republican government. This involved a succession of retreats and an undermining of their initial revolutionary gains, both in the Militias and in control of public order in the rearguard.

As we have seen, Control Patrols made up of militians drawn from a range of anti-fascist organizations—CNT,

---

5 For further information about attempts to overhaul housing stock in Barcelona during the civil war, see Francesc Roca, *Política, economia y espacio. La política territorial en Cataluna (1936–1939)* (Barcelona: Ediciones del Serbal, 1983).

POUM, PSUC, and the Esquerra—was set up on 11 August. CNT militants were the majority, making up roughly half the 711 patrol personnel at that point.

In October 1936, the CNT's entry into the Generalidad government led to the establishment of an Internal Security Council characterized by a problematic dual command of public order forces by the CNT and the Generalidad government. The Control Patrols were losing their autonomy and decision-making capability, whereas the Public Order Commissariat, controlled by the PSUC and the Esquerra, was adding to coercive power, breathing fresh life into the Assault Guards and the Republican National Guard (the former Civil Guard). In late January 1937, PSUC-UGT militias quit the Control Patrols, their places being filled by CNT, Esquerra, and POUM personnel. The disappearance of the Control Patrols, and their absorption into a new unified Security Corps (as decreed on 4 March 1937), implied the end of the CNT's hegemony in police and repressive operations.

Against the backdrop of the fragile political and armed balance in the Barcelona rearguard in the spring of 1937, the expansion in and threat from bourgeois forces hell bent on securing a monopoly on violence, inspired the reorganization and preparation of defense committees at the barrio level, in anticipation of what looked like an inevitable show-down.

But by November-December 1936, the defense committees had become a hindrance to the pro-government policy of the CNT's higher committees; this required putting them to sleep and making them subordinate to the unions, mere armed adjuncts, however bothersome and useless.

In July 1936, the defense committees, having become revolutionary barrio committees in Barcelona and local revolutionary committees across Catalonia, were potentially organs of the power of the working class. They could have become everything had the revolutionary situation of 19 July spread and deepened. In the process of anti-fascist collaboration with the Generalidad government, the ward revolutionary committees lost all title to that description, and the functions of the defense committees were limited and reduced to armed struggle of the trade unions. Revolution or collaborationism. All or almost nothing.

10

The Bread War: Comorera versus the Barrio Committees

On 20 December 1936, the PSUC's Joan Comorera, head of the Supplies Department, made an important speech in Catalan[1] at the Gran Price hall in Barcelona.[2] It was reprinted in part in the Generalidad government's daily gazette the same day and, over the ensuing days, it appeared in the newspapers, generally in the form of a summary, which did not quite convey the importance, provocativeness, and harshness of what he had to say. But plenty of prominence was given, sometimes as a postscript to the speech, to what he had to say about the almost complete dearth of food supplies in Barcelona city.[3]

Comorera opened his speech with an admission that the PSUC had deliberately caused the recent crisis in the Generalidad cabinet, its specific purpose having been to drive the POUM from the government, militarize the militias, and bolster the Generalidad by means of a CNT-UGT compact.

He recalled the importance of the CNT-UGT Liaison Committee back in October, which had ensured that the Collectivizations decree got passed on 24 October 1936, along with the decree on General Mobilization, Militarization of

---

1   See *Treball* (21 December 1936).

2   Antonio Sesé, José del Barrio and Joan Comorera *Our Present Political Position. Speeches Delivered at the Gran Price on 20 December 1936.* Pamphlet (in Spanish) PSUC-UGT, undated.

3   "Wheat shortage," *La Vanguardia* (22 December 1936), 3.

the People's Militias, and the decree ordering that arms in the rearguard be handed in. He recalled how a trade union unity meeting was held the next day (25 October) at the Monumental bullring, at which Comorera had his chance to explain "to that vast multitude of brethren, Marxists and anarchists alike," the implications of the resolutions passed regarding collectivizations, militarization, and the calling in of arms "that were in the hands of groups calling themselves mavericks, but who are essentially parasitical groups fastening upon the revolution. And not merely parasitical groups—more or less passive as they live off the revolution—but often out-and-out gangsters of revolution."

But, Comorera lamented, those decrees "had been written on damp paper," since the mobilization decree and the decree calling in arms in the rearguard had not been implemented "and, right on the front lines no less, we have seen a sort of edict against the mobilization decree and the decree unifying the militias."[4]

Comorera asked whether such a slap in face of the government could be tolerated. He recounted the efforts made to bring the situation under control: "At the Generalidad there was a sort of a Grand Council meeting held, under the chairmanship of President Companys and involving all the department heads and leadership committees of all the organizations represented in the government, a plenary session that concluded with a note of complete confidence in the Council, but which was obviously little more than empty verbiage ["*pura literatura*"], given the situation that exists."[5]

---

4   The allusion is to a letter of objection to militarization, dated 1 November 1936 and issued by Durruti, and to the address he broadcast over the radio on 4 November 1936. See Agustín Guillamón, *Barricadas en Barcelona* (Barcelona: Espartaco Internacional, 2007), 127–138.

5   A reference to the extra-ordinary Generalidad Council meeting of 5–6 November 1936. See *Barricadas en Barcelona*, 127–138.

After reviewing the efforts to thrash out a joint policy with the CNT, one that could grapple successfully with the serious problems posed by the war, Comorera pointed out that, on 24 November, the PSUC had presented "to the CNT and FAI comrades a paper signed by the PSUC and the UGT," proposing "a government streamlining" that would "do away with all hints of systematic discord and revolutionary infantalism." He insisted that, "under the new Council [i.e. Generalidad cabinet] no part should be played by any representative of the Trotskyist faction, which has hijacked a responsible movement not of its making."

Comorera argued that it was right and proper for the POUM to be excluded "on many grounds. Because this Trotskyist faction has systematically pursued a policy of divisiveness. It has maliciously reminded us, and the CNT, of everything that might separate us, everything that might bring us into conflict with one another, everything that might compel us, if it continued, to break ranks with the unity pact we had signed."

Speaking about the POUM, Comorera was uncompromising: "Trotskyism: the source of discord in a movement it did not create." He charged the POUM with carrying out counter-revolutionary activity, "heightening the diffidence and mistrust felt then, and perhaps still felt now, by some members of the CNT leadership," by telling them that eventually, once fascism was beaten, the International Brigades would become a tool in the hands of the Communist Party against the anarchists, as had happened in Russia. Such "systematic" efforts by the POUM were designed simply to thwart "collaboration between the two trade union centrals, without which the war against fascism was as good as lost."

After a lengthy rant against the POUM's international policy, which he said was designed solely "to undermine the anti-fascist front," he summed up the essential cause of the crisis in the Generalidad government (in December 1936), a crisis triggered by the PSUC, as the need to ensure a homogeneous government enjoying both full powers and some prestige in the eyes of the working class.

Comorera argued that such a strong government, with full powers, had to be able to enforce decrees so that they did not remain dead letters, as they had under the first Tarradellas government, in which the POUM's Nin had held a post. They needed a strong government with the means to implement an effective military policy embracing all the forces on the front lines.

Turning to the economy, Comorera argued that "we have to ensure that nobody breaches or circumvents the collectivizations decree," in clear reference to the CNT's industrial unions, which were out to socialize entire sectors of production; "the time for initiatives from small groups has passed, and we need to have a holistic view of the problem" and build faith in collectivism.

He claimed that "today, economic policy confronts us with some worrisome issues," because Catalonia had, in just a few short months, squandered "the wealth built up over preceding generations," and now the "party" was over. After noting that Catalan industry had failed to make up abroad for the markets it had lost within Spain due to the Fascist rebellion and the disappearance of other industries, he offered, as a solution "strict adherence—not one iota added—to the collectivizations decree, which has an economic rationale that, if it is followed, will ensure that we build our economy at a fast rate." Comorera also broached the problem of redistributing work, warning workers that, with the crushing of the fascists, an entire world, an entire economic structure had vanished. The bourgeoisie had vanished and with it had gone many trades and professions. "Parasitical industries have vanished for good." The workforce from industries now gone—or, like construction, disabled during war-time—should be redeployed elsewhere.

Moreover, Comorera argued that a fiscal policy and municipalization of public services were needed if they were to meet the pressing needs of the war.

It was not possible for unemployed workers to be paid a full week's wages, while those who actually put in three days a week got only three days' pay. He stated that "over the five months this war has lasted, the Generalidad has forked over upwards of ninety million pesetas in wages and wage supplements. It has paid all sorts of wages. It has even paid a wage to the 'queers' (*invertidos*) in Chinatown. Let's not proclaim that too loudly!" All of this was now doomed, he noted, because the Generalidad had run out of money. He summed up what he had been saying with a slogan of sorts: "A new fiscal policy closely bound up with an economic policy were the foundations of a sound military policy."

After that, Comorera's diatribe, a high-falutin' political speech better suited to a Generalidad president than to the head of department, confined itself to Supply policy, the responsibility of the department he now headed. His oratory became more concrete, but much more aggressive as well.

"I took over as councillor in charge of Supplies a day ago, and I find that in Catalonia there is no wheat, in Catalonia there are no eggs, in Catalonia there is no meat, Catalonia is all but out of fish, Catalonia has little milk. In Barcelona, I find endless queues where our female comrades are tormented by delays and anxiety, by disappointment when it comes to bread, milk, eggs, meat, all of which are basic necessities. What has happened? What has happened is that we have used up all, or nearly all, of our wealth on a party over these past five months—and that it will be difficult, not simply to rebuild our old economy, but to alleviate this almost complete dearth of basic necessities."

In a manner both populist and rabble-rousing, Comorera made a direct connection between the shortage of basic necessities and the abundance of committees, especially the ward defense committees and their supply warehouses in Barcelona, as well as the revolutionary committees in every locality outside of Barcelona:

Comrades: I have come across an extraordinary number of committees [...] issuing orders that products needed in Barcelona are not to leave their comarca, even though there may be a surplus of them in certain villages; committees that will not allow the free circulation of goods that are not only vital to sustain the energy levels of women and men who live and fight for the war effort, but the very dearth of which places the lives of our children in jeopardy. Committees even in Barcelona: some fantastic defense committees that only defend the situations of privilege they established at the outset of this revolution, this war. Defenses committees that, each and every one, have set up their own little supply warehouses, while working-class women in Barcelona are forced to queue up and return home without any bread for their children. Defense committees that have, to the detriment of the community, replaced the old intermediaries, because those making up those committees in Barcelona and beyond Barcelona think they are entitled to levy taxes on every package a citizen carries. Hence the rise in basic living costs in Barcelona. The rising costs are not, as is routinely argued, down to small retailers: because the unbelievable difference between the price paid to the farmer and the price paid by the consumer, that fantastic margin ends up, not in the retailer's hands, but almost wholly in the hands of these committees.

So Comorera was pinning the blame for the lack and high cost of food on the defense committees, rather than on hoarding or speculation by retailers. His speech justified and endorsed the slogan on placards and leaflets at the housewives' demonstrations of late 1936 and early 1937: "More bread and fewer committees," they read. The demonstrations were sponsored and manipulated by the PSUC. There was an obvious clash between two opposing Supplies policies: the PSUC line and the line of the CNT's Foodstuffs Union. Through thirteen ward supply warehouses overseen by the barrio revolutionary committees (or, rather, by their defense sections) the Foodstuffs Union supplied rations, free of charge, to the people's kitchens which were accessible to the unemployed and their family members; in addition, they maintained centers for the care of refugees who, by April 1937, numbered 220,000 in Barcelona. This was a network of outlets rivalling the retailers (who operated strictly in accordance with the law of supply and demand) and it was designed primarily to ensure that products remained affordable since rising prices would render them inaccessible to workers, and of course to the unemployed and refugees. Retailers were deeply involved in the black market and raked in huge profits thanks to the (literal) hunger of the majority. Comorera's bread war on the ward supplies committees had no purpose other than to wrest any vestige of power from the defense committees, even if the result of that war was a Barcelona low on rations and facing food shortages.

Comorera's strategy over the ensuing months added to military policy (militarization of the People's Militias), economic policy (strict enforcement of the collectivization decree, pre-empting socialization of entire industries and giving the Generalidad control of all companies), and financial policy (the S'Agaro financial decrees issued by Tarradellas in January 1937 as an instrument of state control of the entire Catalan economy) a "relentless supplies policy" that would do away with the revolutionary committees' and defense committees' distribution network and introduce a retailer-dominated free market. What was required to implement these policies was a strong government—the purging of the POUM being a first step—a government capable of turning decrees into orders and effective measures that were actually implemented.

The way to that strong government was through unification of the two trade union associations. According to Comorera, that policy "Is not opposed by the UGT, nor by the PSUC, nor by the ERC, nor by the Unio de Rabassaires. Nor is the CNT opposed to it. This I know and let me state it loud and clear in all sincerity. From our dealings and association with them, we know that the men representing the CNT are making honest, loyal, magnificent efforts so as to work with us on creating these new conditions. I acknowledge and proclaim that because it is the truth."

Outstanding orator that he was, Comorera then posed a rhetorical, but loaded, question to his audience: "Who could oppose all of this, which we all want [anti-fascist unity], coming to pass?," only to answer that

for a start, the pseudo-revolutionary rabble-rousing that, by precipitating events, and seeking to accelerate the revolution, poses a threat to victory. The parasites on the back of the revolution who do not want to see conditions changed, who do not want a change in the present situation. Agents provocateurs, agents provocateurs who might as easily be found in our ranks as in any other organization, agents provocateurs who spill our comrades' blood in the rearguard [...] who operate at grassroots levels, poisoning militants' minds; agents provocateurs who lie in wait for you around a bend in the road, or attack homes in the night and murder those who get in their way.

To the rabble-rousers and agents provocateurs, Comorera added gangsters:

And then there is the gangster of revolution. The gangster, the man who cashes in, the bandit, a phenomenon found in every revolution, in every period of revolution. The man who does not want revolution unless it serves his personal interests [...] The cacique, the new satrap to be found in so many comarcas around Catalonia. Petty satraps surrounded by their mercenaries, better armed than the men in the front lines. Petty satraps who say they want no dictatorship, but who have, right where they are, imposed the dictatorship of their irresponsibility.

Oddly, but maybe this was part of his excellent oratory, Comorera barely mentioned the buzzword of the day, and steered clear of harping on "uncontrollables," although his audience certainly would have expected to hear that word mentioned at some point during his address. Instead he deployed a motley spectrum of synonyms, talking about rabble-rousers, agents provocateurs, and gangsters—that is, mavericks.

Comorera closed his speech with an appeal to the sense of responsibility of every organization, for the sake of achieving a steely anti-fascist unity. To comprehend his speech, we need to bear in mind the strategy pushed by Erno Gero[6]: of adopting a *nuanced* approach to the anarchist movement, by drawing its leaders into the machinery of state while ferociously repressing its more revolutionary elements, who

---

6   Translator's note: Erno Gero (1898–1980), joined Hungarian CP in 1918, implicated in the Soviet Republic in Hungary in 1919. Acted for Comintern in France before being sent to Spain where he was known as Pedro. His brief was to crush the POUM, exploit differences between the CNT-FAI rank and file and more compliant leaders of those organisations and to promote the PSUC in Catalonia. By 1945 he was back in Hungary serving as Interior minister in 1953 and party general secretary in 1956 before fleeing to the USSR following the Hungarian Uprising. In 1962 he was expelled from the party and died in March 1980.

were foully slandered as uncontrollables, gangsters, murderers, agents provocateurs, and mavericks.[7] Comorera very plainly pointed to the defense committees as fitting that bill.

The barrio committees versus Comorera

In the 29 December 1936 edition of *Solidaridad Obrera* the Liaison Commission published a "communiqué to public opinion" on the bread issue, a statement first published in *La Vanguardia* a couple of days before.[8]

Before commenting on the significance of this statement, we need to explain what this Liaison Commission was. On Sunday 26 July 1936, as the Plenum of Regionals and Comarcals was definitively endorsing, once and for all, the CNT's entry into the Central Antifascist Militias Committee (up until then the CNT's involvement had been only a temporary expedient), it was also agreed that a Central Supplies Committee should be established as a vital adjunct to the CAMC.

The Central Supplies Committee was a revolutionary body, formed by the various barrio supplies committees, which, in turn, were merely sections or departments of the ward revolutionary committees. Barcelona had thirteen ward supply warehouses that ensured Barcelona was kept stocked with basic provisions. These had grown out of the logistical arrangements for supplies accessible to each barrio defense committee, prior to and during the revolutionary upheaval of 19 and 20 July.

The Generalidad's 21 July 1936 decree endorsing Citizen Militias answerable to and controlled by the Generalidad government, was eclipsed by the actual formation of a CAMC under the sway of the CNT-FAI, a collaborative body

---

7   See Agustín Guillamón "The NKVD and the SIM in Barcelona. Some of Gero's reports on the war in Spain" (in Spanish), *Balance*, No 22 (November 2001).

8   *La Vanguardia* (27 December 1936) 2; and *Solidaridad Obrera* (29 December 1936), 6.

involving the trade unions, the workers' parties, the bourgeois parties, and the Generalidad government. Its task was primarily to oversee the war effort and public order. As an important auxiliary to the CAMC, the Central Supplies Committee had been launched under the exclusive control and direction of the barrio revolutionary committees: it amounted to a new name adopted by the barrio defense committees following their armed victory. After 19–20 July 1936, the supplies committees and defense committees became sections of the ward revolutionary committees. They wielded real power, which the Generalidad's decrees sought to disguise and avoid mentioning, although there was an attempt to subsume them into the machinery of the state.

This Central Supplies Committee operated in concert with the Barcelona City Council's Supplies Department and with the other organizations that belonged to the CAMC, whether in handing over municipal premises for use as public kitchens or issuing vouchers from the mayoral offices.

The 26 July 1936 Plenum of Comarcals and Locals unanimously agreed that the CNT would work with the rest of the anti-fascist organizations and with the Generalidad government through the CAMC. As a vital adjunct to the CAMC, a Central Supplies Committee was set up: its aim was to keep the militias on the Aragon front supplied, to feed the militias' families (in the absence of the wage-earner) and the many penniless unemployed. The free people's canteens were the revolution's very first achievement, since for many families it was their very first time "eating out at a restaurant," but above all it resolved an ongoing worry of the volunteer militians: ensuring that their families could survive while they themselves were on the front lines. Not until mid-September did the militias begin to receive their soldier's pay. So the Central Supplies Committee was a revolutionary agency meeting an essential requirement of the volunteer militias during the early days. Comorera would later refer to this as a squandering of resources and "partying" in the early days. The Order of 26 July 1936 spelled out the importance of the Central Supplies Committee as an auxiliary to the CAMC.[9]

Given the importance of the work being done by these supplies committees, there was no way that they could be circumvented in the establishment of the Supplies Department after the dissolution of the CAMC in early October 1936.

The Supplies Department was created by a decree of 4 August 1936, but to all intents and purposes it existed only on paper until 14 October following the dissolution of the CAMC and local committees, when orders were issued for the effective organization of the Supplies Department, which the CNT's Doménech had been appointed to head. Collaboration with the ward supplies committees was vital to ensure the efficient operation of the Supplies Department in the new revolutionary situation that arose after the revolutionary days of July.

Article 12 of the organic decree governing organization of the Supplies Department had this to say of the need to work with the ward supplies committees in Barcelona: "The Local Liaison Bureau will be composed of representatives from the appropriate Department of Barcelona City Council and each of the city's ward supplies committees. Said Committee will be a *rapporteur* in all matters relating to supplies in Barcelona city."[10] That (Barcelona) Local Bureau would comprise a chief and a number of officials acting on his instructions.

Once the CAMC had been done away with, the dissolution of the Central Supplies Committee became imperative, but this did not happen until 20 October. However, given the

---

9   That Order appears in Agustín Guillamón, *Barricadas en Barcelona*, 224–225.

10 Decree of 6 October 1936. See *Diari Oficial de la Generalitat de Catalunya*, No. 288 (14 October 1936).

need to rely upon the real, irreplaceable, and unassimilating ward supplies committees, the decision was made to integrate them into the Local Liaison Bureau: "Hereby decreed: Article 1. The Central Supplies Committee is dissolved. Article 2. The functions performed by said Committee shall, dating from the publication of this present decree, fall under the remit of the Local Liaison Bureau as established under Article 12 of the Supplies Department' organic decree."[11]

Another decree from the same date set up the Catering Council to look after "sustenance of jobless, indigent persons and refugees." The revolutionary people's kitchens of July and August 1936 that had fed militias, their families, and the unemployed, gave way to a bourgeois charity that made no bones about classifying the population as a notorious mish-mash of jobless, refugees, tramps, and indigents.

So the Liaison Commission that addressed public opinion through that article more or less represented the revolutionary committees and their supplies sections in the wards around Barcelona, the last remaining bastion of the erstwhile Central Supplies Committee, that revolutionary body and adjunct of the CAMC.[12]

The Liaison Commission opened its piece with a telling introduction to who they were:

> Independent of any party politics and bound up with the needs of the people and the revolution, the Liaison Commission must speak out publicly against certain

---

11 Decree of 17 October 1936: see *Diari Oficial de la Generalitat de Catalunya*, No 294 (20 October 1936).

12 In his detailed and interesting biography of Comorera, Caminal is wide of the mark when he confuses this "Commission liaising between the revolutionary (and supply) committees of Barcelona's barrios and the Supplies Department" with the "CNT-UGT Liaison Committee." See Miquel Caminal, *Joan Comorera. Guerra i revolució (1936–1939)*, Vol. II, 79 et seq.

comments and charges levelled by persons whose sole interest, they have revealed, is to court a popularity that, in revolutionary terms, they do not merit—and, to achieve it, must turn the streets of Barcelona into a "battleground" where UGT and CNT comrades must squabble over that which is by and for us all.

That is not going to happen, despite Comorera, despite Vachier[13] and all those dangerously and irresponsibly provoking bloody clashes between the workers of Catalonia and Spain.[14]

Comorera had already hinted in his address at the Gran Price on 20 December at who the main enemy was: the defense committees. In this article, the Liaison Commission, which is to say the ward revolutionary committee representatives on the Barcelona city council (along with their defense and supplies sections), likewise identified their chief enemy: the PSUC leader, Joan Comorera. The enemies plainly identified each other within days of the PSUC leader's taking charge of the Supplies Department. The gloves were off: it was Comorera versus the defense committees. And the battleground was ready as well: Barcelona's food supply, especially its bread supply.

The Liaison Commission recalled that it had reported to the incoming chief of the Supplies Department, Comorera, "to offer its cooperation." The response was disappointing: "We were received by Vachier who, with hypocritical words

---

13 Jaume Vachier Pallé was appointed director-general of Supplies by Comorera. In 1934 Vachier had been chief of Traffic and City Police at Barcelona city hall. Consistent with the anti-CNT, repressive outlook of Dencàs and Badía, he had issued the city police with short arms.

14 *Solidaridad Obrera* (29 December 1936), 6. *La Vanguardia* of 27 December 1936 (p. 2) reprinted the same statement, but set amid a more wide-ranging article on kindred matters.

(as his latest comments have demonstrated), led us to understand that it was only logical that a change of chief would mean a change in Supplies policy."

The Supplies Commission then asked bluntly about its own status. Vachier's response was as honest as it was brutal: "I cannot tell you anything," he replied, "because that is a matter for Comorera to resolve: although I can tell you that, strictly speaking, your Commission has not performed the function laid down in the Decree that gave it lawful status, and also that the ward committees, which have been operating so efficiently to date, have to go: those institutions and bodies that survive at public expense and which are today doing nothing must fall into line with the revolution."[15]

Vachier was clearly spelling out what the Liaison Commission was and who it represented: the ward committees (with their defense and supplies sections). His argument was odd and provocative, acknowledging as it did the proven efficiency of the ward committees in keeping the city of Barcelona supplied since 19 July 1936, only to arbitrarily point out that the time had come for them to bow out—when there was as yet no one to step into their shoes.

The Liaison Commission asked Vachier: "Do you know how the ward committees function?" To which Vachier replied: "Yes, and tomorrow, after the Council has met, we will tell you what the new Supplies plan is and what your functions will be." The Liaison Commission noted: "We haven't been told a thing."

Comorera quite simply intended to dispense with those committees completely and to create a brand new distribution network wholly controlled by the [Generalidad's] Supplies Department. This was a risky and a provocative undertaking at a time of food shortages and, since even

---

15 Unless otherwise stated, the quotation is taken from *Solidaridad Obrera* of 29 December 1936 (p. 6).

Vachier had acknowledged the efficiency shown by the barrio committees, its entire purpose was to hand over political control of supplies distribution to the PSUC and abolish the committees at any price.

The secretary to the Liaison Commission, Bonet, used this opportunity to explain the operation of the revolutionary barrio committees to a wider public:

> Across Barcelona, there are thirteen distribution warehouses, meaning one for each ward: each of these is staffed by four or five workers who load and unload the sacks; insofar as they can, they see to it that food is set aside for the infirm and milk for the children; that coal, potatoes, sugar, etc., are on sale at the most reasonable prices; and, in the absence of a "ration book," lots of people obtain theirs via the workshop or factory where they are employed. All in all, the Ward Supplies Committees add up to less than a hundred of the "bureaucrats" (of which Vachier spoke), and many get only four potatoes and an occasional kilo of rice. As to other matters, the Liaison Commission needs to state not merely that "distribution" to the ward, and thence to retailers, is made on a fair and proportional basis, but that anyone querying the honesty of the men of the CNT and FAI can have ready access to the books, which will show that it is not they who make up the "new rich," but those hell bent on becoming such.

Bonet put his finger on one of the key points of friction with the PSUC. The supply depots of the barrio committees monitored what, how, and how much was supplied to retailers for sale to the public, and at what price, once the "revolutionary" needs of the barrio (i.e. the needs of its sick, its children, its unemployed, its people's canteens, and so on) had been met. Comorera was lobbying for the abolition of these revolutionary barrio committees and for a free market.

He also knew that these two things went hand in glove, and that a free market would be a delusion unless the defense committees were done away with.

Nonetheless, Bonet was trying to broker a solution to avert a head-on clash with Comorera. On the one hand, he blamed Vachier for any lack of understanding between the Department and the committees; and on the other, he suggested that the barrio committees, hitherto 100 percent CNT, might accommodate a percentage of UGT personnel, mentioning a figure of thirty percent.

Somewhat innocently, Bonet asked: "Why should these distribution depots be done away with? So that new ones can be set up?" and, adopting a more realistic, but just as naive, tone, he asked: "Can the correctness of Comorera's supply policy be demonstrated by holding a rally and labelling those who are to cooperate with it as 'gangsters,' 'speculators,' 'parasites,' and 'cowards'?" So Bonet still believed that collaboration with Comorera was feasible even after, at that rally at the Price theatre, Comorera had already announced loud and clear that he intended to do away with all committees, starting with the defense committees.

Stalinism was a new phenomenon, hard to comprehend and without precedent. For that reason, Bonet could not believe that the UGT, the other "workers" union in the CNT's world view, would not raise its voice with the CNT and repudiate Comorera: "This is not the time for speechifying. Not the time for pinning the blame on others. We are short of bread and must find some. Without bread there will not be any UGT, CNT, Comorera, or any other councillor who can restrain the people, the women with their babes-in-arms clamouring for bread. So we, in concert with these women, will identify the guilty parties, if there are any to be found."

Yet despite Bonet's populist rhetoric, women's demonstrations clamouring for "more bread and fewer committees" and displaying other PSUC slogans were already underway.

Bonet concluded his statement by rebutting Vachier's claim that there were 1,200 bureaucrats on the barrio committees, closing with an appeal for a cooperation and mutual respect that the ensuing months would show to be impossible: "What Vachier has said about 1,200 bureaucrats and about this Commission's unwillingness to accept any direction from the councillor and about our being the speculators of the day is knowingly false [...] And we honestly regret that such things are happening when we should be united in a common purpose, namely, COLLABORATION and respect for one another."

The article was signed by P. Bonet as Liaison Commission secretary. Comorera had clearly identified the enemy he was out to destroy: the defense committees. But the latter, even though they had identified Comorera as a deadly foe, still clung to their illusions about the chances of collaboration between the UGT and the CNT, because they firmly believed that it was a question of agreement between workers at grassroots levels.

They had not yet grasped that Comorera's "bread war" saw a provision-less Barcelona as preferable to the barrio committees' retaining the slightest vestige of power. The sole aim the Stalinists of the PSUC had set themselves was the destruction of all the defense committees, even if that resulted in bread shortages.

The Economic and Political Roots of the Bread War

Rational, planned, adequate provisioning of Barcelona and of Catalonia would have meant deferring to ideas of CNT Economic Councillor, Joan P. Fábregas, who struggled in vain at Generalidad Council meetings from September through to December 1936, to secure a monopoly on foreign trade, in the face of opposition from every other political faction.[16] Meanwhile, on the Paris grain market, ten or twelve private Catalan wholesalers were bidding against one another, forcing prices up. But a monopoly on foreign trade, which was not even a revolutionary step, but simply an appropriate measure in an emergency war situation, was an affront to the free-market philosophy peddled by Comorera.

There was a direct link between bread lines in Barcelona and the senseless competition between the private wholesalers on the European grain, armaments, or raw materials markets. It is very curious that the official histories stress that, on 17 December 1936, following a government crisis triggered by the PSUC, the POUM's Nin was expelled from the government over his denunciation of stalinism; whereas we find scarcely any mention of the fact that the CNT's Fábregas—the very man who had drawn up the Collectivizations and Workers' Control Decree passed on 24 October was also expelled.

Fábregas's departure from the government meant that the Decree would be rolled out, not by its author, but by Tarradellas and Comorera, who denatured and manipulated it to an incredible extent, turning it into an instrument for Generalidad control over the Catalan economy and all collectivized undertakings. The Generalidad was able to appoint an all-powerful receiver-director at its whim and, above all, had the power to sink maverick or recalcitrant firms by withholding the funds to pay wages and buy raw materials, without which firms were doomed to grind to a complete halt.

Fábregas's removal also meant the removal of the principal champion of the establishment of a vital monopoly on foreign trade, a monopoly that was to be replaced by a free market. Comorera had *carte blanche* to impose a

---

16 Juan P Fábregas, *Los factores económicos de la Revolución Española* (Barcelona: Oficinas de Propaganda CNT-FAI, 1937).

dictatorship of shopkeepers, who grew fat on the hunger of the workers.

The Stalinist programme, based on defending bourgeois interests and championing a strong state capable of enforcing its decrees and winning the war, turned the PSUC into the vanguard of the counter-revolution.

11

The Barcelona FAI Radicalized by the Defense Committees

The Barcelona Confederal Defense Committee drafted an "Organizational Plan for Defense Cadres and Committees" which, while undated, seems to have been written during the second half of March 1937.[1]

The plan dealt with defensive readiness at a time when, given the "wholesale breakdown of parties and systems, all that remains is the Revolutionary Proletariat with its programme for reorganizing work and economic and social equality."

It noted the ineffectuality and uselessness of the CNT personnel "who represent us" on the Generalidad Council, but who had not managed to do anything "in the face of looming decrees that threaten to stifle every hint of revolution."

They had enough manpower to stand up to any counter-revolutionary revolt, but their preparedness had been inadequate. What was needed was intense and effective training for defense cadres. For this to happen, the Barcelona Defense Committee had to be given everything it needed: competent staff, appropriate equipment and training in the materials and methods of fighting, as well as proper tactics.

What was needed was a pavilion attached to the CNT's Military Training School where trustworthy comrades might receive training.

---

1   "Plan de estructuración de los Comités de Defensa," Comité de Defensa Confederal de Barcelona.

The ward defense committees would carry out undercover and detailed reconnaissance of all locations occupied by the police and the political parties, plus off-duty premises.

Each comrade had to have a specific, concrete assignment, keeping in mind that "efficient organization is essential to support a prolonged campaign."

These five objectives were set:

1. Study and training in fighting materials, from guns to electrically triggered explosives.

2. Study and preparation of workshops for the manufacture of weapons.

3. Training in the handling of motorized vehicles, setting up communications, radio transmitters, wireless telephony, etc.

4. Aquisition of sufficient and suitable equipment to arm all the defense cadres.

5. Organization on a barrio-by-barrio basis, with each comrade in every cadre having a specific part to play, "so that from the very outset we have well-rounded fighting teams to rely upon."

These defense cadres were to be organized and trained as follows:

A. To be effective, cadres would have to consist of fifteen comrades: seven riflemen, four dynamiters or grenadiers, plus four auxiliaries.

B. Every machine gun would have a fifteen-man service team: nine covering transport and vehicle servicing: three grenadiers offering cover, and three men to "feed" the latter.

C. "One comrade will be in charge of each of these teams, assisted by however many auxiliaries are required for communications or other necessary services, such as provision of rations, tending of the wounded, etc., etc."

D. In each ward, a rough map would be drawn up with the following, appropriately numbered and sketched in differently colored inks:

1. Police stations, barracks, and government premises.
2. Premises occupied by political parties and other organizations.
3. Premises held by the Organization, trade unions, *ateneos*, ward committees, etc.

Thus, one would need only refer to "ward X, letter X," and what needed to be done—and nobody without access to the sketchmap would understand the message.

The report closed with a couple of considerations aimed at the unions:

First: That the defense committees would only be as effective as the assistance and funding they received would allow.

Second: Only the people could bring down the counter-revolution. And that was as much a life-and-death issue now as it had been yesterday. "Also, as noted at the outset of this report, our collaborationist stance does not inspire much hope that we can make our revolution with the State: quite the opposite. We have to do all in our power gradually to recover our own revolutionary identity."

In view of the government crisis, but especially to counter the weakening and threatened dissolution of the Control Patrols, and given the hostility coming from this new Unified Security Corps—an amalgamation of the old, bourgeois, anti-worker repressive forces of the Assault Guards and Civil Guard—we once more face an overriding need to overhaul, bolster, and breathe new life into the barrio defense committees.

We have already witnessed, in late November and early December 1936, the defense committees being placed in a sort of cold storage by the unions, because the unions thought they were redundant, given the existence of the institutionalized "revolutionary police force" of the Control Patrols, in which the CNT was by far the main force.

In the latter half of March, the Barcelona Defense Committee urged a reorganization of the barrio defense committees, painstakingly readying them for what looked like an imminent confrontation, as it worked out a very specific and detailed plan of insurrection.

At a rally held in the Monumental bullring on Sunday 11 April [1937], placards were displayed calling for Maroto to be freed, along with the numerous antifascists in captivity, most of them CNT personnel.[2] Federica Montseny found herself heckled and jeered by the crowd. Time and again voices called out for the prisoners to be set free. The higher committees pinned the blame for such "sabotage" on the Friends of Durruti Group. A very annoyed Federica threatened that she would never again attend a rally in Barcelona.

On Monday 12 April 1937, at the Casa CNT-FAI, the second session of the local plenum of Barcelona anarchist groups got underway, "with the confederal defense groups and Libertarian youth in attendance."[3]

---

2   Maroto was the delegate of the column of militians that bore his name. The column waged a successful campaign in Córdoba and Granada, but failed to take Granada due to a shortage of weaponry. He clashed with the governor of Almería, Gabriel Morón, who he criticized at a rally in February 1937. Maroto was jailed to the great indignation of the libertarian movement, which insisted that he be set free. On 1 May 1937, he was pardoned, but was stripped of command of his column.

3   Second session of the local plenum of the Barcelona Anarchist Groups [...] arranged for the meeting rooms at the Casa

The proceedings involved Sánchez from the Los Mismos group, who chaired the meeting, Liberto Alfonso from the Acracia confederal defense groups, as recording secretary, and Vicente Micó as master of ceremonies.

Juan Santana Calero, from the Devenir anarchist group, referred to the wishy-washy nature of the report drafted at the previous meeting, because "the principle core to organizations of like mind to the anarchist movement is being thrown overboard."[4] In his reckoning, "the counter-revolution has gained significant ground, despite our collaboration in government, which is why, he argued, collaboration is counter-productive and ineffective." According to whoever minuted that second session, Santana Calero "asked that the drafting team spell out what it meant by 'collaboration' and by 'anarchist principles.'" He compared the drafting team's stance on governmentalism with that of the POUM. Santana Calero was pushing the widening gulf between action and principles to absurd limits by making an exaggerated but telling comparison, laying out "the current dilemma: we either burn all the anarchist writings that have informed our activity and conduct for so long, or we set off in search of a 'cosy niche' in governments."

Santana Calero summed up what he was proposing: "No ministerial or departmental collaboration; collaboration only with respect to military oversight of the anti-fascist struggle in which we are engaged, and on issues of public order, but in a responsible manner, without our painting ourselves into ridiculous bourgeois corners, or merely politicking after the fashion of petit bourgeois parties." He declared that ministerial collaboration had completely failed.

Santana Calero closed by touching on matters of the press and prisoners. He denounced as "disgraceful" the

CNT-FAI and attended by the confederal defense groups and Libertarian Youth. Barcelona 24 April 1937.

4   Juan Santana Calero had been active in the Libertarian Youth in Málaga. After May 1937, he joined the Friends of Durruti.

heavy-handed methods used against the confederal press for its criticism of the Organization's collaborationist policy and its condemnation of top committees' abandonment of the prisoners.

Grupo 12, a barrio defense group from the Gracia district, complained that the drafting team reports almost never reflected a delegate's position as the mandate he has received, but as his personal opinion. The Grupo 12's delegate stated that "the majority of delegates have spoken against politics and in favor of Revolution. We are anarchists and we do not have the strength to break the vicious circle in which we are trapped." He rejected the drafting team report because it solved nothing. He brought up the events in Cullera (Valencia), where "more than a thousand Assault Guards, superbly arrayed with all manner of weaponry, mustered and stormed the town's Amalgamated Trades Union. They ransacked and doled out beatings and did as they pleased with our comrades. That is fascism and our comrades from the Departments and Valencia acquiesce to it."

He rejected the mechanical discipline of soldiering and called for "complete socialization of industry, trade, and agriculture" because "otherwise, there will be no winning this war." He said there was no way to carry out revolutionary work "without colliding with capitalism," whatever form it took. He concluded that "it would be better for us to stay anarchists and face up to them all," because that might actually increase their chances of succeeding.

The Galeotes por la Libertad anarchist group agreed with Santana Calero and called for more brevity from all speakers. The Chair asked for speakers solely "from those opposed to the drafting team and from the members of that drafting team." Pérez, from the drafting team, denied that "they had slipped their own view into the proposition." Clemente reasserted the Armonía anarchist group's anti-political viewpoint and moved "that a revolutionary committee be formed." And went on to state: "Those who joined the government ought to have done away with the repressive Civil and Assault Guards, but they have not; they lack the courage, and so they have failed."

The Libertarian Youth's local federation moved that "lest our ideals come to naught," "we should set ourselves up as a revolutionary Convention." Greatly contradicting himself, he went on to say "collaboration is necessary, but so is maintaining our anarchist conduct at all times." And in any case, if that is not possible, "we set should ourselves up as a revolutionary Convention as [was] mentioned earlier."

The Eliseo Reclus anarchist group tried to introduce a note of common sense into a session that struck it as dominated by an extremism as unwitting as it was vague: "extreme stances were all well and good when we were wrapped in the people's embrace. Now nobody embraces us, and making such decisions is dangerous." He concluded that the only thing that should be asked of the top committees was "greater accountability in everything."

The Constancia anarchist group reaffirmed its stance, which it thought had not been reflected in the previous day's minutes; it had "asked that our representatives in government pull out and that a <u>central committee</u> be appointed from among the ward committees."[5]

The significance of this motion from the Constancia anarchist group was extraordinary because it married withdrawal of anarcho-syndicalists from the Generalidad government and the formation of a Central Committee constituted by ward committees. A Central Committee of barrio committees would have represented a new revolutionary authority in opposition and as an alternative to the Generalidad. The revolutionary events of May 1937 erupted within days.

Caudet from the Constancia group talked about what had happened at the rally at the Monumental bullring on Sunday

---

5   The underlining is in the original.

11 April 1937 (when Federica Montseny had been jeered). At that rally there had been mass chanting of the slogan "To hell with politics, to hell with government," which, according to Caudet, "was the voice of the people, a backlash against the changes that have occurred inside our organizations. A backlash against the performance of those holding down Public Order posts because of their bullying and arrests not merely of hostile and questionable elements, but of comrades."

Caudet also spoke of "the agreement to withhold pay, due to a shortage of funds, from those standing guard on the defense committees"; he described this as "a ploy." He also referred to "incidents triggered by some CNT collectives' attempts to raise the prices of basic necessities," a move he reckoned was unpopular.

Abril from the Acracia confederal defense groups said that a change in direction was needed because federalism and anarchism "have vanished from our ranks," adding "those primarily responsible for that are our ministers, who have undergone a complete transformation." He said government was still "a tyranny against the people." He explained that "bourgeois morality and practices" were still rampant in anarchist circles, while beggars still "plead for public charity." He noted that "there are positions of self-styled responsibility utterly bereft of morality." He mentioned the incidents in Vinalesa (Valencia), where "more than 150 comrades—the only real, true anarchists—were ordered to be shot. A handful of them [were]. If one captain with a modicum of humanity had not stepped in, a barbarous injustice would have taken place." And he closed with this radical and pessimistic judgement: "If this is what organization looks like, and if these are what pass for ideas, then we have shown that they are not worth a damn."

The Libertarian Youth Local Federation stated that it had to go, and also reported that, outside its premises, "comrades were being frisked and disarmed by Civil and Assault Guards the other night." They would issue a manifesto and patrol the streets seeking help from the different anarchist groups "to avoid such incidents."

Miguel, from the Convicción y Firmeza group, said that "the creeping advance of the bourgeoisie" was plain to be seen and that "we must act with intelligence and in a manner consistent with our principles."

Grunfeld, from the C group, opposed "pulling out of politics" and argued that "if we take to the streets we may well lose rather than increase ground gained by anarchism."[6] He maintained that they had to do their best to instill an effective economic outlook in the unions "so as to demonstrate the effectiveness of Libertarian Communism." He closed by rejecting violent, emotional solutions.

Alcalà from the Bulgarian group, read a proposal regarding the CNT councillors in the Generalidad government: "That our councillors be reminded that their mission in the Generalidad is to promote all working class initiatives for social progress, to prevent politicians from obstructing the onward march of the social revolution and to keep the CNT-FAI appraised of everything going on in the Generalidad that help or hinders the revolution and the war."

For Alcalà, anarchists' and anarcho-syndicalists' mission was the same as ever: giving the people the whole truth, speaking out against injustices and making them public, ensuring that no gulf opened up between the people and the CNT-FAI, wooing the workers away from the UGT and the bourgeoisie, and ensuring utter unity between the CNT and the FAI by "steering clear of things like the jeering of Federica Montseny at the Monumental, which only benefits the right-wing."

After several other points, Alcalà suggested, as a resolution to the problem posed by Toryho's running the *Solidaridad Obrera*, "setting up a combative anarchist newspaper, if *Soli*

---

6 The A and C anarchist groups were part of an anti-Nosotros front that took its lead from the Nervio group headed by Abad de Santillán and Pedro Herrera.

fails to publish the notes it receives regarding things going on behind the scenes."

Alcalà had thrown his weight behind a classic orthodox position as far from the growing libertarian chorus of criticism as from the worst aberrations of the higher committees's bureaucracy. His basic aim was to head off the growing chances of a split (as clearly seen at the 11 April 1937 Monumental rally), and to preserve the unity between the CNT and the FAI at any price.

The Humanidad anarchist group argued that "19 July was the start of a counter-revolution, not a revolution. And it is still happening." He discussed the evolution of the CNT's stances since July, and of how the anarchists had gone back into the unions to avoid losing their influence, the Local Federation of Catalonia's anarchist groups having successfully "put a different slant on some of the accords reached at the recent CNT congress." He deplored the unwarranted proliferation of plenums and accords that had virtually no practical impact, and advocated "the need for collaboration," insisting upon the utmost accountability from those holding office.

Jiménez from the A anarchist group spoke out against those who were critical of "ministerial collaboration."[7] He called the Libertarian Youth's motion to establish a Convention "tyrannical and arbitrary," and that "breaking with the Antifascist Front was out of the question." He suggested "outlining a program" that would encapsulate "most" libertarian "aspirations," and that could then be "submitted" to the Generalidad government "for its consideration." He closed by arguing for "the need for collaboration to carry on,

---

7   The A and C groups were extensions of the Nervio group led by Abad de Santillán and Pedro Herrera. Most of the Argentinean anarchists who came to Barcelona were active in these three groups. They were the hard core of collaborationism, and virtually all held significant posts in the Generalidad government or inside the Organization.

but on a strictly business basis, without us delving into the thought processes of other political representatives."

Die-hard defense of ministerial collaborationism and of anti-fascist unity had a strong presence within the anarcho-syndicalist movement. The ideological fracture within the CNT-FAI was clear and plain for all to see. The issue was whether that fracture would turn into an organizational split. So far, the various stands of anti-collaborationism had gone no further than criticizing the higher committees, offering no alternative to possibilism and resignation, in the face of the progressive retreat from "the revolutionary gains of July" and the unrelenting violation of principles. The higher committees that backed collaborationism faced growing internal trade union opposition and barely controlled their own grassroots. That was the underlying cause of the "social indiscipline" that worried Companys and the Generalidad government, and the source of the relentless attacks on that nebulous myth, "the uncontrollables." A solution to this was taking shape in the approaching battle over control of Public Order.

The anarchist group Devenir lamented the fact that its suggestion "to pull out of leadership positions responsible for war and Public Order matters" had not been tackled. It deplored the "reek of Marxism" in some of the speeches, and cited Malatesta in support of its proposals. The Zarathustra anarchist group endorsed the Devenir group. Anarchist group 27 stated that "the only ones opposing the Resolution" were the Devenir and Constancia groups. It called either for the Resolution of the drafting team to be passed or for a fresh one to be drafted for discussion.[8]

Ordaz from the Los Indomables anarchist group provocatively declared that "fear has become a factor in the CNT-FAI."

---

8   At anarchist plenums, resolutions were traditionally passed on the basis of unanimity or consensus.

He insisted that "we [CNT folk] should have made an armed stand against all this, but cowardice plays a part." He sided with those challenging the Resolution, and said no to collaboration: "We have to have arm ourselves for the sake of the revolution. We have squandered so much time here on arguments, because we lack the courage and valor to take to the streets."

The chair intervened to clarify what a vote for or against the Resolution meant: "If the Resolution is carried, collaboration will be endorsed. If defeated, our representatives must pull out of the government." So he called for "a definite and clear-cut decision to be made."

Ordaz extended and built upon the chair's clarification: "Given the outrages our representatives have acquiesced to, given the ineptitude of all the politicians favoring homegrown and international capitalism, we need to arrive at some concrete and emphatic agreement." He suggested that "in some further gathering, where we are the majority, a panel be appointed so that, in the event of any provocation, it can immediately bark back on behalf of society in Catalonia."

Group 12 from Gracia presented a written motion:

Having, after a full discussion, fully considered the outcome of nine months of ministerial politics and noting the impossibility of winning the armed struggle against fascism without subordinating all economic, political, and social interests to the over-riding aim of the war; given that only through the complete social ownership of industry, trade, and agriculture can fascism feasibly be crushed; given that any form of government is, by its very essence, reactionary, and therefore contrary to any social revolution, this Plenum agrees:
1) To withdraw everyone currently occupying positions in the anti-fascist government machine.
2) To set about building a revolutionary anti-fascist committee to coordinate the armed struggle against fascism

3) To immediately take social ownership of industry, trade, and agriculture.

4) To proceed with the introduction of the producer's card. To implement a general mobilization of all men fit to bear arms and work tools for front-line or rearguard service.

5) And finally, to bring the inflexible weight of revolutionary discipline to bear upon each and every person as a guarantee that there would be consequences for toying with the social revolution's interests.

This text, in which the influence of legal jargon can be detected, studded as it is with "notings" and "givens," was tantamount to a manifesto, without actually being one. It was, in any event, a bold and splendid resolution from the anarchist revolutionaries and, above all, a revolutionary program and concrete plan of action to compete with the anti-fascist collaborationism prevalent in libertarian ranks. A necessary part of that program was a call for comprehensive socialization of the economy as against the industrial and peasant collectivization that had proved itself to be an instrument of the government to exercise centralized, state control of companies, collectives, and entire sectors that had been expropriated from July to September 1936.

The plenum accepted Group 12's motion unanimously—and considered Ordaz's motion to be covered in the endorsed motion.

The chair concluded that with the passage of this motion "our representatives should pull out of the government of Catalonia." He then asked the Plenum "if the motion should apply also to the rest of the country" since "we also have representatives in the central government."

That sparked some debate and a "minor incident" on which the writer of the minutes offers no further details. Ordaz, from the Los Indomables group, stated that "when accords are reached there is always somebody who tries to apply the brakes." He made it clear "we are only in Barcelona here"; that is, the motion was valid only locally, but he did add that "it might be the spark that lights the torch for Iberia," expressing the possibility, and his desire, that the motion might be extended to cover the whole of republican Spain.

Estrada raised an organizational problem, noting that it was not the FAI groups that had representatives in the government but the CNT's unions. Pablo Ruiz moved that "a Central Revolutionary Committee [be formed] from among all the defense committees."[9] The Local Federation of Anarchist Groups, seeing how the gathering was slipping from its control, countered by saying it would not take responsibility for the motion unless issued with "guidelines for interpreting the accords arrived at." The chair joined in, saying that the important thing now was to avert a clash between the CNT and the FAI "over what we have just agreed to." Caudet moved that a commission be appointed for that very purpose.

Ordaz explored the worry displayed by the Local Federation's representative, taking him to task for the fact that, having convened the plenary "inviting the attendance of the Confederal Defense Groups and the Libertarian Youth," now that "a strong motion has been passed on an item put on the agenda by the Local Federation itself, it is refusing to be answerable to it." Ordaz proudly pointed out that "it is the anarchists that have passed this motion." And, in a major gaffe and, even more, politically incorrectly, he went on to say that "the CNT is a force with obligations to the outlook the anarchists provide it with, rather than to whatever might be most convenient for it. He rejected Caudet's suggestion that a commission be appointed. And in a contradictory turn of

---

9   Pablo Ruiz, a militiaman from the Durruti Column's No 4 Agrupación in Gelsa, was one of the founders of the Friends of Durruti Group in early March 1937.

events, in defiance of the motion just passed, as championed by himself, he stated plainly "that our comrades should not stand down from government. No need for that. What we should do is appoint assistants for them so that, some day, they can get a handle on the situation."

Ordaz was making a travesty of the motion passed at the Plenum, which ordered a withdrawal from all government posts, by embracing the option championed by Escorza and Herrera, which favored setting up technical commissions in every Department so that CNT personnel might control them all.

Pérez, from the Armonia anarchist group, complained of the existence of "a pronounced interest in hobbling the smooth running of the confederal organization" and warned that "nobody should let himself be carried away by the guile or malice of certain comrades who have an distorted view of the situation." He made it clear that "I am not suggesting that they should be treated like fascists, but rather as witless and ill-intentioned." But this clarification sounded to everybody like an accusation, especially when he went on to say that "this is what we have at this plenum." He closed his remarks, urging that "before a resolution is passed on a given issue, we should look at the political and social backgrounds of whoever is moving it, so as to ensure that those attending the plenum are not being bamboozled for any such [political/social] purposes." In response to such grave allegations, the chair asked Pérez to "point out the comrades to whom he is referring." Pérez once again made it plain "that he had not accused anybody of being fractious," and added that he would accept the accords and "will step down from his post."

Codina suggested "that the motions passed be put into immediate effect and that comrades and committees take appropriate action on this matter." A comrade from the Gracia-based Group 12 noted that, back on 19 July 1936, "at the hour of revolution [the anarchist leaders of the CNT-FAI] were caught off guard and insistently called for collaboration. Had we remembered on that memorable date that we were against governments, we would never have been in this position."

The Hispano Suiza anarchist group offered a written motion reporting the arrest of three male comrades from the Ortiz Column and of one female comrade, urging the anarchist groups present to lobby the Public Order Commissariat as soon as the Plenum was over to secure their release. He also warned the defense committees to mount armed patrols from that night on "to ensure that they are not disarmed by the Civil Guard and Assault Guards."

Pressed about the reason for the arrest of these comrades, the Sants Defense Committee said it had to do with "an altercation between the comrades and several members of the Assault Guards." It was agreed to send a team—made up of Ordaz, Santana Calero, and Griells—to see what was going on at Police Headquarters. The plenum unanimously agreed that, as proposed by the Hispano Suiza group, the defense committees be placed on armed alert.

The Local Federation representative defended the fact that it had convened the Plenum, the intention having been "to rally anarchism's finest assets." He regretted that its first session had coincided with the rally at the Monumental bullring, and reiterated: "I still await clarification about what needs to be done in light of the motions passed."

Papiol explained why he voted against the motion, arguing that, at a regional congress and at other plenums, similar motions had already been passed but never put into effect. He stated that "some comrades are convinced that none of the motions passed here will be put into effect." He attributed passing the motion to "feelings running extraordinarily high," and took a few people to task for having changed their minds since the previous session on 11 April. He said that it would have been more practical and "maybe even more revolutionary in an economic sense" to focus on other goals that "might move things a lot further along than these present accords, which will have us labelled as crackpots." He predicted "that we will be frittering a lot of energy away on internecine rearguard fighting." Which was actually a full compendium of arguments encouraging anarchists to defer to the dictates of anti-fascist unity.

The Acracia group stated that the accords should have been reached earlier and in different circumstances. After various digressions, he concluded by saying that "our movement should stand by the sincerity of our anarchist principles."

Sosa, from the Prácticos group, found it deplorable that "the anarchist groups had convened this plenum." He said that "if those in office are not up to the job," they need simply be replaced. "But our representatives should never have been withdrawn once and for all." He pointed out that the letter from Maroto "contradicts the report on his arrest drawn up by the CNT National Committee," and called for the National Committee to resign over its "misguided and false report." His view was that "the entire CNT" had been thrown into jail with Maroto, since he [Maroto] "represented the true feelings of the confederation." Sosa noted the growing "divergence" between the CNT and the FAI, putting this down "to the performance of those representing our higher committees," and insisting that what they needed to debate was "a purging of positions" rather than a permanent and definitive abolition of those posts.

Toryho, the director of *Solidaridad Obrera*, denied that there was any "local organization of anarchist groups" at the Plenum. He denied the "organizational legitimacy" of any of the accords reached. He declared that "the Barcelona FAI has not passed this accord, because most of those gathered here do not belong to the anarchist groups, but to the Confederal Defense Cadres—and the latter do not constitute a responsible body, so any accords they may have arrived at carry no weight."[10]

The Barcelona Local Federation of Anarchist Groups "made it clear that they [the Local Federation] had summoned the Plenum by agreement with the Local Committee of Defense Groups and the Libertarian Youth."[11]

Toryho insisted that "the anarchist groups are not represented at this Plenum" and that the Confederal Defense Committees "are not within their rights to set themselves up as a separate organization." He reiterated that this was "no gathering of anarchist groups," and thus he "does not acknowledge any accords reached because they are worthless."[12]

The chair, rebutting Toryho, merely read out "the circular issued to all the groups," making it clear "that the Plenum was self-evidently convened by the Local Federation of Anarchist Groups."

The Regional Committee of Anarchist Groups repudiated incidents like the ones that had erupted during the last few contributions, because they were unbecoming of anarchists. It was stated that "these resolutions cannot be accepted," and that the intention was to rescind them at a regional plenum shortly to be convened.

---

10 Toryho's objection was based on the defense committees' being completely subordinate to the CNT regional committee, an idea doggedly argued ever since their formation, in order to pre-empt autonomous military decision-making outside of the organizational control of the unions. However, it was nonetheless a desperately bureaucratic response to the decision made by the gathering.

11 The Barcelona Local Federation of Anarchist Groups was answering Toryho by stating that they had convened the Plenum jointly with the Barcelona Defense Committee, in which case it was entirely valid in organizational terms.

12 Toryho's crude opposition flew in the face of the radicalization of the gathering by the defense committees, that is, by the revolutionary ward committees.

That statement created a great stir. After it had abated, Ordaz reported on the findings of the commission sent to Police Headquarters over the arrest of the four comrades. The three Ortiz Column comrades would be brought to the courthouse the following day and "may well be set free immediately." The case of the female comrade was a lot more delicate, being a matter "of organization" and further comment would have to be reserved "given the seriousness of the matter."

The Dinamo anarchist group moved that "a drafting group be appointed to detail and thoroughly explore the contents of the resolution that has been passed, in the light of the atmosphere at the Plenum," to ensure that the resolutions passed by the gathering would be acted upon immediately, "following due notice given to the relevant Committees, so that the latter might get word out to their Groups." His motion was passed unanimously. After which, they moved on to appointing the working party, made up of five people: Iglesias, Caudet from the Constancia group, the Cultura y Acción Group, the Móvil Group, plus Mariano Ros from the Luz y Cultura Group.[13]

The proceedings wound up at 2:30 AM. The minutes were signed off on by Liberto Alfonso from the Grupos de Defensa Confederal de Acracia in Barcelona on 12 April 1937. "Once the proceedings were over, the German anarcho-syndicalist DAS group made the following proposal: 'that a peninsular plenum of the Iberian Anarchist Federation be held in order to lay down specific proposals and coordinate efforts.'"[14] It suggested that this be held on May 1st, in Valencia. The German DAS group's proposal was carried and approval was given for

---

13 The final draft of the Resolution was dated 24 April 1937.

14 For more about the DAS see the book by Nelles, Piotrowski, Linse, and Garcia: *Antifascistas alemanes en Barcelona (1933–1939)* (Barcelona: Sintra, 2010).

"corresponding messages to be issued so that this suggestion might be implemented."[15]

This meeting had slipped through the grip of the faísta bureaucrats. Critics of the motions passed were of that
opinion when they referred to the "strange atmosphere" of
the gathering or to "an abnormal appreciation of the situation." The local plenum of anarchist groups was nothing
other than the authentic Barcelona FAI. We say "authentic"
because it was the only place where the affinity groups were
able to come together and freely express their views without
the crushing weight of the bureaucracy ensconced in organizational and/or government posts; it was a place where, in
theory at any rate, they had the power to determine the strategy of the anarchists of the Barcelona FAI.

The Barcelona Defense Committees, or (it amounts
to the same thing) the delegates from the revolutionary
ward committees and Libertarian Youth, took part in the
Plenum, no doubt making the accords that much more radical. This anarchist gathering was held in a revolutionary
climate, and reflected the desperate situation on the streets
due to food shortages and price-fixing that made food unaf-
fordable. It amounted to a protest against bureaucrats like
the jeering of Federica Montseny at the Monumental bullring on 11 April 1937, where placards calling for Maroto's
release were displayed and chants were heard calling for
a walk-out from government and the release of numerous
other anarchist prisoners.

---

15 The suggestion from the German DAS group that a peninsular plenum be called at such short notice had two obvious purposes. First, to prevent a regional plenum from rescinding the
accords in a painstakingly prepared attempt by the bureaucracy in order to outflank the revolutionaries. Second, to build on
the accords reached in Barcelona, regarding the repudiation of
collaborationism, pulling out of the government, and setting
up a revolutionary committee covering the whole of Spain.

Along with the defense sections of the ward revolutionary committees and Libertarian Youth, and despite the scandalized and hysterical opposition from some bureaucrats, this Barcelona FAI had decided to end collaborationism, to pull anarchist councillors out of the Generalidad government, and to set up a revolutionary committee to direct the war against fascism—which was a crucial step in the direction of the revolutionary uprising that erupted on 3 May 1937.

Furthermore, the Plenum registered an ideological fall-out, not so much between the CNT and the FAI, as between revolutionaries and collaborationists. This pointed to an organizational split within the libertarian movement in Barcelona evidenced in the growing opposition and yawning difference in aims between the ward committees' and Libertarian Youth's defense sections, on the one hand, and the top committees on the other.

This radicalization was the product of an increasingly untenable situation in the streets. On 14 April, a housewives' demonstration, this one not manipulated by the PSUC, set off from La Torrassa on a tour of the various markets in Collblanc, Sants, and Hostafrancs, protesting at the price of bread and other food. It called upon the Revolutionary Committee based in the Plaza de España to intervene in the matter, but the committee told them that it was not within its purview. The demonstrations and protests spread to nearly every market in the city. And they were repeated, albeit rather less heatedly and with fewer disturbances, in a variety of markets. A number of shops and bakeries were attacked. Hunger in the working class districts of Barcelona had led to a demonstration of outrage, demanding solutions.

12

The Defense Committees in May 1937 and Their Final Dissolution

Sometime around 2:45 PM on Monday 3 May 1937, three truckloads of heavily-armed Assault Guards pulled up outside the Telephone Exchange in the Plaza de Cataluña. They were led by Eusebio Rodríguez Salas, the UGT member and dyed-in-the-wool Stalinist formally in charge of the Public Order Commissariat. The Telephone Exchange had been commandeered by the CNT on 19 July 1936. The monitoring of telephone calls, the guarding of the border, and the control patrols were three bones of contention that, since January 1937, had triggered a number of incidents between the Generalidad's republican government and the CNT masses. A clash between the republican machinery of state, with its insistence upon absolute control over everything that fell under "its" remit, and the CNT's defense of the "gains" made on 19 July 1936 was inevitable. Rodríguez Salas meant to take possession of the Telephone Exchange building. The CNT personnel on the lower floors, caught unawares, let themselves be disarmed; but tough resistance was offered on the upper floors thanks to a strategically positioned machine gun. The news spread like wildfire. Barricades were immediately erected all over the city. This was not a spontaneous backlash from the Barcelona working class: its general strike, armed clashes with police, and the barricades themselves were the result of initiative taken by the defense committees—quickly backed up thanks to tremendously widespread discontent, the growing difficulty of making ends meet with a soaring cost of living, the queues and the rationing, as well as the tension that existed among the rank-and-file CNT membership between collaborationists and revolutionaries. The street-fighting was galvanized and mounted from the barrio defense committees (and partly, and to a lesser extent, by one segment of the control patrols). The fact that no orders to mobilize and erect barricades across the city had come from the CNT's higher committees (who were serving as ministers in the Valencia and Barcelona governments) or from some other organization does not mean that those barricades were simply spontaneous creations: they resulted from instructions from the defense committees.[1]

Manuel Escorza had spoken up at a CNT-FAI gathering on 21 July 1936 to argue for a third approach, in contrast to García Oliver's option of "going for broke" (which everyone present regarded as advocating an "anarchist dictatorship") and the overriding majority line of Abad de Santillán and Federica Montseny (that backed loyal collaboration with the Generalidad government). Escorza lobbied for the Generalidad government to be used as a tool to socialize the economy, a tool to be cast aside as soon as it outlived its usefulness to the CNT. Escorza was in charge of the CNT-FAI Investigation Services, handling all sorts of enforcement tasks from July 1936 onwards, as well as espionage and

---

1 Gorkín states: "In actual fact the uprising was entirely spontaneous. Of course, that very relative spontaneity needs explaining: since 19 July, pretty much everywhere, in Barcelona and across Catalonia, defense committees had been set up, organized primarily by rank-and-file CNT and FAI personnel. The committees were fairly dormant for a time, however, it was they who mobilized the working class on 3 May. They were the movement's action groups. We know that no general strike order was issued by either of the two main trade union centrals." CF. Julián Gorkín, "Réunion du sous-secretariat international du POUM—14 mai 1937."

intelligence work. The Services had maintained their own organizational structures that were autonomous and independent both of the Generalidad government and of the CAMC when it existed. They were directly answerable to the CNT-FAI's higher committees (the CNT and FAI regional committees) and they coordinated among the barrio defense committees and CNT members with functions or positions in the Public Order Commissariat and control patrols: people like José Asens, Dionisio Eroles, Aurelio Fernández, 'Portela' and such.

In April 1937, Pedro Herrera "Councillor" (Minister) of Health in the second Tarradellas cabinet, and Manuel Escorza were responsible for negotiating with Lluís Companys (the Generalidad president) to find a way out of the cabinet crisis that had broken out in early March 1937 over the stepping down of the Defense "councillor," the CNT's Isgleas.[2] Companys decided to abandon the tactics of Tarradellas—who could not conceive of a government that was not an anti-fascist unity government—and resolved to end the CNT's role, opting instead for what Comorera, the PSUC secretary had been calling for: the imposition of a "strong" government with no tolerance for the CNT's inability to hold its own, so-called "uncontrollable" militants in check. Companys made up his mind to break away from the increasingly difficult policy of making pacts with the CNT and, thanks to PSUC and Soviet support, reckoned that the time had come for the authority and decision-making of the Generalidad government to be imposed by force. As

---

2   Isgleas had resigned over the plan for the Karl Marx Division, controlled by the PSUC, to switch from the Aragon front to the Madrid front, and not, as some historians maintain, over yet another decree calling for the disarming of the rearguard, which nobody took seriously. Isgleas was against the weakening of the Aragon front. It was a side-swipe at Companys's plans to disarm and control the rearguard.

events showed, however, the government was not yet power-ful enough to stop negotiations with the CNT. The collapse of Companys's conversations with Escorza and Herrera,[3] in which two months of conversations produced no political solution, directly resulted—despite the short-lived new gov-ernment line-up of 16 April[4]—in the May 1937 armed clash-es in Barcelona. Without a word of warning to Tarradellas (much less to Escorza and Herrera), Companys ordered the "councillor" in charge of the Interior Department, Artemi Aiguadé, to take over the Telephone Exchange building. Those orders were carried out by Rodríguez Salas, the Public Order commissar, at 2:45 PM on 3 May 1937.

The seizure of the Telephone Exchange was an irrational response to CNT demands[5] and to a contempt for the nego-tiations, conducted throughout April with Manuel Escorza and Pedro Herrera as the CNT representatives directly en-gaging Companys (who had expressly barred Tarradellas from them).[6] Escorza had the motive and ability to respond immediately on behalf of the CNT Regional Committee to Companys's provocation, marshalling the ward defense

---

3   Minutes of Companys's meetings with Herrera and Escorza on 11 and 13 April 1937.

4   The CNT councillors in that government (which lasted from 16 April to 4 May) were Isgleas (at Defense), Capdevila (Public Services), and Aurelio Fernández (Health and Public Assistance).

5   Herrera and Escorza argued for setting up advisory commis-sions attached to each of the Generalidad departments, which would monitor what was being done in every government department—especially the ones under PSUC control—as a guarantee against future clashes between the various anti-fascist organizations. Their model was the Economic Council and the War Industries Commission that had, according to Escorza and Herrera, proven themselves so effective.

6   Josep Tarradellas, "The political crisis in the run-up to the May Events. 26 days of un-government at the Generalitat." Report.

committees and the CNT officers in the various public order departments. This was probably the trigger behind the armed clashes during the May Events.

However, whatever role was played by a few leaders in the run-up to May, they were all quickly overwhelmed and swept along. It was the barrio committees that unleashed and spearheaded the uprising from 3 to 7 May 1937 in Barcelona. And the barrio defense committees should not be mistaken for the ambiguous and vague notion of the "spontaneity of the masses" peddled by official historiography.

This was how Nin,[7] the political secretary of the POUM, characterized it on 19 May 1937: "The May events in Barcelona breathed life back into certain bodies that, over recent months, had played a certain role in the Catalan capital and in a number of important localities: the Defense Committees. These are chiefly technical-military bodies formed by the CNT unions. In actual fact, it is they who have directed the struggle, and in each barrio they are a rallying point and an organizing center for revolutionary workers."[8]

The Friends of Durruti did not initiate the uprising but they were the most active combatants on the barricades, completely dominating the Plaza Macià (the Plaza Real today), where they sealed off every access with barricades, and the entire length of Calle Hospital. At the junction of

---

7 For a critique of the stances of Nin and the POUM, See Agustín Guillamón, "Josep Rebull de 1937 a 1939. La critica interna a la political del CE del POUM sobre la Guerra de España," *Balance* 19 and 20 (2000), Barcelona.

8 "The problem of organs of power in the Spanish Revolution," article by Nin, dated Barcelona 19 May 1937 and published originally in French in the single issue publication *Juillet. Revue Internationale du POUM*, No 1 (June 1937), Barcelona-Paris. A Spanish translation by Agustín Guillamón was published in *Balance* No 2 (1995). For a critique of Nin's and the POUM's stance, see Agustín Guillamón "Josep Rebull from 1937 to 1939."

the Ramblas and Calle Hospital, under a huge portrait of Durruti affixed to the façade of the apartment building where the Friends of Durruti Grouping had its headquarters, they erected a barricade and made it the chief operations center. Their complete domination of the Calle Hospital was right next to the Confederal Defense Committee headquarters (the HQ of the defense committees) in the Los Escolapios building on the Ronda San Pablo.[9] This linked up with the Brecha de San Pablo, which was captured by about forty militians from the Roja y Negra Column who, under the command of Durruti Column member Máximo Franco, had "travelled down to Barcelona" to "observe and gather intelligence" after both the Roja y Negra and the Lenin Column (the latter under the POUM's Rovira) had caved into pressure to return their respective units to the front lines—as urged by Abad de Santillán and Molina, i.e. the CNT personnel giving orders in the Generalidad's Defense Department in Isgleas's absence.

The toughest and most decisive fighting took place on 4 and 5 May. The working-class barrios had been under CNT-FAI control from the outset. For instance, in the center of Pueblo Nuevo, the barricades were erected to control entry and departure from the city via the Mataró road, but there was perfect peace. In those barrios where fighting was necessary, the battle quickly tilted in favor of the defense committees. This is what happened in Sants, where the defense committee, ensconced in the Hotel Olímpic, stormed the neighbouring Assault Guard barracks (600 men) in the Plaza de España. They next took, as a pre-emptive measure, the National (formerly Civil) Guard's Cararromona barracks (were the Caixa Forum is today), which was held by a party of

---

9   "Pedro" (Erno Gerö) in his reports to Moscow cited Los Escolapios as the center directing the May 1937 uprising. See Agustín Guillamón, "The NKVD and SIM in Barcelona. Some of Gerö's dispatches from the War in Spain," (in Spanish) *Balance*, No 22 (November 2001).

eighty men, the remainder of the 400-man garrison having marched out with orders to capture the radio station in the Ramblas. On reaching Los Escolapios, those Guards were thrashed and took to their heels. In Pueblo Seco, the defense committee used artillery to dislodge some sixty of these National Guards from the América cinema, where they had darted as they retreated toward their barracks.

The CNT workers, thrown by the call from their leaders—the same leaders as back on 19 July 1936!—eventually opted to give up the fight, although they had initially ignored the CNT's leadership's appeals for harmony and an end to the fighting for the sake of anti-fascist unity.

The Defense Committees Finally Disbanded

Even though the May Events were a terrific political defeat for the revolutionaries, as would become apparent after 16 June 1937 with the arrest of the POUM Executive Committee and the outlawing of that party, the military might of the Barcelona city defense committees remained intact.

From then on there would be a selective crackdown on the CNT, with the unleashing of a judicial onslaught on several fronts:[10]

1. Against the local revolutionary committees established during 19 and 20 July.

2. Against those who had any hand in the May 1937 rebellion.

3. Against thought crime, the reading of the clandestine press, defeatist sentiments, or the bearing of arms without a permit.

---

10 François Godichea: *Répression et Ordre Public en Catalogne pendant la guerre civil (1936–1939)*, (Thesis, École des Hautes Études en Sciences Sociales 2001), three volumes, passim.

4. Against certain prominent CNT leaders like Aurelio Fernández, Barriobero, Eroles, Devesa, etc.

Nonetheless, by the end of May 1937, the defense committees were still strong enough to raise a number of armed companies controlled by the ward defense committees. A letter-cum-circular of 27 May 1937 from the Barcelona Confederal Defense Committee—addressed to the Poblet, Clot, and San Martin de Provensals barrio committees— offered a briefing on the decision taken by a plenum of defense committee delegates to approve the resolution put forward by the Armonia Ward Defense Committee (previously known as the San Andres ward committee): that one company be armed and raised in the Sagrera, Hispano, Vilapiscina, Verdun, 19 de Julio (formerly Trinidad) barrios, in addition to Group X, and two companies in the Armonia barrio.[11] "Each company is to be made up of fifty comrades in addition to those holding posts of responsibility within them." Each company was to have a machine-gunner section, a grenadier section, and three squads of riflemen. "The companies are to heed no instructions other than those coming from the war Defense Committee, which is to assume complete command of them." This circular closed with an invitation to the Poblet, Clot, and Martín de Provensals barrios to abide by the initiative endorsed at the [district] plenum of defense committee delegates.

An analysis entitled "Accepting a plan for conspiratorial organization" and dated Barcelona, May 1937, assessed the mistakes of the May Events and prepared the defense committees for strictly clandestine operating conditions by overhauling their organization and setting up a National Defense Committee: "The importance of the recent hard lesson, in

---

11 Barcelona Confederal Defense Committee, "Defense Committee of the Poblet, Clot, and Martin de Provensals Ward, greetings," Barcelona, 27 May 1937.

which provocation surfaced in particularly unfavorable circumstances, the pointed, surreptitious, and emphatic way that it did so, and the breadth of its aims (which even included the utter extermination of our organization), must be kept in mind. That meant the annihilation of the proletariat's revolutionary gains and, therefore, the loss of its freedom."[12]

The barrio revolutionary committees in Barcelona popped up on 19–20 July 1936 and lasted until 7 June 1937 at least. At that point, the revivified Generalidad forces of public order disbanded and took over the various centers belonging to the Control Patrols and a number of defense committee offices, like those in the Las Corts barrio.[13] Despite the decree demanding an end to all armed groups, the majority held out until September 1937, when they were systematically disbanded and their buildings stormed one after another. The last, most significant, and strongest to be overrun was the HQ of the Centre Defense Committee in the Escolapios de San Antonio building. It was stormed on 21 September 1937 by public order troops, who deployed an entire arsenal of machine guns, tanks, and grenades. However, the resistance offered by Los Escolapios was overcome, not by firepower, but by eviction orders issued by the regional committee.

From then on, the defense committees went into hiding, behind titles such as CNT coordination and intelligence sections, dedicated solely to clandestine investigatory and intelligence-gathering tasks, as they had prior to 19 July 1936, but now (in 1938) in a clearly counter-revolutionary setting.

However, they were still strong and combative enough to publish a clandestine mouthpiece entitled *Alerta!*, of which seven issues were printed between October and December 1937. Constant themes of the publication were solidarity

---

12 "Accepting a plan for Conspiratorial Organization" (in Spanish), Barcelona May 1937.

13 Sara Berenguer, *Entre el sol y la tormenta* (Calella: Seuba, 1988). See also the author's correspondence with Sara Berenguer.

with "revolutionary prisoners," demanding their release and denouncing the management and abuses of the Modelo prison; the criticism of collaborationism and of the politicization of the FAI; condemning the catastrophic war policies of the Negrín-Prieto government, and of Stalinist pre-dominance within the Army and the state. The paper sent fraternal greetings out to the Libertarian Youth and the Friends of Durruti Group. One unforgettable feature of the paper was its constant incitements to "make the revolution" and for the higher committees to abandon all posts: "Revolution cannot be launched FROM THE STATE, but only AGAINST THE STATE."[14] In its last edition, dated 4 December 1937, *Alerta!* denounced the communist chekas and the brutal persecution visited upon CNT personnel in the Cerdaña.

Alerta!, which had built up a wide readership, ceased publication by virtue of a decision reached at a gathering of delegates from the barrio committees around Barcelona, succumbing to both pressure from the Local Federation of Anarchist Groups and arguments about the need to consolidate the press, but it threatened to resume publication if the new confederal press kowtowed to unacceptable political compromises or fell short of the requirement to tell it like it was.[15]

Conclusions

The defense committees were the CNT's armed organization, heavily dependent on the unions. Not an agency of the FAI.

They started out handling self-defense issues in the face of the brutal crackdown during the years of *pistolerismo* (1919–1923). In 1934, they stood up to fascistic Catalanists Dencàs and Badía's police meddling in strikes, an example

14 "Today we say," *Alerta!* No 2 (30 October 1937).

15 François Godicheau, *Répression et Ordre Public,* Volume 2, 338–341.

of how the Generalidad's Interior Department and Public Order Commissariat handled their duties prior to the dissolution of those offices in the wake of the separatist uprising on 6 October 1934.

Looking past the bourgeois caricature of the "man of action" and the idea that CNT and FAI were synonymous with gun-and-bomb terrorism, the anarcho-syndicalist movement in the 1920s and 1930s was characterized by enthusiasm for culture and education as paths to progress and emancipation of the proletariat. In its day to day experiences, the libertarian "world" acted out the values of solidarity and anti-capitalism deeply rooted in the popular consciousness of those who were already living in an alternative and parallel community within the bourgeois society of the day—*Vivere est militare* (To live is to militate). The words militate, militant, militia, and militian all derive from the same Latin root. The militant served in the trade union, cultural, and community spheres, as well as in the armed sphere, because they are all part and parcel of the same struggle, the same existence.

The democratic Republic proved incapable of consolidating the slightest reform or of devising solutions to the grave problems of the day, the results of a worldwide economic depression that triggered massive and lingering unemployment. There were a number of working-class insurrections against this futile reformism; and that reformism was hampered by an inflexible right wing and decrepit, obsolete institutions, the Army and the Church foremost among them.

The Nosotros group took issue with the rest of the anarchist groups in Catalonia between April and June 1936, when it was already apparent that military preparations for a coup d'état were under way. Bitter arguments erupted over the two basic precepts of the "seizure of power" and the "revolutionary army." The Nosotros group was up to its neck in laying the groundwork for insurrection, whereas most of the FAI groups, their outlook based upon anarchist doctrinal purism, accused them of militarism, and of being anarcho-bolsheviks. There was a widening gulf between theory and practice. In the Nosotros group's plan, the defense committees were the basis of the clandestine army of the revolution.

In July 1936, these defense groups fought off the army mutineers and turned into revolutionary barrio committees, taking on governmental tasks ranging from raising of militia columns on the front and watch patrols in the rear to food supply, the upkeep of free hospitals and kitchens, the running of schools, the collection of revolutionary taxes, public works schemes to ease unemployment, confiscation of buildings, barracks, hotels, churches, and monasteries—not to mention the expropriation and collectivization of firms, industries, and businesses.

Once the army was routed, a revolutionary situation emerged. The CNT membership had to choose between two options: the anarchist dictatorship proposed by García Oliver, with his ambiguous talk of "going for broke," or collaboration with the Generalidad government and other worker and bourgeois organizations, as suggested by Federica Montseny and Abad de Santillán's Nervio group. In actuality, there was a third option, argued by Manuel Escorza who proposed "hitting the pause button" on the revolutionary situation, hanging on to armed dominance in the militias at street level, until the time was right to do away with the Generalidad. In the end, this option became indistinguishable from the case for collaborationism.

The authentic revolutionary alternative, based on power being taken by the barrio committees and trade unions, loomed rather fleetingly and belatedly some months later. That revolutionary alternative was somewhat disjointedly articulated in the demands that the barrio committees put to Marcos Alcón; it carried the day at the FAI plenum on 12 April 1937, where delegates, radicalized by the barrio committees, approved the withdrawal of CNT personnel from all government and the formation of an insurrectionist Revolutionary Committee; and it was clearly articulated in the Friends of Durruti poster put up in the streets and squares of Barcelona in late April 1937.

The CNT's retreat from revolution, and its embrace of collaborationism with other anti-fascist organizations and partnership in government, rendered the revolutionary and governance functions that the revolutionary barrio committees had initially assumed in July 1936 obsolete. The Control Patrols had a monopoly over revolutionary violence in the rearguard, hijacking such tasks from the defense committees. By November–December 1936, the defense committees found themselves dependent upon the unions again, and in enforced hibernation. Between December 1936 and March 1937, Comorera, from his position as head of the Supplies Department, unleashed the "bread war" on the defense committees in Barcelona's barrios, the object being to utterly annihilate these potential organs of worker power.

In the spring of 1937, the Control Patrols were being brought to heel and eclipsed by the Unified Security Corps, which revitalized and unified the older bourgeois public order agencies: the Assault Guards and Civil Guard. At the same time, this strengthening and unification of the old government forces of repression triggered a revival in and rearmament of the defense committees, which, slipping out of the control of the higher CNT committees, became the detonator and chief protagonists of the May 1937 Events.

Defeat for the May 1937 Events, a result of the CNT leadership's ceasefire order, guaranteed the armed victory of the Stalinist-led counter-revolution, which moved in early June to disband the Control Patrols and used armed force in late September to snuff out all the district defense committees. The ideology of anti-fascist unity that brought together the Generalidad government, Stalinists, republicans, and higher committees—though they were united only for the goal of winning the war and crushing the revolution—was the driving force behind a ferocious crackdown on the anarcho-syndicalist movement, the SBLE (Spanish Bolshevik-Leninist Section/Trotskyists), and the POUM.

In October–December 1937, the defense committees were still capable of publishing a press organ that championed solidarity with revolutionary prisoners and attacked collaborationism.

By 1938, revolutionaries were already buried, behind bars, or driven deep underground. It was Negrín's Republic rather than Franco's dictatorship that defeated the Revolution.

These days, academic historians base their supposed objectivity upon their ability to view and evaluate the past from the vantage point of today's Spanish democracy and the "universal and eternal" (though class-based) validity of human rights and democratic principles. They cannot see the a-chronicity, senselessness, and prejudice encapsulated by this view, because the immediate consequence of the Civil War was not (capitalist) democracy but Franco's bloodthirsty and ruthless dictatorship. The revolutionary situation that arose in July 1936 in Catalonia, thanks to the CNT defense committees' victory over the army and the fascists, can only be appreciated when viewed through the worldview and values of the revolutionary proletariat, and from the defense of its historic interest in the abolition of all class distinctions. The fighting, the killing, the suffering, and the dying was not done for the sake of a Republic or for democracy, but for the emancipation of labor and a better, freer, and fairer society, one that actually seemed within reach. It was a revolutionary, anti-capitalist fight that cannot be understood, accepted, or furthered by those who depend for their very existence upon the system, and who are paid to plead its case; and who still defend, to this day, the Stalinists and the republican Generalidad government of 1937.

Let me ask the reader, perhaps bewildered by this questioning of a number of sacred cows, and perhaps disturbed by some of the historical conflicts and phenomena revealed in these pages, to ponder the splendid and unsettling response of Morpheus in the famous *Matrix* trilogy: "I never said it was going to be easy, Neo. I merely said that it would be the truth."

Agustín Guillamón, Barcelona, February 2011.

Documentary Appendix 1:
The Division of Labour among
the Six-member Defense Cadre[1]

1. Secretary: liaising with other cadres, formation of new groups, reports.

2. Gathering intelligence about personnel: gauging the danger posed by enemies.

3. Gathering intelligence about buildings: drawing up plans and compiling figures.

4. Reconnaissance of strategic points and street-fighting tactics.

5. Keeping tabs on public services.

6. Looking into the sourcing of weapons, money, and supplies.

---

1   According to the October 1934 working party report.

Documentary Appendix 2: "The Friends of Durruti Group. To the Working Class."[1]

The Friends of Durruti Group. To the Working Class.

1. The immediate formation of a Revolutionary Junta made up of urban and rural workers and combatants.

2. Family wage. Ration cards. The economy to be directed and distribution overseen by the trade unions.

3. Liquidation of the counter-revolution.

4. Creation of a revolutionary army.

5. Public Order to be under the complete control of the working class.

6. Steadfast opposition to any armistice.

7. Proletarian justice.

8. An end to the trading of individuals. [The practice of prisoners being exchanged between fascist Spain and republican Spain.]

Attention, workers: our Group is against the continued advance of counter-revolution.

---

1   Poster pasted on the walls and trees in Barcelona, late April 1937.

The Public Order decrees sponsored by Aiguadé will not be enforced. We insist upon the release of Maroto and other arrested comrades.

All power to the working class.

All economic power to the unions.

A Revolutionary Junta instead of the Generalidad.

* * *

The programme set out by the Friends of Durruti *prior* to May 1937 was marked by the stress laid on the unions assuming command of the economy, the criticism of all parties and their connivance with the state, as well as a degree of reversion to purist anarchist doctrine. The Friends of Durruti spelled out their program in a poster that covered the walls in Barcelona in late April 1937. *Well before the May events*, those posters urged the necessity of *replacing* the bourgeois government of the Generalitat of Catalonia with a Revolutionary Junta. The April 1937 poster anticipated and explained the leaflet issued during the May events and touched upon many of the themes and concerns dealt with by Jaime Balius in articles carried in *Solidaridad Obrera*, *La Noche*, and *Ideas* (relating to revolutionary justice, prisoner swaps, the need for the rearguard to live for the war, etc.). For the very first time, the need for a Revolutionary Junta to supplant the bourgeois Generalidad government was raised. That Revolutionary Junta was described as a revolutionary government made up of the workers, peasants, and militians who had, back on 19–20 July 1936, routed fascism from the streets of Barcelona (leaving out the PSUC, which was only founded on 24 July). But the most significant thing was the closing three-line set of watchwords. Replacement of the bourgeois Generalidad government appeared alongside "All power to the working class" and "All economic power to the unions." The political program articulated in that poster just prior to the May events made them without doubt the most advanced and clear-sighted of all the existing proletarian groups and turned the Group into the Spanish proletariat's revolutionary vanguard at that critical and decisive time. As the POUM and the Bolshevik-Leninist Section of Spain acknowledged in their press.

Bibliography

Books, Documents, and Pamphlets

ABAD DE SANTILLÁN, Diego. *Por qué perdimos la guerra*. Esplugues del Llobregat: Plaza Y Janes, 1977.

ALCÓN, Marcos: "Remembering 19 July. The intuition of the anonymous member." *Espoir* (20 July 1975).

Barcelona Confederal Defense Committee. "Poblet-Clot-Martín de Provensals Ward Defense Committee, greetings." Barcelona, 27 May 1937. In Spanish.

BERENGUER, Sara. *Entre el sol y la tormenta*. Calella: Seuba Ediciones, 1988.

Bill of indictment against Antonio Conesa Martínez, José Conesa Martínez, and Antonio Ordaz Lázaro. In Spanish.

CAMINAL, Miguel. *Joan Comorera. Guerr i revolució (1936–1939)*, Vol. II. Barcelona: Empuries, 1984.

_____ CORRESPONDENCE with A. Guillamón.

DALMAU, Marc and MIRÓ, Iván. *Les cooperatives obreres de Sants. Autogestió proletaria en un barri de Barcelona (1870–1939)*. Barcelona: La Ciutat Invisible, 2010.

EALHAM, Chris. *Class, Culture and Conflict in Barcelona, 1898–1937*. London: Routledge, 2005. Also available as *Anarchism and the City: Revolution and Counter-revolution in Barcelona, 1898–1937*. Oakland: AK Press, 2010.

FAI. "Report Submitted by the Anarchist Groups of Catalonia's Liaison Committee to the Comrades in the Region." March 1937? In Spanish.

FONTANA, José María. *Los catalanes en la guerra de España*. Barcelona: Acervo, 1977.

GARCÍA OLIVER, Juan. "What 19 July Was Like." *Le Libertaire* (18 August 1936). In French.

_____ *El Eco de los pasos*. Paris: Ruedo Ibérico, 1978.

_____ (Interviewed by Freddy Gomez) *My Revolutionary Life*. London: Kate Sharpley Library, 2008.

GODICHEAU, François. *Répression et Ordre Public en Catalogne pendant la guerre civile (1936–1939)*. Three Volumes. Thesis. École des Hautes Études en Sciences Sociales, 2001.

GORKÍN, Julián. "Meeting of the POUM's International Under-Secretariat—14 May 1937." In French.

GUILLAMÓN, Agustín. "Josep Rebull, 1937 to 1939. Internal Criticism of the POUM Executive Committee's Policy on the War in Spain." *Balance* Nos 19 & 20 (2000). In Spanish.

_____ "The NKVD and the SIM in Barcelona. Some of Gerö's dispatches on the War in Spain." *Balance*, No 22 (November 2001). In Spanish.

_____ *Barricadas en Barcelona*. Barcelona: Espartaco Internacional, 2007). Also available in French from Editions Spartacus, Paris 2009.

Handwritten statement made by Servando Meana Miranda, Air Force captain. In Spanish.

Indomables, Nervio, Nosotros, Tierra Libre and Germen Anarchist Groups. "Local Revolutionary Preparedness Committee." Motion put to the Barcelona Local Federation of Anarchist Groups in January 1935. In Spanish.

IWA. "Report on the activities of the CNT of Spain (16 December 1932–26 February 1933." Report drawn up by A. Shapiro with help from E. Carbó. Introduction and notes by Frank Mintz. Fondation Pierre Besnard (2005). In French.

LACRUZ, Francisco. *El alzamiento, la revolución y el terror en Barcelona*. Barcelona: Librería Arysel, 1943.

MARÍN, Dolors. *Anarquistas. Un siglo de movimiento libertario en España*. Barcelona: Ariel, 2010.

MÁRQUEZ, José Manuel and GALLARDO, Juan José. *Ortiz. General sin dios ni amo*. Barcelona: Hacer, 1999.

Meeting of committees, held on 2 December 1936.

Memorandum on War Industry. Document No 4. In Spanish.

Minutes of Local Plenum of Barcelona Anarchist Groups held on [*illegible*] June 1936.

Minutes of meetings between Companys and Herrera and Escorza, 11 to 13 April 1937.

Minutes of Plenum of Barcelona Militants held on 5 December 1936.

Minutes of Plenum of Trade Unions and Wards held on 20 November 1936 at 10:00 AM.

MUNIS, G. *Jalones de derrota, promesa de Victoria. Crítica y teoría de la revolución española (1930–1939)*. Brenes: Muñoz Moya, 2003.

National Committee of Defense Committees. "Resolution on establishment of Defense Committees (11 October 1934)." In Spanish.

NELLES, Dieter with LINSE, Ulrich, PIOTROWSKI, Harald and GARCIA, Carlos. *Antifascistas alemanes en Barcelona (1933–1939). El grupo DAS: sus actividades contra la red nazi y en el frente de Aragón*. Barcelona: Sintra, 2010.

NIN, Andrés: "The problem of organs of power in the Spanish Revolution." *Juillet. Revue Internationale du POUM*, No 1 (June 1937), Barcelona-Paris. In French. Available in Spanish translation by Agustín Guillamón in *Balance*, No 2 (1995).

Notes on the meeting held on 3 January 1937. [Control Patrols Secretariat]

PAZ, Abel. *Durruti in the Spanish Revolution*. Oakland: AK Press, 2006.

PEIRATS, Josep: *De mi paso por la vida. Memorias*. Barcelona: Flor del Viento, 2009.

ROCA, Francesc: *Política, economía y espacio. La política territorial en Cataluña (1936–1939)*. Barcelona: Ediciones del Serbal, 1983.

ROMERO, Luis: *Tres días de Julio*. Barcelona: Ariel, 1976. Novel.

SANZ, Carles: *La CNT en pie*. Barcelona-Sabadell: Anomia, 2010.

SANZ, Ricardo: "Francisco Ascaso Morio." Typescript.

Scheme for conspiratorial organisation passed (Barcelona, May 1937).

Second session of the local plenum of Barcelona Anarchist groups [...] held in the assembly rooms of the Casa CNT-FAI, attended by the confederal Defense groups and Libertarian Youth (Barcelona, 24 April 1937). In Spanish.

SESÉ, Antonio, BARRIO José del and COMORERA, Juan: *Nuestra situación política actual. Discursos pronunciados en el Gran Price el día 20 de diciembre de 1936.* Pamphlet published by PSUC-UGT, undated.

TARRADELLAS, Josep: "The political crisis prior to the May Events. 26 days of un-government at the Generalitat." Report in Catalan.

Newspapers

Alerta ...! (1937)
Diari Oficial de la Generalitat de Catalunya (1936–1938)
Más Lejos (1936)
Solidaridad Obrera (1936–1938)
Treball (1936–1938)
La Vanguardia (1936–1938)

Author's Glossary

AIGUADÉ, Artemi: One of three *Esquerra Republicana De Cataluña* (ERC) representatives on the CAMC, with Jaume Miravitlles and Joan Pons. After the CAMC was disbanded, he was appointed to head the Internal Security Department in the first Tarradellas government, chairing the Internal Security Council, the agency charged with managing Public Order, and thus, the Control Patrols. In May 1937, he could rely upon support from Comorera and Vidiella of the PSUC in his attempt to oust the anarchists from the government. The upshot was that the Generalidad government was stripped of its Public Order powers. In 1939, he left for exile in France, living in Paris up until it was occupied by the Germans. In 1941, he made it out to Mexico.

ALCÓN, Marcos (1902–1997): Anarchist active in the Glass-workers' Union. He was involved with the CAMC, standing in for Durruti when he left for the front, and was in charge of War Transport. In 1937, he was asked by the defense committees to take over the general secretaryship of the CNT. He went into exile in Mexico, where he was closely associated with Katia Landau and a leading member of the group publishing *Tierra y Libertad*.

ANARCHISM (State Anarchism and Revolutionary Anarchism): During the civil war, the political project of State anarchism, with anarchism organized along parliamentary party lines and as a bureaucratic organization, proved a resounding failure in every realm. But revolutionary anarchism, a social movement involving management of the economy, revolutionary popular initiatives, and proletarian autonomy produced a light that shines to this very day, heralding a future radically different from capitalist barbarism, fascist horrors, and

Stalinist enslavement. Although that revolutionary anarchism ultimately succumbed to repression coming from the State, the Stalinists, and the higher committees, it bequeathed us the example, and the battles, of a few minorities such as the Friends of Durruti, the Libertarian Youth, and a number of anarchist groups affiliated to the Barcelona Local Federation of Anarchist Groups, allowing us today to theorize about their experiences, learn from their mistakes, and claim their struggles and their history as our own.

ASCASO, Francisco (1901–1936): The youngest child of an anarchist family in Aragon. Baker and waiter by trade. From a very early age he was active in the Aragonese action groups. In December 1920, he was jailed over his brother Domingo's attempt on the life of a reporter from *El Heraldo de Aragón*—who denounced soldiers who had rebelled in the El Carmen barracks that January. He spent two years in prison, emerging with his health shattered by the mistreatment received. In 1922, he left for Barcelona, joining the Los Solidarios anarchist group alongside Durruti, García Oliver, Aurelio Fernández, Gregorio Jover, Ricardo Sanz, etc. He was implicated in many armed actions and attacks. In June 1923 he was arrested and jailed, but managed to escape that December. During the Primo de Rivera dictatorship he lived in exile in Paris. In December 1924, along with Durruti, he embarked on a "tour" of South America that included numerous bank raids in various countries to raise funds to secure the release of anarchist prisoners in Spain. In May 1926 he was back in Paris and that July was arrested, with Jover and Durruti, for planning an attempt on the life of Alfonso XIII, and spent a year behind bars. Thanks to an intensive popular campaign for his release, he dodged extradition to Argentina and Spain. He led a clandestine existence in a number of countries. At the beginning of 1929, he obtained a permit allowing him to live in Brussels. He returned to Barcelona right after the Republic was proclaimed on 14 April 1931. He joined the "Nosotros" group (the name that the erstwhile "Los Solidarios" group had to adopt upon discovering that there was already another group with the same name) with Durruti and García Oliver, to name but two. He regularly wrote for *Solidaridad Obrera* and belonged to the Barcelona Textile Union. Deported to the Canary Islands and Guinea in February 1932 for his role in the January 1932 uprising in the Upper Llobregat, he was freed in September 1932. He served on the Revolutionary Committee that steered the 8 January 1933 uprising in Barcelona. Arrested in April 1933 with Durruti, they both were committed to the Puerto de Santa María prison until he was released that October.

He worked as a waiter and was involved in the abstentionist campaign during the November 1933 elections and was the driving force behind the December 1933 uprising. At the start of 1934 he was appointed general secretary of the CNT, backing the general strike in Zaragoza.

Ascaso came out against the Asturias CNT signing a Workers' Alliance pact with the UGT. On 6 October 1934, he called off the general strike that was supposed to support the Generalidad government in its confrontation with the central government, and for this was removed from his post as general secretary. He took part in the Zaragoza Congress (May 1936), representing the Barcelona Textile Union. As a member of the Confederal Defense Committee, he was one of the leaders of the worker uprising against the army mutiny on 19 July 1936 in Barcelona, throwing himself into the street fighting, displaying mad daring and rashness. On 20 July, he was killed, shot in the head during the storming of the Atarazanas barracks.

ASENS, José: In July 1936 Asens was secretary of the Barcelona Local Federation of Unions, a member of the CNT's Regional Committee, and of the Confederal Defense Committee. He was one of three CNT representatives on the CAMC, with Durruti and García Oliver. He headed the Control Patrols Agency and made numerous trips out of the country for the purpose of buying arms. In April 1938 he was the CNT representative on the

Executive Committee of the Libertarian Movement.[1] Disinclined to comply with the bourgeois republican courts, which called him to account for his stewardship of the Patrols, he went into exile in France. This led to him being, in June 1938, "banned" from holding any post within the Organization. When the civil war was over he was readmitted to the CNT with full rights and took part in its reconstruction in France. Asens died in 1985.

ASTURIAS, INSURRECTION IN 1934: Following the defeat of the left in the November 1933 elections, a number of rightist governments formed. But the entry of CEDA (Confederación Española de Derechas Autónomas, led by its "*Jefe*," Gil Robles) ministers into the government was deemed a fascist coup d'état on a par with recent developments in Vienna. The workers' uprising, scheduled to take place throughout the country, was confined to an armed worker uprising in Asturias—where the CNT and the UGT appeared to be united under the umbrella of the Workers' Alliance—and a nationalist revolt in Catalonia in which the CNT played no part. The Asturian workers' uprising was crushed by African troops led by General Franco.

---

1 Translator's note: The Executive Committee of the Libertarian Movement was a ten-man body established in Catalonia to enforce and impose uniform discipline upon all CNT members, committees, trade unions, and federations. It was a sign that the CNT's federalism was being jettisoned as cumbersome, that the leading militants were wedded to collaboration in politics, with some moving towards the emergence (in all but name) of a libertarian political party. The ECLM (or LMEC) was largely self-appointed from among the organizations making up the Libertarian Movement (i.e. the CNT, the FAI, and the Libertarian Youth), each of these organizations having lost something of its separate identity. All pretense of elected delegates representing the grassroots was abandoned: "names" were nominated and then a label (CNT or FAI) hung on them. For reasons of survival, it was more or less a body that *purported* to represent all the organizations but which was largely *un*representative, with a broad hint of some sort of "apostolic succession" to ensure that the CNT identity did not vanish entirely.

BALIUS, Jaime (1904–1980): Balius walked with a limp and suffered spasms in one arm as a result of a degenerative illness. In his younger days, he was a nationalist, taking part in the attempt on the life of Alfonso XIII in Garraf, and for a few months he was with the BOC (Worker-Peasant Bloc). In 1933, he joined the anarchist movement while in prison. On 21 July 1936, he issued a flyer as a supplement to *Solidaridad Obrera*. With Pablo Ruiz and Francisco Carreño, he founded the Friends of Durruti Group. Atop a barricade in May 1937, he read out a manifesto calling for active solidarity from French workers.

In 1939, in exile in France, he joined with Ridel, Prud-hommeaux, and some French anarchists to launch the French-Spanish Chapter of the Friends of Durruti that, in the review *Révision* and in a triple edition of *L'Espagne nouvelle* (Nos 67–69, July–September 1939) published a maverick analysis and some rigorous reflections on why the Spanish revolution failed. After the Nazi invasion of France, he spent many years as an exile in Mexico, including a few months in Munis's home. He later spent two years in the Sanatorio Español, his condition having deteriorated, and, in of utter poverty, corresponded with California-based historian Burnett Bolloten, who gave him moral and financial support. During the 1960s, he managed to relocate to France. From 1964 on, he was a contributor to *Le Combat syndicaliste*. He died in Hyères in the "Bon Séjour" home for Spanish republicans in exile.

BARCELONA LOCAL FEDERATION OF ANARCHIST GROUPS: The authentic FAI in the city of Barcelona, or, if you will, the only forum for Barcelona anarchist groups to articulate their disagreements with and critiques of the official policy of collaborationism.

BARRIOBERO, Eduardo (1880–1939): Republican lawyer, politician, federalist, and freemason. Madrid-based. He was regarded as the organizer of the assassination of Dato, which took the Spanish prime minister's life in March 1921. Barriobero was twice exiled during the Primo de Rivera dictatorship. He was elected a deputy to the Republic's Constituent Cortes, standing out for his scathing criticism of the government over the Casas Viejas incident. He acted as attorney for CNT personnel. On 21 July 1936, he moved to Barcelona to replace Ángel Samblancat as head of the Courts Office, the functions of which he strengthened and broadened. In this work, he was assisted by Antonio Devesa from the CNT Prisoners' Aid Committee, and by José Batlle, liaison with the Centre Ward's Defense Committee.

From June 1937 onwards he defended numerous CNT members charged in connection with the May Events. In October 1937, he himself was jailed over alleged irregularities at the Courts Office. The republican authorities failed to release him when Barcelona fell to the Francoists and he was shot by the Francoists.

BARRIO REVOLUTIONARY COMMITTEES in the city of Barcelona: The barrio-level revolutionary committees in Barcelona city, along with a range of local committees in the remainder of Catalonia, were potential organs of working class power. They called for socialization of the economy and opposed militarization of the militias as well as collaboration with government and the anti-fascist parties. Being armed, they amounted to the clandestine army of the revolution. Their main failing was their inability to organize themselves and to liaise with one another outside of the CNT apparatus. The "higher" committees swamped the revolutionary committees politically and organizationally. And the revolutionary committees became the higher committees' worst enemies and the greatest impediment to their desired and necessary absorption into the machinery of the bourgeois State as the ultimate aim of a process of institutionalization. Comorera declared war on the revolutionary committees, content to see the residents of Barcelona face bread shortages, as long as the committees were destroyed.

BERNERI, Camillo: Active in the Young Socialists as a youth, he was a Great War veteran, professor of humanities at the

University of Florence, and a member of the Italian Anarchist Union (UAI). Berneri was exiled from Italy following the fascist take-over, arriving in Spain in July 1936. With Carlo Rosselli, he raised the very first column of Italian volunteers to fight in Aragon. His own hearing difficulties prevented him from remaining at the front. In Barcelona, he published the Italian-language newspaper *Guerra di Classe*. He was hyper-critical of collaborationism and his open letter to Federica Montseny became very famous and widely read. He also contributed to CNT-FAI radio broadcasts. During the May Events in 1937, he and Francesco Barbieri were murdered by the Stalinists.

BOC (Bloc Obrero y Campesino/Worker-Peasant Bloc): A breakaway from the PCE, in 1931. Its leader was Maurín. In 1935, it amalgamated with the ICE to form the POUM.

BREAD WAR: This expression covers three phenomena:

(a) The confrontation between Comorera, the PSUC's head of the Supplies Department, and the ward supplies committees, spilling over also into the Barcelona Union of Cooperatives.

(b) The war between three different networks for the distribution of flour and bread (and the rationing thereof): one run by the *barrio* committees, one by the cooperatives, and Comorera's projected but non-existent network, which he ordered Barcelona Corporation to conjure out of nothing. The "war" lasted from 20 December 1936 until the events of May 1937.

(c) PSUC-manipulated demonstrations by women carrying placards with such counter-revolutionary slogans as "More bread, fewer committees."

CAMC (Central Antifascist Militias Committee): Short-lived government agency embracing revolutionary organizations, reformists and counter-revolutionaries, parties and labor unions, and anti-fascist bourgeois. Established in Barcelona on 21 July 1936 as the bitter fruits of the successful uprising to counter the army revolt and of the CNT's refusal to seize power. It was a class collaborationist body that lasted a mere nine weeks. Many historians mistakenly refer to the CAMC as a dual power organ.

CARBÓ, Eusebio (1883–1958): Anarcho-syndicalist journalist. At the CNT's 1919 congress he defended the Russian revolution and CNT entry into the Third International. He made frequent trips around Europe between 1917 and 1920, spending long periods in Italy where he met Malatesta, Fabbri and Borghi, escorting the latter to many trade union rallies. From 1930 he was on the editorial board of *Solidaridad Obrera*. Carbó founded the weekly *Más Lejos*. During the civil war he held posts with the Generalidad's Propaganda Commissariat and on the Economic Council. On the CNT's behalf he wrote the draft for the Collectivizations Decree promulgated by Joan Pau Fábregas. He died in exile in Mexico.

CARREÑO, Francisco: Rationalist schoolteacher, leading militant and public speaker in the 1930s. A member of the Durruti Column's War Committee and co-founder of the Friends of Durruti Grouping with Jaime Balius and Pablo Ruiz.

CASARES QUIROGA, Santiago: Spanish prime minister at the time of the army mutiny, on 17 July 1936, that was to grow into a civil war. Unable to treat it with the significance that it deserved or to stand up to the rebellion, he resigned and was replaced by Martínez Barrio who never actually took office as leader of the government and, finally, by José Giral. Casares refused to issue weapons to the workers' organizations. During the civil war he held no further office, leaving for France with Azaña and Martínez Barrio after the fall of Catalonia. He died in exile in 1950. His daughter, María Casares knew a measure of success in France as an actress.

CASAS VIEJAS: The Casas Viejas incidents is how the massacre of anarchists by a sizable detachment of Assault Guards under orders to "aim for the guts" has gone down in history. What occurred in a small hamlet in the province of Cadiz between 10 and 12 January 1933 was one of the most tragic events of the Second Spanish Republic. It ushered in a huge political crisis during the Republic's first two years and started the ball rolling when it came to the loss of political and social support;

months later, this would lead to the downfall of Manuel Azaña's republican-socialist coalition cabinet.

CENTRAL SUPPLIES COMMITTEE: The Central Supplies Committee popped up as an indispensable complement to the CAMC. It was chaired by Doménech and segued "naturally" into the first Tarradellas government's Supplies Department, which Doménech also headed. Its foundation and strength derived from coordination and cooperation with the Barcelona city ward committees and local committees across Catalonia.

CNT (Confederación Nacional del Trabajo/ National Confederation of Labor): Anarcho-syndicalist trade union, founded in 1910, in which four-fifths of the Catalan proletariat was active by July 1936. Overwhelmingly in the majority in Barcelona city.

COMPANYS, Lluís: President of the Generalidad of Catalonia, successor to Macià, the very first president of the republican Generalidad back in 1931. Companys had held office as mayor of Barcelona, civil governor, and Minister of the Marine in the government of the Republic. A friend of Salvador Seguí and a lawyer, he was very often used by anarcho-syndicalists. In November 1936, CNT personnel unearthed an Estat Catalá plan for a pro-independence coup targeting Companys on the grounds that he was not enough of a Catalanist and rather too well-disposed toward alliance with the CNT. In exile in France, he was arrested by the Gestapo and extradited to Spain. In October 1940 he was shot in the ditches of the castle of Montjuich in Barcelona.

COMORERA, Joan (1895–1958): Represented the USC (Unió Socialista de Catalunya) in the Catalan Parliament. Served as head of the Agricultural and Economic Departments in the government formed by Companys in 1934. Secretary of the PSUC from its foundation on 24 July 1936. During the civil war, he occupied one department after another. In concert with the Hungarian Gerö (aka Pedro), he led the PSUC in a personalist, authoritarian manner. In 1949, he was expelled from the PSUC on charges of "Titoism." In 1951, he smuggled himself back into Catalonia. Arrested in 1954, he was tried and imprisoned. He died in Burgos prison in 1958.

CONESA, Antonio: Part of an action group led by Antonio Ordaz Lazaro, the lieutenant or right-hand man of Aurelio Fernández. Antonio Conesa's bullying behavior plus his extravagant demands for special attention while in the hospital grew out of his membership of an action group "backed" by Aurelio Fernández's authority. Conesa was arrested and tried in connection with the disappearance of Martí Puig. Puig was suspected of having tried to assassinate Conesa, whom he accused of abusing his authority and demanding special treatment as a patient.

CONTROL PATROLS: The Control Patrols were established between 21 July and mid-August 1936 as a "revolutionary" police force answerable to the CAMC. Only about half the patrolmen held CNT membership cards or were from the FAI: the other half were affiliated to the other organizations making up the CAMC: the POUM, the ERC, the PSUC, essentially. Of eleven section delegates, only four were from the CNT—the working class barrios of Pueblo Nuevo, Sants, San Andres (Armonía) and Clot—another four were from the ERC, three from the PSUC, and none from the POUM. The Control Patrols answered to the CAMC's Investigation Committee, headed by Aurelio Fernández (FAI) and Salvador González (PSUC). The delegates directly in charge of overseeing the Control Patrols were José Asens (FAI) and Tomás Fábregas (from the Acció Catalana party). The patrolmen's wages (ten pesetas a day) were covered by the Generalidad. Even though arrests were made by every section and some detainees were interrogated at the former Casa Cambó by Manuel Escorza, the central prison was in the San Elías former convent of the Poor Clare nuns. When the CAMC was disbanded, the Patrols fell under the command of a Security Council that CNT personnel argued was autonomous, but that the PSUC, ERC, and Generalidad government regarded as subordinate to the head of the Security Department, Artemi Aiguadé.

CRTC: Regional Labor Confederation of Catalonia, usually, but wrongly referred to as the CNT of Catalonia.

DECREE ON COLLECTIVIZATIONS AND WORKERS' CONTROL: On 24 October 1936, the CNT's Joan Pau Fábregas, Economy Minister, promulgated the Collectivizations and Workers' Control Decree. It resulted from negotiations between the CNT and every other anti-fascist faction, and with the Generalidad government. It slowed down and launched the regulation of the spontaneous process of expropriation that the workers had launched following the defeat of the July 1936 mutiny. When Joan Pau Fábregas left the Generalidad cabinet formed on 17 December 1936, the actual implementation of the decree was shaped and manipulated by Josep Tarradellas through fifty-eight funding and taxation orders passed in January 1937. The Collectivizations Decree became a tool in the hands of the Generalidad for effectively controlling every venture and plan for the Catalan economy. The workers' revolution, won on the streets, was being lost in offices.

DECREE DISSOLVING LOCAL COMMITTEES: The decree of 9 October 1936, complemented by the one published on the 12th, announced the disbanding of all the local committees that had emerged on 19 July. They were to be replaced by new town councils. Despite resistance from many local committees to their disbandment, and the several months' delay in setting up the new town councils, this represented a deadly blow from which there would be no recovery. Resistance from the CNT membership, which ignored the instructions from the higher committees or orders from the Generalidad government, posed a threat to the anti-fascist compact.

DECREE MILITARIZING THE MILITIAS: The decrees signed on 24 October 1936 regarding militarization of the militias from 1 November onwards, plus the promulgation of the Collectivizations Decree completed the disastrous record of the CAMC. Together they meant the switch from worker militias made up of anti-fascist volunteers to a bourgeois army in the classic mode, bound by the monarchist military code of justice and led by the Generalidad; and the switch from expropriation and worker control of the factories to a centralized economy controlled and directed by the Generalidad.

DIFFERENTIATING BETWEEN The Confederation, The Specific, and The Organization:

The Confederation: refers to the trade union confederation or CNT.

The Specific: refers to the FAI, i.e. the anarchists' own, exclusive or specific organization.

The Organization: In the 1930s, given the *trabazón* (working arrangement) between the unions and "the specific," this referred to the overall organization of the CNT plus FAI and, in common parlance, it eclipsed "Confederation," the term that had been in use since well before the foundation of the FAI.

DIRECT ACTION: In 1918, direct action was understood to mean direct negotiation between the *sindicato único* and each entrepreneur, with no intermediaries of any kind, be they State or local authorities or Employers' Federation. This rendered the CNT extraordinarily powerful as it tackled each firm separately. In 1919, the response from the employers was State terrorism and the hiring of gunmen to wipe out the syndicalists.

DOMÉNECH, Josep J. (1900–1979): Trade unionist and cooperativist, served as secretary of the CRTC in 1934 and in 1937. He headed the Central Supplies Committee and was later head of the Generalidad's Supplies Department. In December 1936 he was head of the Public Services Department, at loggerheads with Comorera and his bread war against the barrio committees. In April 1937 he served for a few days as head of the Economy Department. Exiled in France, he returned to Barcelona in 1975.

DURRUTI, Buenaventura (Leon 1896–Madrid 1936): Mechanic involved in the labor movement's social struggles from a very young age. His pugnacious involvement in the August 1917 general strike led to his expulsion from the UGT. A few weeks after that, he left for exile in France in order to avoid military service. In October 1922, with Francisco Ascaso, García Oliver, Aurelio Fernández, Ricardo Sanz, and others, he set up the "Los Solidarios" anarchist group. At the beginning of 1923, he was arrested in Madrid, but freed that June. On 1 September the same year, he had a hand in the hold-up of the Gijon branch of the Banco de España. After Primo de Rivera proclaimed himself dictator on 23 September, he decided to leave the country again. In January 1924, Ascaso and Durruti settled in Paris. In November 1924, they were implicated in the Vera de Bidasoa plot, a plan for small guerrilla groups to infiltrate Spain. After that failed in December 1924, Durruti and Ascaso left for South America, where they combined work at a variety of trades with hold-ups that raised funds for the release of prisoners, the founding of rationalist schools, and other schemes, in an odyssey that brought them to New York, Mexico, Cuba, Chile, Argentina, and Uruguay before they wound up back in Paris in May 1926. In July 1926, Durruti, Ascaso, and Jover were arrested and charged with plotting an attempt on the life of Alonso XIII, who was on a visit to Paris on 14 July 1926. An intense and massive popular campaign was launched to stop the Spanish anarchists' extradition to Argentina or Spain, and this won their release in July 1927. After going underground for a time, and repeated expulsions from the French-Belgian border, Durruti had been granted right of lawful residence in Brussels in early 1929.

With the proclamation of the Republic in April 1931, Durruti returned to Barcelona, living in the working class Pueblo Nuevo barrio. He formed the "Nosotros" group with García Oliver, Francisco Ascaso, Ricardo Sanz, etc.

In February 1932 he was deported to the Canary Islands and to Guinea as punishment for his part in the January 1932 uprising in the Upper Llobregat. On his release in September 1932, he served on the Revolutionary Committee that orchestrated the 8 January 1933 uprising in Barcelona. Arrested in April 1933 with Francisco Ascaso, the pair of them were jailed in Puerto de Santa María prison until they were released in October.

He worked as a mechanic and took part in the campaign calling for abstention in the November 1933 elections. He was a driving force behind the December 1933 uprising, which earned him arrest and imprisonment in Burgos prison, where he remained until the April 1934 amnesty. That June, he took part in the CNT National Plenum that rejected the Workers' Alliance that the Asturian CNT had signed with the UGT. He was arrested in connection with the events of 6 October 1934 in Catalonia, even though he had had nothing to do with them. He was held in Barcelona's Modelo Prison until April 1935. For the remainder of that year, he was in and out of prison for short stays. In July 1936, he was on the Confederal Defense Committee that defeated the army. On 20 July 1936, he was part of a delegation that met with Companys and took the provisional decision to set up the CAMC. He was appointed delegate of the Column that set off to capture Zaragoza on 24 July. He was against militarization of the militias and participation in the government. Part of the Durruti Column was relocated to Madrid, which was in danger of falling to the Francoists. On 19 November 1936, he was wounded on the Madrid front, dying the following day of the gunshot wound. His funeral in Barcelona on Sunday 23 November was impressive and massively attended. Within a year of his death, Stalinist propaganda was falsely crediting him with a slogan that its own propaganda machine went on to make famous: "We renounce everything, save victory."

ECONOMIC COUNCIL: The revolutionary situation in Barcelona in the wake of the victorious uprising of 19 and 20 July 1936 was quickly fleshed out in three brand new bodies: the CAMC, the Central Supplies Committee, and the Economic Council. There were others such as the CENU (New Unified Schooling Council) and the War Industries Commission, but the first three were the most important ones, and they articulated the new "revolutionary order." The third, the Economic Council, was charged with regulating and coordinating the collectivizations and Catalan economic planning. Two members of that Council would finish up as the first two anarchist ministers in history to join any government: Antonio García Birlán and Joan Pau Fábregas.

ERC (*Esquerra Republicana De Cataluña*/Republican Left of Catalonia): Republican Catalanist party of the petite bourgeoisie, with some workerist leanings. Led by Macià and Companys, it scored a great election victory in the April 1931 elections. The party provided two Generalidad presidents: Macià (who died on Christmas 1933) and Companys (who replaced him in the position).

EROLES, Dionisio: CNT militant from the Barcelona Sants barrio action groups. He was given a twenty-year jail term for an attack mounted during the days of *pistolerismo*, and spent the entire Primo de Rivera dictatorship years behind bars. Eroles took part in the uprisings of January 1932 and January 1933. During the civil war, he held the post of secretary of the Workers' and Soldiers' Council (a body charged with purging the army, Civil Guard, and police) and in October 1936 was Chief of Services of the Internal Security Council, in fierce competition and confrontation with the Commissariat-General and Security Department which were dominated by Stalinists and ERC members. After May 1937, he served for a few months as acting regional secretary of the CRTC. He was murdered in exile in 1940.

ESCORZA, Manuel (1912–1968): A bout of polio left him permanently paralyzed. Because of his wasted legs, he used huge lifts inside his shoes, as well as crutches that made him look grievously deformed and maimed, despite being highly intelligent, very tenacious, and cultivated. He was active in the Libertarian Youth and came to serve on the FAI's Peninsular Committee. At the CNT-FAI meeting held on 20 July 1936, he advocated a "third way" between García Oliver's "go for broke" line and the collaborationist policy advocated by Montseny and Santillán: it amounted to using the Generalidad government as an instrument to socialize the economy, one that the CNT could shrug off once they had no further use for it. He was in charge of

217

the CNT-FAI's Investigation Services that carried out all sorts of repressive missions after July 1936, as well as espionage and intelligence-gathering. He was feared and despised by his own people and outsiders because of his powers. In the summer of 1936, he participated in talks between the CAMC and Moroccan independence fighters in an attempt to deny Francoists access to Moroccan volunteers, by granting them independence. In October 1936, he signed the CNT-UGT-PSUC-FAI unity agreement along with Eroles and Herrera. In April 1937, with Pedro Herrera, he negotiated directly with Companys to find a way out of the Generalidad government crisis. He went into exile in Chile.

ESTAT CATALÀ: A nationalist, pro-independence, right-wing, radical political party that was formed in June 1936 when several tiny Catalanist organizations amalgamated. It did not serve on the CAMC, and was undermined by multiple personal rivalries. Its very first secretary escaped to Italy as he felt that he was under threat. His successor, Torres Picart, was arrested in November 1936 for his part in a hare-brained attempted coup against Companys, intended to physically dispose of CNT personnel like Aurelio Fernández or Dionisio Eroles and end "anarchist influence" in the Generalidad government. Cornudella, the replacement secretary, encouraged the party's visceral opposition to the CNT, a rapprochement with the PSUC, and support for the Generalidad government. In May 1937 the party was involved in lots of street-fighting against CNT personnel and in defense of its headquarters.

FÁBREGAS, Joan Pau (1894–1966): CNT member and economist. During his eighty days (26 September–16 December 1936) in charge of the Economy Department he tried to plan and accomplish three aims, succeeding in one of them, but only on paper: legalizing the expropriation of factories, firms, and workshops, by means of a Decree on Collectivizations and Workers' Control. The decree was rolled out later, in January 1937, through orders and provisions drawn up by Tarradellas, to whom the credit belongs for its actual enforcement in a manner entirely at odds with the spirit and the letter of the decree Fábregas passed.

His other two aims never got past the draft stage: The scheme for civic mobilization of the rearguard workforce, something about which the workers had strong feelings, and for which they had been lobbying; and the Foreign Trade Council which tried to impose a monopoly on foreign trade so as to pre-empt rising costs of food, arms, and raw materials procured abroad.

Fábregas was dropped from the government at the same time as Nin, on 17 December 1936, with not a voice raised in his defense. The historians usually highlight the political significance of Nin's departure, but make no mention of Fábregas's, which had greater economic, political, and social implications. Fábregas had made himself enemies, both inside the government (Companys and Comorera) and within the CNT (Santillán and the "Nervio" group).

FAI: Iberian Anarchist Federation, aka "The Specific."

FAISTAS: FAI militants. The term was also used scornfully to describe those who supported uprisings regardless of objective conditions, in the belief that mere example might spread to the people thanks to the daring displayed by the revolutionary action groups. The *treintistas*, or reformists, took exception to FAI meddling in the unions, advocating a gradualist trade union activity and, at any rate, painstaking preparation of uprisings—which they believed had to be massive and organized in an objective context favorable to their spreading across the nation and throughout society.

FASCISM OR DEMOCRACY? Whether in its fascist or democratic variety, the capitalist State has to be destroyed. The proletariat cannot enter into a compact with the republican (or democratic) bourgeoisie in order to defeat the fascist bourgeoisie, because such a compact of itself implies that the revolutionary alternative has already failed, and that the revolutionary programme of the proletariat (and the methods of

struggle peculiar to it) has been jettisoned in favor of a programme of anti-fascist unity with the democratic bourgeoisie
for the sake of winning the war against fascism.

FERNÁNDEZ SÁNCHEZ, Aurelio: Born in Oviedo in 1897. A
mechanic by trade, he moved to Barcelona in 1922. Belonged to
the "Los Solidarios" group. Attempted to assassinate Martínez
Anido. On 1 September 1923, he was involved in the hold-up
at the Gijon branch of the Banco de España, the proceeds from
which were to be used to buy arms. During the Primo de Rivera
dictatorship, he was in exile in Paris. In July 1926, he was involved
in the attempted assassination of Alfonso XIII in Paris. In October, he crossed into Belgium. Shortly after that he was picked up
in Madrid with bombs and weapons. He was held in Cartagena
prison up until the Republic was proclaimed in April 1931. He
then joined the "Nosotros" group and had a hand in various revolutionary uprisings, such as the one in January 1933. He served
on the Catalonian Regional Defense Committee. He was the
FAI representative on the CAMC and handled the Investigation
and Watch Department. He organized the Control Patrols. After
October 1936, he was general secretary of Catalonia's Internal
Security Council, continually running afoul of the Stalinists and
councillor Artemi Aiguadé. In April 1937, he was made Health
Councillor in the Generalidad government. In April 1937, he was
detained in the Modelo prison, tried on several counts, not least
for making an attempt on the life of the president of the High
Court, Andreu Abelló, of which he was found innocent. But before he could leave the prison, he was hit with charges of murder
and defrauding the Marist brothers. Thanks to García Oliver's
intervention, he walked free on 6 January 1938. In April 1938, he
joined the Executive Committee of the Libertarian Movement, as
FAI representative. In 1939, he left for exile in Mexico.

FOUS (*Federación Obrera de Unidad Sindical*/ Trade Union Unity
Labor Federation): with a foothold mainly in Catalonia, FOUS
had a presence across Spain and was under POUM influence.
In September 1936, Nin ordered it to amalgamate with the UGT

in an unsuccessful attempt to wean it away from the PSUC. In July 1936, its membership stood at some 50,000.

FRIENDS OF DURRUTI: The Friends of Durruti *Agrupación* was a large anarchist grouping with about 5,000 members. Founded in March 1937, they were against militarization and very critical of the CNT's entry into the republican and Generalidad governments. On 2 March 1937, the newspaper *La Noche* carried a note setting out the aims, characteristics, and membership requirements of the Friends of Durruti, which was formally launched on 17 March. Its leading light, Jaime Balius, was appointed vice-secretary; Pablo Ruiz and Francisco Carreño served on its steering council.

On Sunday 11 April, there was hissing and whistling during Federica Montseny's speech at a rally in the Monumental bullring. The Friends of Durruti were carrying a placard demanding the release of Maroto and imprisoned antifascists. At meetings of the CNT Regional Committee, the Friends of Durruti were accused of having boycotted minister Montseny.

On Sunday 18 April 1937, the Friends of Durruti held a rally in the Poliorama Theatre chaired by Romero and addressed by Francisco Pellicer, Pablo Ruiz, Jaime Balius, Francisco Carreño, and Vicente Pérez 'Combina'.

In late April, a poster from the group appeared on trees and walls throughout Barcelona, advertising its programme: "All power to the working class. All economic power to the unions. Revolutionary Junta instead of Generalidad."

On Sunday 2 May, they held a rally in the Goya Theatre, screening the film "19 *de Julio*," with commentary by Jaime Balius, and with Liberto Callejas and Francisco Carreño also having their say.

On (Wednesday) 5 May, the Friends of Durruti distributed a handbill around the barricades. Over the airwaves, the CNT disowned the Friends of Durruti.

On (Thursday) 6 May, *La Batalla* reprinted the Friends of Durruti handbill. In the same edition, *La Batalla* issued an appeal for the workers to step back. *Solidaridad Obrera* disowned the Friends of Durruti handbill.

On (Saturday) 8 May, the barricades came down, except those barricades belonging to the PSUC that remained up until June, a token of that party's success. The Friends of Durruti circulated a Manifesto analysing the May Events. In that Manifesto, there was reference to the "treachery" of the CNT's leaders. On (Sunday) 9 May, *Solidaridad Obrera* described the Manifesto as rabble-rousing and the members of the group as provocateurs.

19 May saw publication of the heavily censored first issue of *El Amigo del Pueblo*.

On 22 May, there was a Plenum of CNT Local and Comarcal Federations that moved that the Friends of Durruti be expelled. The Sabadell Council agreed to replace councillor (and comarcal delegate of the Generalidad Economic Council) Bruno Lladó for having put up a Friends of Durruti poster in his office.

On 26 May, issue 2 of *El Amigo del Pueblo*—having evaded the censor this time—appeared clandestinely. Within days, Balius was jailed for publication of an article critical of Negrín, following a complaint made by the PSUC.

On 28 May, *La Batalla* was shut down, along with the POUM's radio station and the Friends of Durruti's clubhouse on the Ramblas. *Solidaridad Obrera* carried a call for the expulsion of the Friends of Durruti on its front page.

On 6 June, the Control Patrols were disbanded at gunpoint.

January 1938 saw publication by the Friends of Durruti of a pamphlet, *Towards a Fresh Revolution*, written by Balius. On 1 February 1938, issue 12 (the last) of *El Amigo del Pueblo* was published, after which it was forced underground, rendering publication unfeasible.

GARCÍA OLIVER, Juan (Reus 1901–Guadalajara, Mexico, 1980): Outstanding anarcho-syndicalist activist, waiter by trade. He earned his spurs in social struggles in his hometown and, in 1922, helped set up the "Los Solidarios" group with Durruti, Ascaso, Jover, Sanz, Aurelio Fernández, etc., taking part in many robberies and attacks, notably the killing of Cardinal Soldevila. He served time in Burgos prison. In 1924, he left for exile in Paris, negotiating with Macià's supporters regarding an invasion to end the Primo de Rivera dictatorship, and with some Italian exiles regarding an attempt on Mussolini's life. He joined forces with Durruti, Ascaso, and Jover—just back from their American "tour"—in laying plans for an attempt on the life of Alfonso XIII, and managed to avoid arrest by fleeing to Brussels. He took part in the attempted invasion of Catalonia by Macià's Catalan nationalists. Arrested and convicted, he did not emerge from prison until the Republic was proclaimed in April 1931.

He was involved in the January 1933 uprising. Arrested and tortured, he was freed from prison shortly before the November 1933 elections and joined the "Nosotros" group. In May 1936, he attended the Zaragoza Congress. On 19 and 20 July, he played a very prominent part in the street-fighting, as organizer and strategist from within the "Nosotros" group, which acted as a Confederal Defense Committee. At CAMC meetings, he played a leading role, taking on the secretaryship for War portfolio.

In November 1936, he agreed to take the post of Justice minister in the Largo Caballero government. In May 1937, he was one of the main anarchist leaders calling for a ceasefire.

In the summer of 1937, he served on the Policy Advisory Commission (CAP/*Comisión Asesora Política*) that advised and directed the regional committee of the Catalan CNT. In September 1937, he was lobbying for the CNT rebels holding out at the Escolapios building to surrender to the Stalinists and the police. In 1938, he worked on setting up a Libertarian Movement Executive Committee. Following a short stay in Sweden, he finally went into exile in Guadalajara (Mexico) where he died in 1980. He wrote a controversial book of memoirs, *El Eco de los pasos*, published under the Ruedo Ibérico imprint (Paris).

GELSA: In October 1936, the decree militarizing the People's Militias triggered great unease among the Durruti Column's anarchist militias on the Aragon front. After long and bitter squabbling, in March 1937, several hundred volunteer militias manning the Gelsa sector of the front decided to quit and return to the rearguard. Back in Barcelona, many of them joined the Friends of Durruti Group. Pablo Ruiz played a leading role in this process of active "revolutionary defeatism" by the Gelsa militias.

GENERALIDAD GOVERNMENT: Catalonia's bourgeois, home-rule government, all but completely swept aside by the workers' uprising against the army and the fascists in July 1936. The dissolution of the CAMC on 1 October 1936 paved the way to its re-establishment. The collapse of the central state's apparatus in Catalonia allowed the Generalidad home-rule government to establish its own control of defense, public order, and border control responsibilities, powers not included in the Home Rule Statute for Catalonia. These were lost once and for all in the wake of the events of May 1937 when said functions were recaptured by the central government.

GROUP A: Jacinto Toryho, Jacobo Prince, Abelardo Iglesias Saavedra, Federico Sabaté, Miguel Tardaguila, Palmiro Aranda, Francisco López, Juan Osó, José Jiménez Sánchez, etc.

GROUP NERVIO: Diego Abad de Santillán, Pedro Herrera, Jacobo Maguid, Germinal de Sousa, Adolfo Verde, Ildefonso González, José Mari, Juan Rúa, Vicente Tarin, Horacio Baraco, Simon Radowitzky, etc. Led by Santillán, this group was made up for the most part of Argentineans. With Group A, and others, it made up an anti-Nosotros front. Its members captured many posts inside the Organization as well as within the government administration.

GROUP NOSOTROS: The new name adopted by Los Solidarios Group in the 1930s. It was made up of Buenaventura Durruti, Francisco Ascaso, Juan García Oliver, José Asens, Antonio Ortiz, Aurelio Fernández, Ricardo Sanz, etc., totalling about twenty first-rank militants backed by many collaborators who prepared and facilitated the various activities they mounted. On 19 July 1936, the Nosotros group performed as a Confederal Defense

Committee, leading the worker's uprising and the streetfighting against the army. Later, several of them became column delegates (Durruti, Ortiz), held various military posts (Jover, Sanz) or police posts (Asens and Aurelio Fernández), or even ministerial office (García Oliver).

GROUP SEISDEDOS: Manuel Escorza del Val, Liberato Minué, Abelino Estrada, José Irizalde, Manuel Gallego, etc. Many of them staffed the CNT-FAI's Investigation Service, led by Manuel Escorza.

HERRERA, Pedro: Railway worker active in the Nervio group. A friend of Santillán and Toryho. As FAI representative, he signed the UGT-CNT-PSUC-FAI united action pact in October 1936. From 16 December 1936 until 3 April 1937, he was Health and Social Assistance minister with the Generalidad. In mid-April, with Escorza, he negotiated directly with Companys to find a way out of the Generalidad cabinet crisis.

HIGHER COMMITTEES: The anti-fascist ideology, along with CNT participation in a range of municipal posts, Generalidad departments, and indeed central government ministries generated a bureaucracy of higher committees with interests different from and opposed to those of the revolutionary committees that emerged in the barrios of Barcelona. Whereas the higher committees made victory over fascism the number one priority, the barrio committees clung to a programme of working class revolution.

The institutionalization of these higher CNT and FAI committees turned them into servants of the state whose worst enemies were the revolutionary committees at the barrio level, as the Regional Committee stated bluntly at the get-together of the libertarian higher committees on 25 November 1936. The naïve and simplistic contention that separates the anarcho-syndicalists leaders into traitors or heroes, as if the bulk of the membership was vapid and insipid, explains nothing. The confrontation between the higher committees and the ward revolutionary committees was yet another chapter in the class struggle and it came very close to ending in a split, which was eventually resolved by selective Stalinist repression: the annihilation of the revolutionaries and the absorption of the higher committees into the machinery of the State.

The institutionalization of the CNT had significant and inescapable implications for the CNT's own organizational and ideological character.

The leadership and authority functions performed by the higher committees (a very tiny circle of personnel equipped to perform these) generated a range of interests, methods and aims different from those of the CNT rank-and-file membership. Hence, on the one hand, the widespread disaffection and disappointment among the membership and grassroots militants grappling with food shortages and repression, and left entirely to their own devices by the higher committees. Hence also, the emergence of a revolutionary opposition, essentially embodied by the Friends of Durruti, the Libertarian Youth of Catalonia, a few anarchist groups from the Barcelona Local Federation of Anarchist Groups—especially after May 1937, but already discernible very early on in the summer of 1936, in the barrio and defense committees in the wards of Barcelona.

ICE (*Izquierda Comunista de España*/Communist Left of Spain): Part of the international Trotskyist opposition. In 1932, it broke away from the PCE and began to break free of Trotskyist discipline. Nin and Andrade were flirting with Maurin's BOC, whereas Fersen, Esteban Bilbao, and Munis opposed the foundation of the POUM, regarding it as a centrist, counter-revolutionary party.

JCI (*Juventud Comunista Ibérica*/Iberian Communist Youth): The youth wing of the POUM.

LARGO CABALLERO, Francisco (Madrid 1869–Paris 1946): PSOE and UGT leader. He collaborated with the institutions of the Primo de Rivera dictatorship and was Minister of Labor, 1931–1933. Jailed following the events of October 1934, he was radicalized, becoming leader of the left wing of the PSOE. He

advocated a revolutionary workers' front policy and was nick-
named "the Spanish Lenin." He served as prime minister from
5 September 1936 until 17 May 1937, when he tendered his
resignation over communist pressures. He was marginalized in
the PSOE and UGT and became a refugee in France in 1939. He
was deported to a concentration camp in Germany.

LÉRIDA PEOPLE'S COMMITTEE: The People's Committee of
Lérida, made up of the CNT-FAI, UGT, and POUM—with no
input from the bourgeois of the ERC, and with the CNT having
the preponderant influence—was a fully autonomous government that ignored orders from the Generalidad government
and the CAMC. On 26 September 1936, anarcho-syndicalists
joined the new Generalidad government and on 1 October the
CAMC was formally disbanded once and for all.

The new Generalidad cabinet visited Lerida to bring its
People's Committee to heel. On that visit on 30 September by
Josep Tarradellas (councillor-in-chief), Josep Doménech (Supplies councillor), André Nin (political secretary of the POUM
in charge of the Justice Department), Joan Comrera (PSUC
secretary in charge of the Public Services Department), and a
hundred Assault Guards, the People's Committee was enjoined
to accept the government's dispositions, and the need for a single command, given Lérida's proximity to the Aragon front.

Following the decrees of 9 and 12 October disbanding the
local committees and forming new, Popular Front town councils, Lérida agreed, on 22 October, to the formation of a new
council and to the winding-up of the People's Committee. This
implied the end of the CNT's hegemony and the end of one of
the few power bases enjoyed by the POUM, thereafter replaced
by the strengthened writ of the Generalidad.

MAROTO, Francisco: Delegate of the militia column that bore
his name. The column mounted a successful military campaign
in Córdoba and Granada, failing to take the latter city due to
lack of weapons. Maroto clashed with Gabriel Morón, the governor of Almería, giving him a dressing-down at a meeting in

February 1937. Maroto was jailed, to enormous outrage from the libertarian movement, which called for his release. On 1 May 1937, he was pardoned, but lost command of his column. At the end of the war, he was arrested, tortured, and shot by Falangists in Alicante.

MARTÍNEZ ANIDO, Severiano (1862–1938): Military governor in Barcelona 1920–1922 and leader of the repression targeting workers' organizations, especially the CNT. His policy was characterized by brutality and the use of terrorist methods. He set up the Sindicatos Libres (Free Trade Unions), funded by the bosses, whose purpose was to murder the syndicalists from the CNT. He was Interior minister during the Primo de Rivera dictatorship and Public Order minister in Franco's first cabinet.

He was one of thirty-five high-ranking Francoists named by the Audiencia Nacional in an indictment drawn up by Baltasar Garzón relating to unlawful detention and crimes against humanity carried out during the Spanish civil war and during the early years of the Franco dictatorship.

MAS, Valerio: Acting secretary of the Catalan Regional Committee of Catalonia (CNT) from 20 November 1936 until 2 March 1937. He then served as elected secretary from 2 March until 5 May, at which point he was made a councillor in the provisional government, appointed while the fighting raged during a week of bloodshed in Barcelona in May 1937.

MAURÍN, Joaquín: (1896–1973): Founder of the BOC. Unchallenged leader of the newly founded POUM, the result of the amalgamation with the ICE. He was caught by surprise in Francoist territory by the outbreak of the civil war. His comrades thought him dead, but he was held in Francoist prisons until October 1946. Disillusioned with politics, he gave up militant activity in exile.

MERA, Cipriano (Madrid 1895–Paris 1975): CNT bricklayer. Mera's column became the 14th Division of which he was appointed commander. That division played a telling role in the defense of Madrid in November 1936 and in the battle of

Guadalajara in March 1937, defeating Italian troops. Mera commanded the IV Corps of the Army of the Centre. In 1938, by then promoted to lieutenant-colonel, he set up his HQ in Alcohete (Guadalajara), near the Horche villa, from which he oversaw the entire eastern sector of the capital. He supported Colonel Segismundo Casado's coup d'état of 5 March 1939. And was imprisoned until 1942. He left for exile in France, where he worked as a bricklayer again.

MOLA, General: Emilio Mola was the general who, immediately after the February elections in 1936 that awarded victory to the Popular Front, painstakingly planned what was meant to be a coup d'état on 17 July 1936. The so-called "Mola Plan" ordered that the enemy in the rear be exterminated, this being deemed the only military means available to an army facing hostility from the vast majority of the population.

MONTSENY, Federica (1905–1994): The daughter of anarchist intellectuals, she was a contributor to *La Revista Blanca* (run by her parents "Federico Urales" and "Soledad Gustavo") from a very young age. She wrote a number of "proletarian" novels. The keynotes of her articles were a-politicism and ideological purism. In 1936, she was on the FAI Peninsular Committee. From November 1936 until May 1937, she served as Health minister in the Largo Caballero government. During the May Events of 1937, she took a leading role in dampening down the street-fighting in Barcelona. In exile, she reverted to her anarchist purism and a-politicism. With her partner Germinal Esgleas, she dominated the CNT apparatus in exile, helping to render it decrepit and ineffectual.

MUNIS, G: Nom de plume of Manuel Fernández Grandizo y Martines (1912–1989).

NEGRÍN LÓPEZ, Juan (Las Palmas 1889–Paris 1956): Medical specialist and eminent scientist who had studied in Germany. Professor in Madrid. Finance minister in the Largo Caballero government. He was responsible for shipping the Bank of Spain's gold reserves to Moscow. On 17 May 1937, he took over from Caballero as prime minister. He presided over the "government of Victory," dropping CNT and UGT representatives and relying upon the support of the Stalinists. In August 1937, he disbanded the Council of Aragon. On 31 October 1937, he ordered the government's relocation to Barcelona. In April 1938, he formed a "national unity government," incorporating the CNT and UGT. The bloody battle of the Ebro (July–August 1938) and strict rationing, with lentils as a staple (referred to humorously as "Dr Negrín's pills"), were the earmarks of his time in government. In September 1938, he tried to negotiate an end to the war on the basis of a thirteen-point programme. In October, he decided that the International Brigades should be withdrawn from Spain. With the fall of Catalonia to the fascists, he crossed the border, only to return to the Center-South zone, calling for resistance to the bitter end. Casado's coup on 4 March 1939 sent him scuttling to France. In 1945, he stepped down as prime minister of the Republic.

NIN, André (1892–1937): Started out as a trade unionist in the CNT, serving as its general secretary in 1921. He was an official of the Profintern until 1929, when he was expelled from Russia over his Trotskyist leanings. Back in Barcelona, in 1930 he helped organize the Spanish Trotskyist Opposition which in March 1932 assumed the name ICE. In 1934, he made his final break with Trotsky after a lengthy process of rapprochement with Maurín. He advocated amalgamation with the BOC and in September 1935 co-founded the POUM. The disappearance of Maurín from the scene with the outbreak of the civil war left him as political secretary of the new party. In August 1936, he served on the Economic Council. From 26 September to 16 December 1936, he held the position of Generalidad minister of Justice, undoing the work of Barriobero and ordering the dissolution of the Court Offices. On 30 September, he accompanied Tarradellas and Comorera to a showdown with the Lerida People's Committee. Along with the CNT's Joan Pau Fábregas, he was left out of the Generalidad government set up on 17 December

1936. In January 1937, at the height of the crackdown on the POUM in Madrid, he wrote a letter demanding that his party take part in the talks concerning amalgamating the PSOE and PCE. In May 1937, he did his best to quell the street-fighting and avoid the POUM being isolated, imposing a policy of following the lead of the CNT's higher committees. He turned down the suggestion of a raid against the Generalidad because "this was a political matter, not a military one."

On 16 June, the POUM was outlawed and its central committee arrested. Nin, taken to Alcalá de Henares, was abducted by agents of the Soviet secret police, tortured, and murdered.

NON-INTERVENTION COMMITTEE: The Non-Intervention Committee, known also as the London Committee, was an organization set up in 1936 at the suggestion of France in order to monitor observance of the Non-Intervention Agreement, which was designed to prevent outside intervention in the Spanish Civil War and to avert the internationalization of the conflict at a time when relations between the democracies and the dictatorships were extremely tense. Germany and Italy signed the Non-Intervention Agreement on 8 August 1936. In the end, some twenty-seven European countries, including the Soviet Union, signed it. Whereas the United Kingdom and France refrained from intervening in the war, Germany and Italy systematically and decisively backed the Franco camp, while the Soviet Union dispatched intermittent aid to republican Spain. The Committee was an utter farce that hobbled the lawful, democratic government of the Republic by placing a bunch of would-be, coup-maker military officers on an equal footing with it. Besides, whereas the republican government was prevented from buying arms, the Axis supplied Franco with all the arms and men he could have wanted and right from the outset. The Committee was spawned by the French and British governments' fear of a successful revolution in Spain.

ORDAZ, Antonio (1901–1950): CNT member and FAI propagandist. Deported to Guinea in 1930. He served on the CNT's

Prisoners' Aid Committee. During the civil war he was very active in repressive activities in the rearguard. Some described him as Aurelio Fernández's right hand man. On 29 June 1937, he was jailed in the Modelo prison in Barcelona and stood trial with Aurelio Fernández in connection with the Marist Brothers affair. He figured prominently in many incidents in prison, serving on the Antifascist Prisoners' Committee. In December 1937, he was moved to Manresa from where he managed to escape on 3 January 1938, along with another seventeen CNT members, notably Justo Bueno Perez.

ORTIZ, Antonio (1907–1996): CNT Woodworkers' Union activist. Helped lay the groundwork for the January 1933 uprising, for which he was jailed. In 1931, he joined the Nosotros anarchist group with Durruti, Ascaso, García Oliver, etc. He played a prominent role in the 19–20 July 1936 uprising. On the evening of 25 July 1936, he left by train for the Aragon front as a delegate with the Ortiz or Sur-Ebro Column.

On 14 September 1937, because he opposed the Stalinist General Enrique Líster's break-up of the collectives in Aragon and the dissolution of the Council of Aragon, he was removed as commander of the 25th Division. He was left without a military post for some months. Eventually, in July 1938, he left for exile in France along with Joaquín Ascaso (former president of the Council of Aragon) and several co-workers. He accused the top ranks of the CNT-FAI of having issued orders for himself and Joaquín Ascaso to be murdered. He was interned in the Le Vernet concentration camp in France. Enlisting in an assault battalion in the French army, he saw action in several countries in Africa and Europe, a was decorated a number of times. His most brilliant coup was the liberation of Belfort (France). Ortiz's battalion struck into German territory, capturing Karlsruhe and Pforzheim, where he was wounded. In 1948, he was at the center of an attempt on Franco's life—a plan to use a light aircraft to bomb the Caudillo's yacht. Wanted in France in connection with the assassination attempt, he left for exile in several Latin American countries. He died in a home for the elderly in Barcelona in 1996.

PEIRÓ, Juan (Barcelona 1887–Valencia 1942): Outstanding anarcho-syndicalist leader and glassmaker. In 1918, he took part in the congress in Sants (a working-class area of Barcelona) in the debate on direct action. At the La Comedia Theatre congress in Madrid, he spoke up in favor of Federations of Industry. From June 1920 until late 1921, he was in jail for his trade union activities, and again from January to September 1925, in May 1927, and August to September 1927. He served as CNT general secretary in 1922 and again in 1928–29. In 1931, he signed the *Manifesto of the Thirty*. Under the Republic, he served as Industry minister (1936–1937). An exile in France, he was picked up by the Gestapo and extradited to Spain. The Falangists offered him a position working for them as a union organizer. His rejection of the offer made it inevitable that he would be shot.

PESTAÑA NUÑEZ, Ángel (1886–1937): Outstanding trade union leader and CNT veteran, watchmaker by trade. In 1917 he was director of *Solidaridad Obrera*. The CNT congress in 1919 decided to join the Third International on a provisional basis and dispatched him to Russia to investigate the organization of soviets. Pestaña drafted a report condemning the soviet regime, leading to the CNT pulling out of the Communist International. In 1922, along with Seguí and Viadiu, he signed a declaration endorsing CNT a-politicism. In August that year, gunmen from the Sindicato Libre made an attempt on his life. During the Primo de Rivera dictatorship, he was jailed from 1924 until 1926. In August 1931, he signed the *Manifesto of the Thirty* (Treinta). In March 1933, he was thrown out of the CNT. In April 1934, he launched the Syndicalist Party. With the outbreak of civil war he moved to Madrid. His worsening health, shattered since the assassination attempt in 1924, forced him to withdraw to the little village of Begues (near Badalona), where he died.

PORTELA: Alias used by CNT activist **Vicente Gil**. He was in charge of issuing passports and monitoring the borders, first under the CAMC (July to October 1936) and later as part of the Security Council (October 1936 until March 1937).

POUM (*Partido Obrero de Unificación Marxista*/Workers' Party of Marxist Unification): Founded in September 1935 through the amalgamation of the BOC and the ICE. By July 1936, it had a membership of around 5,000 in Catalonia. A Leninist party, it did not allow factional work, discussion, or debate of any sort—on pain of immediate expulsion—except in the run-up to congresses. It was critical of Stalinism in the Soviet Union. On 16 June 1937, the party was outlawed, its central committee jailed and its membership persecuted. Its political secretary, Nin, was abducted, tortured, and murdered by the Soviets. The Hotel Falcón, where foreign POUM sympathizers were billeted, was turned into a Stalinist prison.

PRIMO DE RIVERA DICTATORSHIP: During the reign of Alfonso XIII, on 13 September 1923, General Miguel Primo de Rivera orchestrated a coup and assumed dictatorial powers. In so doing, he ended the *pistolerismo* in Barcelona and saved the king's embarrassment over his role in the massacre of the Spanish army in Annual (during Spain's war in Morocco). Primo de Rivera persecuted the CNT and reached an accommodation with the UGT. His economic policy was one of spectacular public works and, to some extent, State management. He launched a single party. His son, Jose Antonio Primo de Rivera, founded the Falange. The economic crisis after 1929 undermined the social base upon which he depended. On 28 January 1930, he stepped down and was succeeded by the "*dictablanda*" (soft dictatorship) headed by General Berenguer.

PRODUCER'S CARD: This was a "workerist" measure, revolutionary in character, in April 1937, through which a *carnet de productor* entitled its holder to rations, ensuring that ready access to cash was not the only way to survive. The point was to flush bourgeoisie and those living on private incomes out of their idlers' hiding-places and enrol them in the army, or force them to play an active part in military defense plans. It never actually came into force. Not to be confused with the "work card" (*carta de trabajo*) imposed by the Stalinists in 1938, which was a step toward militarization of the working class and labor relations.

PSOE (*Partido Socialista Obrero Español*/ Spanish Workers' Socialist Party): Reformist party. In Catalonia, the PSOE's Catalan Federation evaporated completely when it amalgamated with three other parties to launch the PSUC. In the Madrid and Valencia governments, the PSOE provided the prime ministers from 5 September 1936 until the end of the war, first was Largo Caballero and later, Negrín (from 16 May 1937), although the latter was heavily influenced by the PCE.

PSUC (*Partido Socialista Unificada de Cataluña*/Unified Socialist Party of Catalonia): The result of the 24 July 1936 amalgamation of four small socialist and communist parties. Its general secretary was Juan Comorera. It was controlled by Moscow through the Hungarian Gerö (aka "Pedro") who, in 1956, deployed tanks to crush the workers' uprising in Budapest. The PSUC was the only party in the Third International formed out of the amalgamation of socialists and communists and it was the only party whose homeland was not possessed of a state of its own.

RABASSAIRE: A a tenant farmer, the duration of whose lease was determined by the lifespan of his vine root. The Unió de Rabassaires (Rabassaires' Union) was a Catalanist peasant party close to the Esquerra (ERC).

REVOLUTIONARY PROGRAMME OF THE PROLETAR- IAT: The proletariat's revolutionary programme incorporates internationalization of the revolution, social ownership of the economy, the laying of sound bases for the abolition of wage labor around the globe, worker oversight of the war and workers' militias, the organization of society along councilist and assembly-based lines, and a proletarian crackdown on bourgeois and petit bourgeois segments of society in order to crush the inevitable armed retaliation from the counter-revolution. The number one theoretical advance made by the Friends of Durruti was the assertion of the totalitarian character of proletarian revolution. It is totalitarian in the sense that it is all-encompassing and must reach into everything—the social, the political, the economic, the cultural, etc—and into every country, overriding national borders. It was also authoritarian in that it was militarily confronting the class enemy, that is, the petite bourgeoisie to which the PSUC was pandering.

RUIZ, Pablo: Pablo Ruiz was a militiaman with the No. 4 Gelsa Group of the Durruti Column and, in early March 1937, among the founders of the Friends of Durruti Group.

SANTANA CALERO, Juan: Juan Santana Calero was active in the Libertarian Youth in Malaga and joined the Friends of Durruti after May 1937.

SANTILLÁN, **Diego Abad de**: The extravagant alias used by the anarchist writer and leader Sinesio Baudilio García Fernández (1897–1983). In 1905, his family, workers and impoverished peasants from the mountains of Leon, emigrated to Argentina. Santillán returned to Spain in 1913, where he passed his baccalaureate and embarked on university studies. Shuttling between Spain and Argentina, he came into contact with the anarchist movement in both countries. He habitually contributed to *La Protesta*, the mouthpiece of the FORA (Argentine Regional Workers' Federation). In 1922, he left for Germany to study medicine and took part in both the Berlin congress of the IWA in 1925 and the Amsterdam congress in 1926. In 1933, he settled in Spain, a fugitive from the Argentinean police. In 1934, he joined the Barcelona editorial board of *Solidaridad Obrera* (organ of the Catalan CNT), directed *Tierra y Libertad* (the FAI mouthpiece), and was the driving force behind *Tiempos Nuevos* review. He set up the Nervio group that marshalled an anti-Nosotros front: Nervio welcomed all the Argentinean anarchists arriving in Barcelona and during the civil war secured significant leadership positions for them.

Although he was not to the fore in the street-fighting, he served in the CAMC's War Department headed by García Oliver. In the summer and autumn of 1936, he amassed countless positions of responsibility, bringing the same ineptitude to his performance in each of them. From December 1936 until April 1937, he was Economic Councillor in the Generalidad government, replacing Joan Pau Fábregas (who has passed the Collectivizations Decree), and was always quick to champion the government viewpoint over the CNT's. In May 1937, he joined those who called for a cease-fire, only to have a change of heart a few days later.

In September 1937, he published a book that assumed that the war was as good as lost. He had no difficulty with the paradox between his writing immaculately purist theoretical articles while engaging in collaborationist political activity favoring CNT participation in government tasks. In the summer of 1938 he launched the prestigious theoretical review *Timón*, returned to his activities as a translator, and resurrected Tierra y Libertad publishers. He lived in exile in Argentina.

SANZ, Ricardo (1898–1986): Textile worker from the Pueblo Nuevo barrio of Barcelona; trade unionist and anarchist. In 1922 he joined the "Los Solidarios" group along with Durruti, Ascaso, García Oliver, etc. He set up an arms cache in Pueblo Nuevo, as well as a bomb-making factory. In 1925, he was taken into preventive detention. In 1926, he was again detained for another twenty-six months. From 1928 to 1930, he was inactive. In 1931, he re-emerged with the organization of the confederal defense cadres. He was on the revolutionary committee overseeing the January 1933 uprising and took part in the street-fighting on 19–20 July 1936. During that summer, he worked on supply lines to the columns on the Aragon front. After Durruti's death, he was chosen to replace him as column delegate (which, come militarization, became the 26th Division). He lived in exile in France.

SBLE (*Sección Bolchevique-Leninista Española*/Spanish Bolshevik-Leninist Section): Orthodox Trotskyist group, the membership of which included Munis, Domenico Sedran (aka 'Carlini'), Hans David Freund (aka "Moulin"), Erwin Wolf, and Jaime Fernández.

SEGUÍ, Salvador (1887–1923): Known by his nickname "*Noi del Sucre*," he was general secretary of the CNT from 1918 to 1923. Born into a working-class family, he arrived in Barcelona at the age of two. He began work at a very early age, as a painter's apprentice. Self-educated, he was drawn to anarcho-syndicalism, and very soon stood out for his oratorical gifts and his ability to attract numbers of workers.

In 1908, a Labor Congress was held in Barcelona; it gave birth to the Catalan Regional Workers' Federation (FROC). As part of the leadership of the Solidaridad Obrera (Workers' Solidarity) organization, Segui had an active hand in organizing workers' resistance during the so-called Tragic Week in Barcelona (1909). Appointed secretary of the Ateneo Sindicalista during the First World War, he toured Spain, publicizing its outlook. In 1916, he managed to broker an agreement between the CNT's and the socialist UGT trade unions; together they called a successful general strike against the soaring cost of living.

At the CNT congress in 1918, he backed the *sindicatos únicos*, an organizational format that strengthened workers in their negotiations with the bosses. During his time as secretary of the CNT, he did his best to curb the more violent members of the organization. He played a major role in the negotiations leading up to the La Canadiense strike, in February and March 1919, with Barcelona under army occupation. His crucial intervention at the Las Arenas bullring rally established him as a speaker and leader: he called for a peaceful end to the general strike, which was regarded as a victory for the workers in that they had secured the eight-hour day, a promise from the employers that those sacked would shortly be re-hired, and the release of imprisoned workers held in captivity by private persons—with the threat of a violent eruption if their demands were not met.

The employers' failure to honor the agreement triggered a further general strike on 24 March that lasted until 17 April, and ended in defeat for the workers. Segui's performance came under severe criticism from those who were for continuing the general strike until every one of its aims had been achieved.

Toward the end of 1919, the employers declared a general lock-out in Barcelona city, deploying police, army, Civil Guard, Somatén militiamen, and hired gunmen against CNT trade unionists, while the Barcelona working class did its best to survive the hunger imposed by rising prices.

In November 1920, Seguí was deported to the La Mola fortress in Mahón (Minorca), where he was held for many months. After his release in April 1922, he joined with Pestaña, Peiró, and Viadiu in signing a "policy statement" that advocated a political function for the unions, although one that side-stepped the traditional parties and parliamentary system.

Seguí was gunned down by the employers' hired guns on 10 March 1923 in Barcelona's Calle de la Cadena while out walking with fellow CNT member Francisco Comas Pagés (aka "Peronas").

SESÉ ARTASO, Antonio: Started out as a CNT member before switching to the Catalan-Balearics Communist Federation and later co-founding the BOC. In 1932, he joined the Partit Comunista de Catalunya and, in July 1936, the PSUC. He took over from José del Barrio (who had been made delegate for the Karl Marx Column) as secretary of the Catalan UGT. In the spring of 1937, he was one of those spearheading the confrontation with the CNT. During the May Events of 1937, he was appointed Councillor without portfolio, but was murdered in a shoot-out on 5 May 1937 in front of the CNT Public Entertainments Union headquarters on Calle Caspe, en route to take up his post at the Generalidad Palace.

SINDICATO DE OFICIOS VARIOS (Amalagamated Trades Union): The *sindicatos únicos* covered each branch of industry. Thus, in Barcelona there were the Woodworkers, Construction-workers, Textile-workers, Hospitality-workers, Healthworkers unions, and so on. But in a small town where the numbers were not available for the various *sindicatos únicos*, *sindicato de oficios varios* popped up, embracing all the workers in the town, regardless of trade. There was also a Sindicato de Oficios Varios in Barcelona; it embraced those workers who could not affiliate to an existing *sindicato de ramo* because there was none, either due to a scarcity of workers in that sector or because the union was still in the gestation process. This was the case with people like intellectuals, artists, etc.

SINDICATO ÚNICO: The Sants Congress of the Regional Labor Confederation of Catalonia met in the Sants barrio of Barcelona from 28 June to 1 July 1918. The main achievements of the congress were its endorsement of direct action, and the *sindicato único* or *sindicato de ramo*. In addition, approval was given to the need to unionize women and end once and for all the exploitation of minors, whatever the cost. A resolution was passed banning overtime as long as there were workers out of work. It was agreed that those trades that had already secured the eight-hour work day would help the those that had not. The aim was a standard wage (*salario único*).

The greatest achievement was the organization of the CNT along *sindicato único* lines. The point was to do away with the old craft organization on the basis of trades with different interests within the same factory or firm setting. Autonomous trades bodies were disbanded and replace by a single, united organization covering all the workers in each branch of industry. In the textile industry, say, separate trade-based organization for spinners, weavers, boilermen, machine-operators, etc. were done away with, and they all came under the umbrella of the single textile union, affording the workers great organizational power vis à vis the employer, who, in the event of a strike, could no longer play one trade within his firm off against the rest. The same went for the *sindicatos únicos* of the Woodworkers, Healthworkers, Construction workers, Bankworkers, etc. The older trades unions were replaced by the *sindicatos únicos* in each branch of industry.

The *sindicato único* meant greater unity when confronting the bosses and it facilitated strategies like the general strike and direct action. The main champions of the *sindicato único* were Salvador Segui and Emilio Mira, who argued: "Workers must demonstrate unity in dealing with the organized solidarity of the employer class."

SOCIALIZATION V. COLLECTIVIZATION: The spring of 1937 saw growing opposition between worker-driven *socialization* and the *collectivization* managed and manipulated by the Generalidad. On the one hand, the Generalidad government, socially dependent upon petit bourgeois sectors—administrative, technical, former-owners, liberal professions, and even Stalinist or right-wing workers, many of them organized in the UGT—mounted an offensive designed to increase its control of firms, invoking the Collectivizations Decree and enforcing a battery of financial decrees that Tarradellas approved in S'Agaró in January 1937. In parallel with this, the radical segment of the CNT membership tried to *socialize* production, which meant boosting the power of the Industrial Unions in those ventures. As far as this radical faction of the CNT was concerned, socialization meant that the running of the Catalan economy would pass into the hands of the unions (the CNT), and it implied a break with the dynamic of trade union capitalism, by introducing a fair distribution of wealth that would end the scandalous differences among workers employed in wealthy collectivized industries, poor ones, and workers not employed at all. The management of a socialized Catalan economy also implied setting up suitable bodies within the CNT—that is, the replacement of the *sindicatos únicos* (suitable to supporting a strike, but not to the running of firms) by Industrial Unions (better equipped to run the various sectors of the economy). This took place in the early months of 1937. Socialization of the Catalan economy presupposed the economy (and the war) being dependent on the CNT and this, in turn, required the abolition of the Generalidad government.

So the Generalidad's counter-revolutionary offensive, designed to boost its control by extending it into every firm, clashed directly with the radical CNT sector's plans to abolish the Generalidad itself.

Over the spring of 1937, a firm-by-firm struggle erupted as the assemblies about to endorse socialization came under pressure and were manipulated in various ways, ranging from the most ruinous political intrigues to the deployment of police strength. In these tough, firm-by-firm battles, which the CNT's higher committees were never willing to coordinate—since that would have meant breaking with the anti-fascist unity agreement— an ever more obvious and "painful" gulf opened up among the trade union membership, between the collaborationist sector and the CNT's radical sector. In this attempt to socialize the Catalan economy, the CNT radicals tried to compete with the collaborationist faction for the support of the union member- ship. But those radical members were almost always a minority at factory meetings, given the huge influx of opportunists in the wake of 19 July, and the blood-letting by the revolution itself among revolutionaries who had enlisted in the militias or risen to positions of responsibility.

Examples of this socialization-versus-collectivization tension, manipulated by the Generalidad, include pamphlets like:

Barcelona Steel & Metalworking Industrial Union, CNT-AIT. ¿Colectivización? ¿Nacionalización? No: Socialización (Primero de mayo printers, Barcelona 1937).

Memoria del Primer Congreso Regional de Sindicatos de la In- dustria de la Edificacion, Madera y Decoracion (Inicial Graphics, Barcelona 1937)

The protagonists themselves write in: *Balances para la his- toria. Las colectivizaciones y la autogestión obrera durante la Guerra civil Española* (Publisher, place and date of publication not indicated).

STATE CAPITALISM AND TRADE UNION CAPI- TALISM: Stalinism was a counter-revolutionary option championing State capitalism and advocating a Stalinist party dictatorship over the proletariat. The State anarchism of the higher libertarian committees was a counter-revolutionary option in that it championed a trade union capitalism and called for further strengthening of the State apparatus, for anti-fascist unity, renouncing the revolution in the name of the single aim of winning the war.

TARRADELLAS, Josep (1899–1988): Bourgeois Catalanist politician. Private secretary to Maciá and husband to his daughter. In 1931, he was elected as a deputy and that December joined the Generalidad government, overseeing the Interior and Health portfolios. Stood trial in connection with the events of October 1934. When the civil war broke out, he placed himself at the disposal of Companys, the Generalidad president, at a point when public office had generally been abandoned by the ERC. In July-September 1936, he headed the Public Services Department. From September 1936 until May 1937, he was prime minister ("Conseller Prima") of the Generalidad Council and was responsible for the Finance Department.

TORYHO, Jacinto: Anarchist journalist. In 1932, he was a staff writer with *Solidaridad Obrera* and *Tierra y Libertad*. In 1933, he joined the A anarchist group. After the revolutionary events of July 1936, he set up a CNT-FAI Press and Propaganda Bureau. In November 1936, he replaced Liberto Callejas as chief editor with *Solidaridad Obrera*, purging the team of long-standing anarchist staffers and replacing them with bourgeois professionals and collaborationist ideologues. He was the very prototype of the bureaucrat ensconced in his post. His ineptitude and bullying, the discontent of the unions, and the irritation of the readership finally ensured, in March 1938, that he was dismissed as *Solidaridad Obrera* director. He went into exile in Argentina.

TREINTISTAS: The *treintistas* described themselves as gradualist revolutionaries and pure syndicalists opposed to the "hare-brained" uprisings of the faístas. Their preference was for long-term trade union activity rather than short-term, hasty insurrectionist activity that brought repression and dis-organization.

The *Manifesto of the Thirty* in August 1931 was signed by, among others, Progreso Alfarache, Roldán Cortada (who finished up in the UGT), Juan Lopez (who served as the Republic's Industry minister), Juan Peiro (a very prominent trade unionist and a man of great prestige), Angel Pestaña, etc.

The main consequence of the *Manifesto of the Thirty* was that the CNT split and the so-called Opposition Unions emerging, which in January 1933 were to launch the Libertarian Syndicalist Federation (FSL) emerging.

In Catalonia, the FSL grew strong in towns like Sabadell, Mataró, Badalona, Manresa, and others. It also was very strong in the Valencia region. It numbered some 65,000 members. Joan Peiró returned to the reunified CNT with his great prestige undiminished.

Ángel Pestaña quit the FSL and founded his minuscule Syndicalist Party in April 1934. This placed him beyond the pale to the rest of the CNT world, and can be regarded as his personal and political failure.

UGT (*Unión General de Trabajadores*/General Union of Workers): The socialist trade union, in the minority in Catalonia in July 1936. Its numbers were greatly inflated by the recruitment of petit-bourgeois, anti-CNT shopkeepers, thanks to the Stalinists' counter-revolutionary policy that made the union a transmission belt passing on the orders from the PSUC.

UNCONTROLLABLES: The higher CNT and FAI committees re-established Public Order, i.e., republican law and order in the streets of Barcelona, cracking down on crime and ferreting out fascist "moles," but also restraining the revolutionary violence of the barrio committees and trade unions. Such confrontation with revolutionary expropriators was brazenly portrayed as determination to stop fascist sympathizers, clergy, and a maverick, opportunistic crime wave (which was, without a doubt, a real, serious problem). All the anti-fascist organizations—the Generalidad government and higher committees included—conflated such criminality with the revolutionary violence coming from the barrio committees and unions that were collectivizing or controlling factories, workshops, and farms; executing fascists, gunmen, right-wingers, military personnel, and clergy; and commandeering housing, cars, luxury dwellings, barracks, churches, monasteries, hospitals, hospices, and other real estate abandoned by fleeing fascists and others

In the eyes of many, the revolutionary process had gone too far. The first step toward dealing with it consisted of halting it in its tracks and ensuring that it would go no further. Reclaiming lost ground would come later. Hence, the emergence of the novel idea of "revolutionary order," which quite simply meant preventing the revolution from going any deeper and interpreting "revolutionary gains" as constituting a new order—the finished product—which had to be defended against revolutionary mavericks, rampant criminality, the dispossessed bourgeoisie, and the fascists.

The success of the term "uncontrollable" precisely depended on this ambiguity embracing and conflating two distinct and different things—the criminal and the revolutionary—in a form discreet and disguised enough to be palatable even to the barrio committees, local committees, and trade union committees, the very people against whom it was directed. It was plain and precise enough to be bandied about by the higher committees, the bourgeois parties, the Stalinists, and the government as they tackled the revolutionaries who became, with the "uncontrollable" label, the focus of their attacks, the object of their snide comments, and their number one target.

The requisite and inescapable crackdown on chaotic, opportunistic, criminality was a superb pretext on which to stem the revolutionary expropriators as well. It also hinted at the true character of the CAMC, which was not quite the Generalidad government, yet the first step towards its reconstruction—which is to say, a class collaborationist body involving all working-class and bourgeois trade union and political organizations, plus representatives of the government. The CAMC's ultimate purpose, conscious or otherwise, was to return full powers to the bourgeois State. It wan an agency suited to controlling and channelling the "July Revolution" and to laying the groundwork for the future rebuilding of the State. The same is true of the Control Patrols. Ensconced in the barracks that had once belonged to the "real" forces of Public Order, i.e. the Civil Guard and Assault Guard, a "revolutionary" police force out to protect this new "revolutionary" order and capable of cracking down on arbitrary criminality, was also capable of "containing" the barrio and trade union committees, with all the contradictions one would assume to be generated by the untenable position of higher committees leading an ideologically anti-State organization while immersed in government business and in rebuilding the capitalist state.

Throughout history, revolutionary movements have never been unblemished and flawless; they have been motley and contradictory, naïve and forward-thinking, irksome and blinkered, surprising and far-sighted, all at the same time.

USC (*Unio Socialista de Catalunya*/Socialist Union of Catalonia): Founded in 1923. Joan Comorera was appointed its general secretary in 1932. It was one of four tiny parties that amalgamated, on 24 July 1936, to launch the PSUC.

VINALESA: On 8 March 1937, violent armed clashes erupted in Vinalesa (Valencia) between militarization-opposing anarchists and the Assault Guards trying to force them back into the front lines; several were killed and wounded on both sides. Upwards of two hundred anarcho-syndicalists were detained, ninety-two of them militias from the Iron Column. In the end, on 21 March, the Iron Column agreed to militarization, becoming the 83rd Brigade.

Index

Support **AK Press!**

AK Press is one of the world's largest and most productive anarchist publishing houses. We're entirely worker-run & democratically managed. We operate without a corporate structure—no boss, no managers, no bullshit. We publish close to twenty books every year, and distribute thousands of other titles published by other like-minded independent presses and projects from around the globe.

The Friends of AK program is a way that you can directly contribute to the continued existence of AK Press, and ensure that we're able to keep publishing great books just like this one! Friends pay $25 a month directly into our publishing account ($30 for Canada, $35 for international), and receive a copy of every book AK Press publishes for the duration of their membership! Friends also receive a discount on anything they order from our website or buy at a table: 50% on AK titles, and 20% on everything else. We've also added a new Friends of AK ebook program: $15 a month gets you an electronic copy of every book we publish for the duration of your membership. Combine it with a print subscription, too!

There's great stuff in the works—so sign up now to become a Friend of AK Press, and let the presses roll!

Won't you be our friend? Email friendsofak@akpress.org for more info, or visit the Friends of AK Press website: www.akpress.org/programs/friendsofak

What is the Kate Sharpley Library?

The Kate Sharpley Library is a library, archive, publishing outfit and affinity group. We preserve and promote anarchist history.

What we've got

Our collection includes anarchist books, pamphlets, newspapers and leaflets from the nineteenth century to the present in over twenty languages. The collection includes manuscripts, badges, audio and video recordings, and photographs, as well as the work of historians and other writers who have documented the anarchist movement.

What we do

We promote the history of anarchism by reprinting original documents from our collection, and translating or publishing new works on anarchism and its history. These appear in our quarterly bulletin or regularly published pamphlets. We have also provided manuscripts to other anarchist publishers. People come and research in the library, or we can send out a limited amount of photocopies.

Why we do it

We don't say one strand of class-struggle anarchism has all the answers. We don't think anarchism can be understood by looking at 'thinkers' in isolation. We do think that what previous generations thought and did, what they wanted and how they tried to get it, is relevant today. We encourage the anarchist movement to think about its own history—not to live on past glories but to get an extra perspective on current and future dangers and opportunities.

How we do it

Everything at the Kate Sharpley Library—acquisitions, cataloguing, preservation work, publishing, answering inquiries is done by volunteers. All our running costs are met by donations (from members of the collective or our subscribers and supporters) or by the small income we make through publishing.

How you can help

Please subscribe to our bulletin to keep up with what we're doing. There are four issues of the Bulletin a year. Or become a Friend, a KSL Friend subscription gets you the Bulletin and all our publications as they come out.

You can send us anarchist material that you don't need any more (from books to badges)—we can pay postage for large loads, but it doesn't have to be large. A couple of pamphlets will be as gratefully received as anything. Even if you send us duplicates we can trade with other archives for material we do not have. If you publish anarchist material, please add us to your mailing list!

You can send us money too. Details are on our website at: http://www.katesharpleylibrary.net/doc/donations

Keep in touch!

www.katesharpleylibrary.net
www.facebook.com/KateSharpleyLibrary
Postal addresses:
Kate Sharpley Library, BM Hurricane, London, WC1N 3XX

Kate Sharpley Library, PMB 820, 2425 Channing Way, Berkeley CA 94704, USA